Some Descendants of

CAPTAIN THOMAS HARRIS

ca 1586–1658

Robert W. Witt

HERITAGE BOOKS
2017

HERITAGE BOOKS

AN IMPRINT OF HERITAGE BOOKS, INC.

Books, CDs, and more—Worldwide

For our listing of thousands of titles see our website
at
www.HeritageBooks.com

Published 2017 by
HERITAGE BOOKS, INC.
Publishing Division
5810 Ruatan Street
Berwyn Heights, Md. 20740

Heritage Books by the author:
Descendants of John Witt, the Virginia Immigrant
Some Descendants of Captain Thomas Harris, ca 1586–1658
The Isle of Wight Cooks

International Standard Book Number
Paperbound: 978-0-7884-5779-1

Table of Contents

First Generation

---

1. Captain Thomas Harris. Born ca 1586 in England. Thomas died in Henrico County, VA, in 1658; he was 72.

There is considerable disagreement about the wives of Thomas. Some insist that he first married a Gurganey and had no children with her; then he second married Audrey Hoare and had the two children with her. He then married Joane Vincent, the widow of his neighbor Wiliam Vincent, but had no children with his third wife [GenForum/Harris and WorldConnect]. Ann Gurganey, widow of Edward Gurganey, left land to Capt. Thomas in her will dated 11 Feb 1619. Possibly they had intended to marry, but she died before they did. Land records would suggest that he was married only twice. A record in Henrico of 25 Feb 1638 refers to Adry Harris as his first wife and another record dated 11 Nov 1635 refers to his wife as Joane Harris (Foley, *Early Virginia Families*, v. 1).

Thomas arrived in Virginia in 1611, first in Jamestown and then Henrico County. He was one of the first burgesses to represent Henrico Co. The first assembly was 6 Jan 1639.

Ca 1623 when Thomas was 37, he first married Audrey Hoare, daughter of Thomas Hoare & Julyan Triplett, in Virginia. Born on 28 Aug 1604 in England. Audrey died ? .

They had the following children:

        2   i.   Mary (1625-1703)

3   ii.   William (1629-1678)

Ca 1634 when Thomas was 48, he second married Joane Vincent, in Henrico County, VA. Born ca 1600 in England. Joane died ? .

Second Generation

2. Mary Harris (Thomas[1]). Born in 1625 in Henrico County, VA. Mary died in 1703; she was 78.

Information about the husband is from Boddie, *Virginia Genealogies;* information about the children is from Mary Ligon's will (Weisiger, *Colonial Wills of Henrico Co.*).

Mary married Thomas Ligon. Born ca 1623. Thomas died ? .

They had the following children:

4	i.	Richard (1657-?)
5	ii.	William (1659-<1703)
6	iii.	Hugh (1661-?)
7	iv.	Mary (1663-?)
8	v.	Johanna

3. William Harris I (Thomas[1]). Born in 1629 in Henrico County, VA. William died in Virginia in 1678; he was 49.

Information about the first marriage is from Ancestry; information about the second marriage is from WorldConnect. Information about the sons is from William's will (Weisiger, *Colonial Wills of Henrico Co.*) and from a land transaction by William Byrd in Henrico Co., 1 Aug 1696 (Weisiger, *Henrico Co. Deeds).*

In 1656 when William was 27, he first married Lucy Stewart, in Henrico County, VA. Born ? . Lucy died ? .

Ca 1670 when William was 41, he second married Alice Stewart, in Henrico County, VA. Born ca 1640 in Virginia. Alice died in New Kent County, VA, aft 1696; she was 56.

They had the following children:

9 i. Thomas (?-1679)

10 ii. William (ca1672-ca1743)

11 iii. Edward (ca1674-?)

---

4. Richard Ligon (Mary Harris[2], Thomas[1]). Born in 1657. Richard died ? .

Information about the marriage is from Lindsay, *Marriages of Henrico Co.* In 1706 Richard sold land left to his mother by her father Thomas Harris (Henrico co., VA, Website).

In 1681 when Richard was 24, he married Mary Worsham, in Henrico County, VA. Born ? . Mary died ? .

5. William Ligon (Mary Harris[2], Thomas[1]). Born in 1659. William died bef 1703; he was 44.

6. Hugh Ligon (Mary Harris[2], Thomas[1]). Born in 1661. Hugh died ? .

Information about the marriage is from Lindsay, *Marriages of Henrico Co.*

In 1689 when Hugh was 28, he married Elizabeth Walthall, in Henrico County, VA. Born ? . Elizabeth died ? .

7. Mary Ligon (Mary Harris[2], Thomas[1]). Born in 1663. Mary died ? .

Information about the husband is from Mary Ligon's will (Weisiger, *Colonial Wills of Henrico Co.*).

Mary married Thomas Farrar. Born ? . Thomas died ? .

8. Johanna Ligon (Mary Harris[2], Thomas[1]).

Information about the husband is from Mary Ligon's will (Weisiger, *Colonial Wills of Henrico Co.*).

Johanna married Robert Hancock. Born ? . Robert died ? .

9. Thomas Harris (William[2], Thomas[1]). Born ? in Virginia. Thomas died in May 1679 in Henrico County, VA.

Thomas's will, 10 Feb 1678, mentions a sister-in-law Love Harris, not identified, and a cousin Richard Lygon (Henrico Co., VA, Website).

10. William Harris II (William[2], Thomas[1]). Born ca 1672 in Henrico County, VA. William died in Hanover County, VA, ca 1743; he was 71.

Information about the wife and children is from *Parish Register of Saint Peter* and WorldConnect.

William married Mary Giles. Born ? . Mary died ? .

They had the following children:

12	i.	Edward (1695-1751)
13	ii.	Thomas (ca1697-1784)
14	iii.	Elizabeth (1698->1770)
15	iv.	William (ca1698-ca1778)
16	v.	George (1701-ca1778)
17	vi.	David (1701-1781)
18	vii.	John (1704-1786)
19	viii.	Stephen (1707->1771)

11. Edward Harris (William[2], Thomas[1]). Born ca 1674 in Hanover County, VA. Edward died ? .

Information about the wife and children is from *Parish Register of Saint Peter.*

Edward married Elizabeth ?. Born ? . Elizabeth died ? .

They had the following children:

20	i.	Anne (1700-?)
21	ii.	Edward (1704-?)
22	iii.	Sarah (1705-?)
23	iv.	Judith (1707-?)
24	v.	John (1710-?)
25	vi.	Thomas (1712-?)

---

12. Edward Harris (William[3], William[2], Thomas[1]). Born in 1695 in Henrico County, VA. Edward died in Prince Edward County, VA, in 1751; he was 56.

Edward received a land patent in Prince Edward Co., 30 Sep 1745 (T.L.C. Genealogy, *Prince Edward Deed Book 1*).

Edward married Ann ?.

13. Thomas Harris (William[3], William[2], Thomas[1]). Born ca 1697 in Hanover County, VA. Thomas died in Prince Edward County, VA, on 16 Feb 1784; he was 87.

Information about the marriage and children is from LDS.

Thomas married Elizabeth Lindsey, in Hanover County, VA. Born ca 1704 in Virginia. Elizabeth died in Prince Edward County, VA, aft 1782; she was 78.

They had the following children:

26	i.	David (ca1726-?)
27	ii.	John (ca1728-?)
28	iii.	Peter (ca1730-?)
29	iv.	Sherwood (Shureed) (ca1732-?)
30	v.	Elizabeth (ca1734-?)
31	vi.	Judith (ca1736-?)

14. Elizabeth Harris (William[3], William[2], Thomas[1]). Born in 1698 in Henrico County, VA. Elizabeth died in Virginia aft 1770; she was 72.

Information about the first husband is from a petition to administer William I's estate (Weisiger, *Colonial Wills of Henrico Co.*); information about the daughter is from Henrico Co., VA, Website. Information about the second husband and the sons is from Prince Edward Co., Va, Website.

Elizabeth first married George Archer. Born ? . George died ? .

They had one child:

32	i.	Elizabeth

In 1714 when Elizabeth was 16, she second married John Hudson, in Virginia. Born in 1690. John died in Hanover County, VA, in 1732; he was 42.

They had the following children:

33	i.	George (1714-?)
34	ii.	Christopher (1716-1779)
35	iii.	John (1717-1801)
36	iv.	William (1719-1800)
37	v.	Thomas (1722-?)
38	vi.	Elizabeth (1722-?)

39	vii.	David (1723-1787)
40	viii.	Cuthbert (1724-1801)
41	ix.	Mary (1726-?)
42	x.	Rebecca (1728-?)
43	xi.	Anna (1732-?)
44	xii.	Charles

15. William Harris III (William[3], William[2], Thomas[1]). Born ca 1698 in Virginia. William died in Virginia ca 1778; he was 80.

Information about the sons is from WorldConnect.

William married ?.

They had the following children:

45	i.	Thomas
46	ii.	Robert C. R.
47	iii.	Harrison

16. George Harris (William[3], William[2], Thomas[1]). Born in Apr 1701 in New Kent County, VA. George died in Hanover County, VA, ca 1778; he was 76.

Information about the son is from Sorelle.

George married ?.

They had one child:

| 48 | i. | William (ca1730-1799) |

17. David Harris (William[3], William[2], Thomas[1]). Born on 27 Apr 1701 in Hanover County, VA. David died in Hanover County, VA, in 1781; he was 79.

Information about the marriage and sons is from LDS. WorldConnect has Jane Harrison as the wife.

In 1727 when David was 25, he married Jane Landy, in Hanover County, VA. Born ca 1704 in Hanover County, VA. Jane died ? .

They had the following children:

        49   i.   Giles (ca1728-ca1775)

        50   ii.   Lewis (1730-1784)

18. John Harris (William[3], William[2], Thomas[1]). Born in Mar 1704 in New Kent County, VA. John died in Prince Edward County, VA, in Dec 1786; he was 82.

Information about the marriage and children is from LDS.

Ca 1730 when John was 25, he married Mary Tinsley, in Prince Edward County, VA. Born ca 1708 in Prince Edward County, VA. Mary died in Hanover County, VA, bef 1786; she was 78.

They had the following children:

        51   i.   Elizabeth (ca1731-1818)

        52   ii.   David (ca1733-?)

19. Stephen Harris (William[3], William[2], Thomas[1]). Born in 1707 in Hanover County, VA. Stephen died in Virginia aft 1771; he was 64.

20. Anne Harris (Edward[3], William[2], Thomas[1]). Born in Nov 1700 in New Kent County, VA. Anne died ? .

21. Edward Harris (Edward[3], William[2], Thomas[1]). Born on 27 Nov 1704 in New Kent County, VA. Edward died ? .

Information about the son is from *Parish Register of Saint Peter.*

Edward married ?.

They had one child:

> **53**   i.   Edward (1727-?)

22. Sarah Harris (Edward[3], William[2], Thomas[1]). Born on 20 Jan 1705 in New Kent County, VA. Sarah died ? .

23. Judith Harris (Edward[3], William[2], Thomas[1]). Born on 5 Jan 1707 in New Kent County, VA. Judith died ? .

24. John Harris (Edward[3], William[2], Thomas[1]). Born on 24 Apr 1710 in New Kent County, VA. John died ? .

Information about the wife and children is from *Parish Register of Saint Peter.*

John married Ann ?. Born ? . Ann died ? .

They had the following children:

> **54**   i.   Richard (1730-?)
>
> **55**   ii.   Mary (1735-?)
>
> **56**   iii.   Ann (1738-?)

25. Thomas Harris (Edward[3], William[2], Thomas[1]). Born on 14 Jun 1712 in New Kent County, VA. Thomas died ? .

---

26. David Harris (Thomas[4], William[3], William[2], Thomas[1]). Born ca 1726 in Hanover County, VA. David died ? .

27. John Harris (Thomas[4], William[3], William[2], Thomas[1]). Born ca 1728 in Hanover County, VA. John died ? .

28. Peter Harris (Thomas[4], William[3], William[2], Thomas[1]). Born ca 1730 in Hanover County, VA. Peter died ? .

29. Sherwood (Shureed) Harris ((Thomas[4], William[3], William[2], Thomas[1]). Born ca 1732 in Hanover County, VA. Sherwood (Shureed) died ? .

30. Elizabeth Harris (Thomas[4], William[3], William[2], Thomas[1]). Born ca 1734 in Hanover County, VA. Elizabeth died ? .

31. Judith Harris (Thomas[4], William[3], William[2], Thomas[1]). Born ca 1736 in Hanover County, VA. Judith died ? .

Information about the marriage is from Knorr, *Marriage Bonds Prince Edward Co.*

On 19 Feb 1796 when Judith was 60, she married Jesse Pryor, in Prince Edward County, VA. Born ? . Jesse died ? .

32. Elizabeth Archer (Elizabeth Harris[4], William[3], William[2], Thomas[1]). Born ? . Elizabeth died ? .

33. George Hudson (Elizabeth Harris[4], William[3], William[2], Thomas[1]). Born in 1714 in Hanover County, VA. George died ? .

Information about the wife is from Hanover Co., VA, Website.

George married Sarah Jennings. Born ? . Sarah died ? .

34. Christopher Hudson (Elizabeth Harris[4], William[3], William[2], Thomas[1]). Born in 1716. Christopher died in 1779; he was 63.

Information about the wife is from Hanover Co., VA, Website.

Christopher married Cary Byrd. Born ? . Cary died ? .

35. John Hudson (Elizabeth Harris[4], William[3], William[2], Thomas[1]). Born in 1717. John died in 1801; he was 84.

Information about the wife is from Hanover Co., VA, Website.

John married Mary Greene. Born ? . Mary died ? .

36. William Hudson (Elizabeth Harris[4], William[3], William[2], Thomas[1]). Born in 1719 in Hanover County, VA. William died in 1800; he was 81.

William refers to his daughter Sarah Harris in his will of 1795 (Prince Edward Co., VA, Website). I have not determined which Harris she married.

William married Frances Greene. Born ? . Frances died ? .

They had one child:

57   i.   Sarah

37. Thomas Hudson (Elizabeth Harris[4], William[3], William[2], Thomas[1]). Born in 1722. Thomas died ? .

38. Elizabeth Hudson (Elizabeth Harris[4], William[3], William[2], Thomas[1]). Born in 1722. Elizabeth died ? .

39. David Hudson (Elizabeth Harris[4], William[3], William[2], Thomas[1]). Born in 1723. David died in 1787; he was 64.

40. Cuthbert Hudson (Elizabeth Harris[4], William[3], William[2], Thomas[1]). Born in 1724. Cuthbert died in Georgia in 1801; he was 77.

Information about the wife is from Hanover Co., VA, Website.

Cuthbert married Elizabeth Hall. Born ? . Elizabeth died ? .

41. Mary Hudson (Elizabeth Harris[4], William[3], William[2], Thomas[1]). Born in 1726. Mary died ? .

42. Rebecca Hudson (Elizabeth Harris[4], William[3], William[2], Thomas[1]). Born in 1728. Rebecca died ? .

43. Anna Hudson (Elizabeth Harris[4], William[3], William[2], Thomas[1]). Born in 1732. Anna died ? .

44. Charles Hudson (Elizabeth Harris[4], William[3], William[2], Thomas[1]). Born ? . Charles died ? .

Information about the wife is from Hanover Co., VA, Website.

Charles married Susannah Patrick. Born ? . Susannah died ? .

45. Thomas Harris (William[4], William[3], William[2], Thomas[1]). Born ? . Thomas died ? .

Information about the wife is from WorldConnect.

Thomas married ? Ebony. Born ? . ? died ? .

46. Robert C. R. Harris (William[4], William[3], William[2], Thomas[1]). Born ? . Robert C. R. died ? .

47. Harrison Harris (William[4], William[3], William[2], Thomas[1]). Born ? . Harrison died ? .Harrison purchased land in Kentucky on the Elk Horn River 4 Aug 1791 (Davis, *Hanover Co., VA, Deeds)*.

48. William Harris (George[4], William[3], William[2], Thomas[1]). Born ca 1730. William died in Prince Edward County, VA, in 1799; he was 69.

Information about the sons is from Prince Edward Co., VA, Website. Ralph and Graves sold William's land in 1805 and moved to Georgia.

William married ?.

They had the following children:

58	i.	Ralph (ca1764-1815)
59	ii.	Graves (ca1765-1826)
60	iii.	George

49. Giles Harris (David[4], William[3], William[2], Thomas[1]). Born ca 1728 in Hanover County, VA. Giles died in Prince Edward County, VA, ca 1775; he was 47.

Information about the first wife and her children is from LDS and WorldConnect. Information about the second wife and her children is from Rucker, *Genealogical Records*.

Giles first married ?.

They had the following children:

61	i.	David (ca1751-?)
62	ii.	Lettice (ca1753-?)

In 1769 when Giles was 41, he second married Ann E. Gray Chandler. Born ? . Ann E. Gray died ? .

They had the following children:

63	i.	Edmond (1770-1835)
64	ii.	Claiborne (1772-ca1862)
65	iii.	Obediah (1774-?)

50. Lewis Harris (David[4], William[3], William[2], Thomas[1]). Born in 1730 in Hanover County, VA. Lewis died in Prince Edward County, VA, in 1784; he was 54.

Information about the marriage and children is from LDS.

In 1763 when Lewis was 33, he married Elizabeth Harris (51) , daughter of John Harris (18) & Mary Tinsley, in Hanover County, VA. Born ca 1731 in Hanover County, VA. Elizabeth died in Prince Edward County, VA, in 1818; she was 87.

They had the following children:

66	i.	Giles (1766-1844)
67	ii.	John (1766-1827)
68	iii.	Patience Elizabeth (1768-<1818)

69	iv.	Lewis (1770-1850)
70	v.	Gideon (1772-1860)
71	vi.	Mary Tinsley (1774-1814)
72	vii.	Jane (1778-1829)
73	viii.	David (1781-1864)

51. Elizabeth Harris (John[4], William[3], William[2], Thomas[1]). Born ca 1731 in Hanover County, VA. Elizabeth died in Prince Edward County, VA, in 1818; she was 87.

In 1763 when Elizabeth was 32, she married Lewis Harris (50) , son of David Harris (17) & Jane Landy, in Hanover County, VA. Born in 1730 in Hanover County, VA. Lewis died in Prince Edward County, VA, in 1784; he was 54.

They had the following children:

66	i.	Giles (1766-1844)
67	ii.	John (1766-1827)
68	iii.	Patience Elizabeth (1768-<1818)
69	iv.	Lewis (1770-1850)
70	v.	Gideon (1772-1860)
71	vi.	Mary Tinsley (1774-1814)
72	vii.	Jane (1778-1829)
73	viii.	David (1781-1864)

52. David Harris (John[4], William[3], William[2], Thomas[1]). Born ca 1733 in Hanover County, VA. David died ? .

Information about the wife is from WorldConnect.

David married Ann Watkins. Born ? . Ann died ? .

53. Edward Harris (Edward[4], Edward[3], William[2], Thomas[1]). Born on 6 Feb 1727 in New Kent County, VA. Edward died ? .

54. Richard Harris (John[4], Edward[3], William[2], Thomas[1]). Born on 20 Feb 1730 in New Kent County, VA. Richard died ? .

55. Mary Harris (John[4], Edward[3], William[2], Thomas[1]). Born on 7 Mar 1735 in New Kent County, VA. Mary died ? .

56. Ann Harris (John[4], Edward[3], William[2], Thomas[1]). Born on 15 Oct 1738 in New Kent County, VA. Ann died ? .

Sixth Generation

57. Sarah Hudson (William[5], Elizabeth Harris[4], William[3], William[2], Thomas[1]). Born ? . Sarah died ? .

58. Ralph Harris (William[5], George[4], William[3], William[2], Thomas[1]). Born ca 1764 in Hanover County, VA. Ralph died in Georgia in 1815; he was 51.

Information about the marriage is from Knorr, *Marriage Bonds Prince Edward Co.*

In Dec 1790 when Ralph was 26, he married Agnes Baldwin, daughter of John Baldwin & Susannah Peak, in Prince Edward County, VA. Born ? . Agnes died ? .

59. Graves Harris (William[5], George[4], William[3], William[2], Thomas[1]). Born ca 1765 in Hanover County, VA. Graves died in Georgia in 1826; he was 61.

Information about the marriage is from Knorr, *Marriage Bonds Prince Edward Co.*

On 20 Nov 1787 when Graves was 22, he married Elizabeth Baldwin, daughter of John Baldwin & Susannah Peak, in Prince Edward County, VA. Born ? . Elizabeth died ? .

60. George Harris (William[5], George[4], William[3], William[2], Thomas[1]). Born ? . George died ? .

61. David Harris (Giles[5], David[4], William[3], William[2], Thomas[1]). Born ca 1751 in Prince Edward County, VA. David died ? .

62. Lettice Harris (Giles[5], David[4], William[3], William[2], Thomas[1]). Born ca 1753 in Prince Edward County, VA. Lettice died ? .

Information about the husband is from WorldConnect.

Lettice married Thomas Gray. Born ? . Thomas died ? .

63. Edmond Harris (Giles[5], David[4], William[3], William[2], Thomas[1]). Born on 3 Aug 1770 in Prince Edward County, VA. Edmond died in Maury County, TN, in 1835; he was 64.

Information about the marriage is from Knorr, *Marriage Bonds Prince Edward Co.* Information about the children is from LDS. Edmond purchased land in Buckingham Co., VA, in 1797 and 1801 and sold land to his brother Claiborne in 1804 (Ward, *Land Tax Summaries*).

On 29 Dec 1791 when Edmond was 21, he married Rhoda Arnold, daughter of John Arnold & Sarah Brown, in Prince Edward County, VA. Born ca 1771 in Prince Edward County, VA. Rhoda died in Maury County, TN, on 20 Apr 1881; she was 110.

They had the following children:

74	i.	William (1793-1814)
75	ii.	Nancye (1796-?)
76	iii.	Elizabeth (1799-1874)
77	iv.	Judith (1801-1881)
78	v.	Virginia (1803-?)
79	vi.	Giles Turner (1806-1866)

80   vii.   Claiborn (1808-1881)

64. Claiborne Harris (Giles[5], David[4], William[3], William[2], Thomas[1]). Born on 24 Aug 1772 in Prince Edward County, VA. Claiborne died in Buckingham County, VA, ca 1862; he was 89.

Information about the marriage is from Kidd and Stinson, *Lost Marriages*; information about the children is from WorldConnect. Claiborne purchased land in Buckingham County, VA, between 1815 and 1840 (Ward, *Land Tax Summaries*, v. 2).

Ca 1804 when Claiborne was 31, he married Mary "Polly" Gannaway, daughter of Gregory Gannaway & Rhoda Robertson, in Buckingham County, VA. Born on 12 Aug 1784 in Buckingham County, VA. Mary "Polly" died in Buckingham County, VA, ca 1874; she was 89.

They had the following children:

> **81**   i.   Giles (1805-1874)
>
> **82**   ii.   Harrison (ca1808-?)
>
> **83**   iii.   John Claiborn (ca1810-1871)
>
> **84**   iv.   Theodoric Carter Gannaway (ca1812->1850)
>
> **85**   v.   William (ca1814-1882)
>
> **86**   vi.   Edmond (ca1816-?)
>
> **87**   vii.   Rhoda (ca1818-?)

27

65. Obediah Harris (Giles[5], David[4], William[3], William[2], Thomas[1]). Born on 2 Nov 1774 in Prince Edward County, VA. Obediah died ? .

Information about the marriage and children is from LDS and Prince Edward Co., VA, Website. Obediah is listed as Capt. in land transactions in Buckingham Co., VA, 1810-1814 (Ward, *Land Tax Summaries*). In the 1850 Census of Buckingham Co., VA, Elizabeth Harris, 23, and Augusta Harris, 21, are members of the household. I assume these are granddaughters.

Ca 1799 when Obediah was 24, he married Elizabeth "Betty" Watkins, in Prince Edward County, VA. Born ca 1778 in Prince Edward County, VA. Elizabeth "Betty" died ? .

They had the following children:

88	i.	Giles (ca1800-?)
89	ii.	Lewis (ca1802-?)
90	iii.	Obediah (ca1811-?)
91	iv.	Robert (ca1810-?)
92	v.	Ammon (1808-1894)
93	vi.	Phoebe (ca1810-?)
94	vii.	Elizabeth (ca1812-?)
95	viii.	Mary (ca1814-?)

66. Giles Harris (Lewis[5], David[4], William[3], William[2], Thomas[1]). Born on 8 Aug 1766 in Prince Edward County, VA. Giles died in Walker County, GA, on 9 Oct 1844; he was 78.

Information about the marriages and children is from LDS.

Bef 1792 when Giles was 25, he first married ? Ward, in Prince Edward County, VA. Born ca 1770. ? died ? .

They had one child:

96   i.   Giles Ward (ca1792-?)

Bef 1794 when Giles was 27, he second married Elizabeth Thurman. Born ca 1770 in Virginia. Elizabeth died ? in Madison County, GA.

They had the following children:

97   i.   Augustus (ca1794-?)

98   ii.   Tinsley (ca1796-?)

99   iii.   Obadiah (ca1798-?)

100   iv.   John (Jack) (ca1800-?)

101   v.   William Austin (ca1803-1838)

102   vi.   Jane Lindsey (1805-1891)

103   vii.   Martha (ca1806-?)

104   viii.   Sarah Giles (1811-1875)

67. John Harris (Lewis[5], David[4], William[3], William[2], Thomas[1]). Born on 8 Aug 1766 in Prince Edward County, VA. John died in Wilson County, TN, in 1827; he was 60.

Information about the wife and children is from John Harris'
will (Partlow, *Wilson Co. Wills*). John was in Wilson Co.,
TN, by January of 1810, when he purchased land there; he
sold land to his brother Gideon in September of 1812
(Partlow, *Wilson Co. Deed Books C-M),* and may have been
there as early as 1804, when a John Harris first appears on
the tax list (Partlow, *Tax Lists of Wilson Co.*).

On 26 Aug John married Elizabeth Winn, in Louisa County,
VA. Born ca 1772 in Louisa County, VA. Elizabeth died ? .

They had the following children:

105	i.	Lewis (ca1795-?)
106	ii.	Richard W. (ca1797-1853)
107	iii.	Snead (ca1799-?)
108	iv.	John (ca1801-?)
109	v.	Mary "Polly" (ca1803-?)
110	vi.	Nancy (ca1805-<1828)
111	vii.	Elizabeth (ca1807-1845)

68. Patience Elizabeth Harris (Lewis[5], David[4], William[3],
William[2], Thomas[1]). Born in 1768 in Prince Edward County,
VA. Patience Elizabeth died bef 1818; she was 50.

Information about the marriage is from Knorr, *Marriage
Bonds Prince Edward Co.* Information about the children is
from LDS.

On 24 Mar 1790 when Patience Elizabeth was 22, she married David Arnold, son of John Arnold & Sarah Brown, in Prince Edward County, VA. Born ca 1765 in Prince Edward County, VA. David died bef 1818; he was 53.

They had the following children:

112	i.	John H. (ca1793-?)
113	ii.	Margaret Elizabeth (ca1795-?)
114	iii.	Mary "Polly" T. (ca1797-?)
115	iv.	Lindsey (1798-1868)

69. Lewis Harris (Lewis[5], David[4], William[3], William[2], Thomas[1]). Born on 10 Aug 1770 in Prince Edward County, VA. Lewis died in Marshall County, TN, on 4 Aug 1850; he was 79.

Information about the marriage is from Porch, *Marriage Records, Marshall Co.*

On 13 Dec 1841 when Lewis was 71, he married Anna Wright, in Marshall County, TN. Born ? in Virginia. Anna died ? in Prince Edward County, VA.

70. Gideon Harris (Lewis[5], David[4], William[3], William[2], Thomas[1]). Born on 30 Jul 1772 in Prince Edward County, VA. Gideon died in Marshall County, TN, on 26 Oct 1860; he was 88. Information about the marriage is from Knorr, *Marriage Bonds Prince Edward Co.* Information about the children is from LDS and W. Lee Harris. Gideon's nephew Lindsey Arnold is living with Gideon in 1860 (Marshall Co.

Census 1860). Gideon was in Wilson Co., TN, by December of 1811, when he purchased land there. He also purchased land from his brother John in September of 1812. He was in Maury Co., TN, by Jan 1822; he sold land in Wilson Co. on Jan 29, 1822 and is listed on the deed as of Maury Co., TN (Partlow, *Wilson Co. Deed Boooks C-M*).

On 25 Dec 1805 when Gideon was 33, he married Martha Taylor Gilliam, daughter of James Gilliam & Frances Hopkins, in Prince Edward County, VA. Born on 3 Feb 1786 in Goochland County, VA. Martha Taylor died in Marshall County, TN, on 14 May 1860; she was 74.

They had the following children:

> **116**   i.   Francis Hopkins (1807-1863)
>
> **117**   ii.   David Rice (1808-1873)
>
> **118**   iii.   Elizabeth Lewis "Betsy" (1809-1885)
>
> **119**   iv.   James Gilliam (1811-1882)
>
> **120**   v.   Gideon Lindsey (1813-1896)
>
> **121**   vi.   Giles Claiborne (1815-1889)
>
> **122**   vii.   John Gardner (1817-1892)

123	viii.	Mary Tinsley (1819-1829)
124	ix.	Sarah Giles (1823-1854)
125	x.	Martha Jane (1826-1914)

71. Mary Tinsley Harris (Lewis[5], David[4], William[3], William[2], Thomas[1]). Born in 1774 in Prince Edward County, VA. Mary Tinsley died in Wilson County, TN, in 1814; she was 40.

72. Jane Harris (Lewis[5], David[4], William[3], William[2], Thomas[1]). Born in 1778 in Prince Edward County, VA. Jane died in Prince Edward County, VA, in 1829; she was 51.

73. David Harris (Lewis[5], David[4], William[3], William[2], Thomas[1]). Born on 31 Dec 1781 in Prince Edward County, VA. David died in Marshall County, TN, on 22 Jun 1864; he was 82.

Information about the marriage is from Ancestry; information about the sons is from LDS.

On 20 Aug 1820 when David was 38, he married Mary C. "Polly" Jesse, in Prince Edward County, VA. Born on 14 Dec 1793 in Prince Edward County, VA. Mary C. "Polly" died in Marshall County, TN, on 2 Jul 1864; she was 70.

They had the following children:

126	i.	William Lindsey (1821-1897)
127	ii.	Lewis Tinsley (1825-1858)

74. William Harris (Edmond[6], Giles[5], David[4], William[3], William[2], Thomas[1]). Born in 1793 in Prince Edward County, VA. William died in Maury County, TN, in 1814; he was 21.

75. Nancye Harris (Edmond[6], Giles[5], David[4], William[3], William[2], Thomas[1]). Born in 1796 in Prince Edward County, VA. Nancye died ? .

Information about the first marriage is from Whitley, *Marriages of Maury Co.* Information about the second husband is from LDS.

On 6 Apr 1815 when Nancye was 19, she first married William McCord, in Maury County, TN. Born ? . William died ? .

Nancye second married William Perry. Born ca 1792. William died ? .

76. Elizabeth Harris (Edmond[6], Giles[5], David[4], William[3], William[2], Thomas[1]). Born on 12 Sep 1799 in Prince Edward County, VA. Elizabeth died in Athens, TN, on 22 Mar 1874; she was 74.

Information about the marriage is from Whitley, Maury Co. Marriages; information about the son is from LDS.

On 7 Apr 1818 when Elizabeth was 18, she married Kirk Prewitt, in Maury County, TN. Born on 24 Dec 1798 in Warren County, GA. Kirk died in Monroe County, MS, on 11 Oct 1879; he was 80.

They had one child:

> **128**   i.   John Brantley (1819-1905)

77. Judith Harris (Edmond[6], Giles[5], David[4], William[3], William[2], Thomas[1]). Born on 10 May 1801 in Prince Edward County, VA. Judith died in Maury County, TN, on 20 May 1881; she was 80.

Information about the marriage is from Whitley, *Marriages of Maury Co.* Information about the children is from LDS.

On 11 Dec 1819 when Judith was 18, she married Richard Ambrose Wilkes, in Maury County, TN. Born on 23 May 1799 in Virginia. Richard Ambrose died in Giles County, TN, on 19 Sep 1867; he was 68.

They had the following children:

> **129**   i.   William Henderson (1821-1895)
>
> **130**   ii.   Franklin C. (1822-1881)
>
> **131**   iii.   Ann Eliza (1825-1854)
>
> **132**   iv.   Martha Virginia (1828-1895)
>
> **133**   v.   Richard Sparks (1829-?)
>
> **134**   vi.   Benjamin Leroy (1832-1862)

135 vii. George Washington (1834-1853)

136 viii. Josephine Castera (1836-1912)

137 ix. James Horace (1838-1912)

138 x. John Summerfield (1841-1908)

78. Virginia Harris (Edmond[6], Giles[5], David[4], William[3], William[2], Thomas[1]). Born in 1803 in Tennessee. Virginia died ? .

Information about the husband is from LDS.

Virginia married William Perry. Born ca 1792. William died ? .

79. Giles Turner Harris (Edmond[6], Giles[5], David[4], William[3], William[2], Thomas[1]). Born in 1806 in Maury County, TN. Giles Turner died in 1866; he was 60.

Information about the first marriage is from Whitley, *Marriages of Maury Co.* Information about the children is from Maury Co. Cemetery Records and Maury Co., TN, Census 1850. Giles' wife in the 1850 Census is Jane. I'm assuming that since there are several years between the birth of William and Robert, Caroline died sometime after the birth of William and that the other children are Jane's.

On 21 Dec 1826 when Giles Turner was 20, he first married Caroline Daniel, in Maury County, TN. Born ? . Caroline died ? .

They had one child:

> **139**   i.   William (ca1828-?)

Giles Turner second married Jane ?. Born ca 1812 in Tennessee.

They had the following children:

> **140**   i.   Robert Giles (1835-1910)
>
> **141**   ii.   Carlos C. (1837-1903)
>
> **142**   iii.   Rowena (ca1839-?)
>
> **143**   iv.   Edmund (ca1839-?)
>
> **144**   v.   Mary (ca1848-?)
>
> **145**   vi.   Alice (1850-?)

80. Claiborn Harris (Edmond[6], Giles[5], David[4], William[3], William[2], Thomas[1]). Born in 1808 in Maury County, TN. Claiborn died in 1881; he was 73.

Information about the wife is from LDS.

Claiborn married ? Smith. Born ? . ? died ? .

81. Giles Harris (Claiborne[6], Giles[5], David[4], William[3], William[2], Thomas[1]). Born on 19 Sep 1805 in Buckingham County, VA. Giles died in Owensboro, KY, on 15 Mar 1874; he was 68.

Information about the marriage is from Ancestry; information about the children is from Cumberland Co., VA, Census 1850 and WorldConnect.

On 16 Dec 1828 when Giles was 23, he married Martha Williamson "Patsy" Bransford, daughter of Benjamin Bransford & Lucy Hatcher, in Cumberland County, VA. Born on 15 Feb 1807 in Cumberland County, VA. Martha Williamson "Patsy" died in Petersburg, VA, on 28 Jul 1856; she was 49.

They had the following children:

146 i. Thomas Woodson (1833-1851)

147 ii. William Bransford (1835-1862)

148 iii. Lucy Hatcher (1837-1860)

149 iv. Mary Robertson "Molly" (1839-1896)

150 v. Sarah Catherine (1841-1918)

151 vi. Frederick Giles (1843-1862)

152 vii. Susan Elizabeth (1846-1925)

153 viii. Martha Virginia (1831-1856)

82. Harrison Harris (Claiborne[6], Giles[5], David[4], William[3], William[2], Thomas[1]). Born ca 1808 in Buckingham County, VA. Harrison died ? .

83. John Claiborn Harris (Claiborne[6], Giles[5], David[4], William[3], William[2], Thomas[1]). Born ca 1810 in Buckingham County, VA. John Claiborn died in North Carolina, in 1871; he was 61.

Information about the marriages is from WorldConnect; information about the children is from Appomattox Co., VA, Census 1860. John has no wife in the 1860 Census; however, his wife in the 1870 Census is Amanda. Either the marriage and death record of the first wife is incorrect, or the third wife's name was also Amanda. There is a marriage record for a John Harris and Amanda Crowe, daughter of Edward Goulsman, on 28 Nov 1861 in Appomattox Co., VA. (Jamerson, *Appomattox Co. Marriages*) Perhaps Amanda was his third wife rather than the first.

In 1835 when John Claiborn was 25, he first married Gouldman Amanda Crowe, in Buckingham County, VA. Born in 1814 in Buckingham County, VA. Gouldman Amanda died ca 1839; she was 25.

In 1839 when John Claiborn was 29, he second married Susan Matthews, in Virginia. Born in 1811 in Virginia. Susan died in 1852; she was 41.

They had the following children:

    154   i.   William Moore (1842-1870)

    155   ii.   Tandy (1844-1927)

    156   iii.   Mary Elizabeth (1847-1913)

John Claiborn third married ? Jones. Born ? . ? died ? .

84. Theodoric Carter Gannaway Harris (Claiborne[6], Giles[5], David[4], William[3], William[2], Thomas[1]). Born ca 1812 in Buckingham County, VA. Theodoric Carter Gannaway died aft 1850; he was 38.

85. William Harris (Claiborne[6], Giles[5], David[4], William[3], William[2], Thomas[1]). Born ca 1814 in Buckingham County, VA. William died in North Carolina, in 1882; he was 68.

86. Edmond Harris (Claiborne[6], Giles[5], David[4], William[3], William[2], Thomas[1]). Born ca 1816 in Buckingham County, VA. Edmond died ? .

Information about the marriage is from WorldConnect; information about the children is from Thomas Harris.

On 8 Jan 1833 when Edmond was 17, he married Sallie Sanderson Fowler, in Campbell County, VA. Born ? in Campbell County, VA. Sallie Sanderson died ? .

They had the following children:

157	i.	Mary Constance
158	ii.	Virginia
159	iii.	Amanda
160	iv.	Nancy
161	v.	Patsy
162	vi.	William
163	vii.	Christopher
164	viii.	John

87. Rhoda Harris (Claiborne[6], Giles[5], David[4], William[3], William[2], Thomas[1]). Born ca 1818 in Buckingham County, VA. Rhoda died ? .

Information about the first husband is from Ancestry; information about the second husband is from WorldConnect.

On 18 Dec 1847 when Rhoda was 29, she first married David Oglesby Jr., in Bedford County, VA. Born ? . David died ? .

Rhoda second married ? Fowler. Born ? . ? died ? .

88. Giles Harris (Obediah[6], Giles[5], David[4], William[3], William[2], Thomas[1]). Born ca 1800 in Prince Edward County, VA. Giles died ? .

Information about the wife is from WorldConnect.

Giles married Mary ?. Born ? . Mary died ? .

89. Lewis Harris (Obediah[6], Giles[5], David[4], William[3], William[2], Thomas[1]). Born ca 1802 in Prince Edward County, VA. Lewis died ? .

90. Obediah Harris (Obediah[6], Giles[5], David[4], William[3], William[2], Thomas[1]). Born ca 1811 in Prince Edward County, VA. Obediah died ? .

Information about the wife and children is from the 1850 Census of Buckingham Co., VA.

Obediah married Eliza ?. Born ca 1813 in Virginia. Eliza died ? .

They had the following children:

166	i.	Giles (ca1841-?)
167	ii.	Susanna (ca1843-?)
168	iii.	Mina Dora (ca1845-?)
169	iv.	Mary (ca1847-?)
170	v.	Emily (ca1849-?)

91. Robert Harris (Obediah[6], Giles[5], David[4], William[3], William[2], Thomas[1]). Born ca 1810 in Prince Edward County, VA. Robert died ? .

92. Ammon Harris (Obediah[6], Giles[5], David[4], William[3], William[2], Thomas[1]). Born on 20 Mar 1808 in Prince Edward County, VA. Ammon died in Missouri on 1 Jun 1894; he was 86.

Information about the marriage and children is from Prince Edward Co., VA, website. In the 1850 Census of Buckingham Co., VA, Ammon is listed with no wife and only Philip in the household. Samuel may have died before the Census was taken, and Josephine and Mary Elizabeth were evidently in a different household.

On 17 Jun 1841 when Ammon was 33, he married Mary Ann Smith Watkins, in Prince Edward County, VA. Born on 8 Sep 1817 in Virginia. Mary Ann Smith died in Virginia ca 1848; she was 30.

They had the following children:

171	i.	Philip Watkins (1842-1906)
172	ii.	Samuel (1844-<1860)
173	iii.	Josephine (1845-1931)
174	iv.	Mary Elizabeth (1847-1924)

93. Phoebe Harris (Obediah[6], Giles[5], David[4], William[3], William[2], Thomas[1]). Born ca 1810 in Prince Edward County, VA. Phoebe died ? .

Information about the husband is from Prince Edward Co., VA, Website.

Phoebe married Nathaniel Carrington. Born ? . Nathaniel died ? .

94. Elizabeth Harris (Obediah[6], Giles[5], David[4], William[3], William[2], Thomas[1]). Born ca 1812 in Prince Edward County, VA. Elizabeth died ? .

Information about the husband is from WorldConnect.

Elizabeth married ? Venable. Born ? . ? died ? .

95. Mary Harris (Obediah[6], Giles[5], David[4], William[3], William[2], Thomas[1]). Born ca 1814 in Virginia. Mary died ? .

Information about the husband is from WorldConnect.

Mary married ? Hurt. Born ? . ? died ? .

96. Giles Ward Harris (Giles[6], Lewis[5], David[4], William[3], William[2], Thomas[1]). Born ca 1792 in Prince Edward County, VA. Giles Ward died ? .

97. Augustus Harris (Giles[6], Lewis[5], David[4], William[3], William[2], Thomas[1]). Born ca 1794 in Virginia. Augustus died ? .

98. Tinsley Harris (Giles[6], Lewis[5], David[4], William[3], William[2], Thomas[1]). Born ca 1796 in Virginia. Tinsley died ? .

99. Obadiah Harris (Giles[6], Lewis[5], David[4], William[3], William[2], Thomas[1]). Born ca 1798 in Virginia. Obadiah died ? .

Information about the marriage is from WorldConnect; information about the children is from Walker Co., GA, Census 1850.

On 17 Oct 1825 when Obadiah was 27, he married Narcissus Aycock. Born on 1 May 1804 in Georgia. Narcissus died in Georgia aft 1870; she was 65.

They had the following children:

175	i.	Penelope (ca1833-?)
176	ii.	William W. (ca1834-?)
177	iii.	Nancy (ca1838-?)
178	iv.	Giles Ward (1839-1877)
179	v.	Augustus G. (ca1842-?)

100. John (Jack) Harris (Giles[6], Lewis[5], David[4], William[3], William[2], Thomas[1]). Born ca 1800 in Virginia. John (Jack) died ? .

101. William Austin Harris (Giles[6], Lewis[5], David[4], William[3], William[2], Thomas[1]). Born ca 1803 in Virginia. William Austin died in Georgia in 1838; he was 35.

Information about the marriage and sons is from LDS and WorldConnect.

In 1827 when William Austin was 24, he married Cynthia Strickland, in Georgia. Born ca 1805. Cynthia died in Monroe County, GA, in 1859; she was 54.

They had the following children:

> **180** i. Luvinia (1831-1899)
>
> **181** ii. William (1833-1863)
>
> **182** iii. Austin Dabney (1835-1881)

102. Jane Lindsey Harris (Giles[6], Lewis[5], David[4], William[3], William[2], Thomas[1]). Born on 22 Jan 1805 in Madison County, GA. Jane Lindsey died in Lamar County, GA, on 1 May 1891; she was 86.

Information about the marriage is from LDS.

On 21 Sep 1828 when Jane Lindsey was 23, she married Samuel Mitchell, in Madison County, GA. Born in 1784 in Londonderry, Ireland. Samuel died in Pike County, GA, on 30 May 1847; he was 63.

103. Martha Harris (Giles[6], Lewis[5], David[4], William[3], William[2], Thomas[1]). Born ca 1806 in Virginia. Martha died ? .

104. Sarah Giles Harris (Giles[6], Lewis[5], David[4], William[3], William[2], Thomas[1]). Born on 10 Oct 1811 in Virginia. Sarah Giles died on 21 Apr 1875; she was 63.

Information about the marriage is from WorldConnect.

On 28 Oct 1830 when Sarah Giles was 19, she married William Myrick. Born in 1794. William died ? .

105. Lewis Harris (John[6], Lewis[5], David[4], William[3], William[2], Thomas[1]). Born ca 1795 in Prince Edward County, VA. Lewis died ? .

106. Richard W. Harris (John[6], Lewis[5], David[4], William[3], William[2], Thomas[1]). Born ca 1797 in Prince Edward County, VA. Richard W. died in Wilson County, TN, in 1853; he was 56.

Information about the wife and children is from Richard's will. Harriet F. and Susan E. were minors at the time of Richard's death, and Susan E. was a minor at the time of Amelia's death (Partlow, *Wilson Co., TN, Miscellaneous Records).*

Richard W. married Amelia ?. Born ? . Amelia died in 1861 in Wilson County, TN.

They had the following children:

183	i.	Mary J.
184	ii.	Sarah B.
185	iii.	Evaline N.
186	iv.	Joseph B.
187	v.	Harriett F.
188	vi.	Susan E.

107. Snead Harris (John[6], Lewis[5], David[4], William[3], William[2], Thomas[1]). Born ca 1799 in Prince Edward County, VA. Snead died ? .

Information about the marriage is from Whitley, *Marriages of Wilson Co.* Snead was involved in several land transactions in Wilson Co., TN, from 1834 to 1841. In one transaction he was with John Tilford, perhaps his father-in-law or brother-in-law (Partlow, *Wilson Co., TN, Deed Books N-Z*).

On 17 Dec 1828 when Snead was 29, he married Fany Tilford, in Wilson County, TN. Born ? . Fany died ? .

108. John Harris (John[6], Lewis[5], David[4], William[3], William[2], Thomas[1]). Born ca 1801 in Prince Edward County, VA. John died ? .

109. Mary "Polly" Harris (John[6], Lewis[5], David[4], William[3], William[2], Thomas[1]). Born ca 1803 in Prince Edward County, VA. Mary "Polly" died ? .

Information about the husband is from LDS.

Mary "Polly" married Henry Ward, in Wilson County, TN. Born in 1799. Henry died ? .

110. Nancy Harris (John[6], Lewis[5], David[4], William[3], William[2], Thomas[1]). Born ca 1805 in Prince Edward County, VA. Nancy died in Wilson County, TN, bef 1828; she was 23.

Information about the husband and children is from John Harris' will (Partlow, *Wilson Co. Wills*).

Nancy married Andrew McDonald, in probably Wilson County, TN. Born ca 1801 in Prince Edward County, VA. Andrew died ? .

They had the following children:

> **189** i. Andrew

190   ii.   Elizabeth A. (ca1827-?)

111. Elizabeth Harris (John[6], Lewis[5], David[4], William[3], William[2], Thomas[1]). Born ca 1807 in Tennessee. Elizabeth died in Wilson County, TN, in 1845; she was 38.

Information about the husband is from John Harris' will (Partlow, *Wilson Co. Wills*).

Elizabeth married Ira Douglas. Born on 17 Nov 1797 in Smith County, TN. Ira Douglas died ? .

112. John H. Arnold (Patience Elizabeth Harris[6], Lewis[5], David[4], William[3], William[2], Thomas[1]). Born ca 1793 in Prince Edward County, VA. John H. died ? .

113. Margaret Elizabeth Arnold (Patience Elizabeth Harris[6], Lewis[5], David[4], William[3], William[2], Thomas[1]). Born ca 1795 in Prince Edward County, VA. Margaret Elizabeth died ? .

Information about the husband is from WorldConnect.

In 1818 when Margaret Elizabeth was 23, she married William B. Hill. Born ? . William B. died ? .

114. Mary "Polly" T. Arnold (Patience Elizabeth Harris[6], Lewis[5], David[4], William[3], William[2], Thomas[1]). Born ca 1797 in Prince Edward County, VA. Mary "Polly" T. died ? .

Information about the husband is from WorldConnect.

Mary "Polly" T. married Joseph A. Royal. Born ? . Joseph A. died ? .

115. Lindsey Arnold (Patience Elizabeth Harris[6], Lewis[5], David[4], William[3], William[2], Thomas[1]). Born on 28 Dec 1798 in Prince

Edward County, VA. Lindsey died in Marshall County, TN, on 11 Aug 1868; he was 69.

116. Francis Hopkins Harris (Gideon[6], Lewis[5], David[4], William[3], William[2], Thomas[1]). Born on 3 Mar 1807 in Prince Edward County, VA. Francis Hopkins died in Marshall County, TN, on 15 Nov 1863; she was 56.

Information about the marriages and children is from W. Lee Harris and Marshall Co., TN, Census 1850.

On 30 Dec 1823 when Francis Hopkins was 16, she first married James A Steele, in Maury County, TN. Born ? in Maury County, TN. James A Steele died ? in Marshall County, TN.

They had one child:

> **191**   i.   Martha Elizabeth (1824-1842)

On 4 Sep 1841 when Francis Hopkins was 34, she second married William Ashley Moore, son of Samuel Moore & Elizabeth Berry, in Marshall County, TN. Born on 19 May 1798 in Marshall County, TN. William Ashley died in Marshall County, TN, on 5 Mar 1881; he was 82.

They had the following children:

> **192**   i.   Gideon Lindsey (1842-ca1862)
>
> **193**   ii.   Robert Hawkins (1844-1918)
>
> **194**   iii.   Elisha (ca1847-?)

117. David Rice Harris (Gideon[6], Lewis[5], David[4], William[3], William[2], Thomas[1]). Born on 4 Aug 1808 in Prince Edward County, VA. David Rice died in Perry County, TN, on 30 Jan 1873; he was 64.

Information about the marriages is from W. Lee Harris. Information about the children is from Perry Co., TN, Census 1850 and 1870.

On 16 Nov 1830 when David Rice was 22, he first married Rebecca Dillard, in Maury County, TN. Born ca 1812 in Tennessee. Rebecca died in Perry County, TN, ca 1858; she was 46.

They had the following children:

> **195**   i.   John R. (ca1833-ca1858)
>
> **196**   ii.   Gideon Lewis (1835-1889)
>
> **197**   iii.   Sarah (ca1837-ca1858)
>
> **198**   iv.   William (ca1839-1862)
>
> **199**   v.   Martha Jane (1840-1895)

In 1860 when David Rice was 51, he second married Elizabeth Roberts, in Perry County, TN. Born ? . Elizabeth died ca 1870 in Perry County, TN.

They had the following children:

> **200**   i.   Giles Tinsley (1861-1950)

201	ii.	Margaret Safronia "Maggie" (1863-1953)
202	iii.	Thomas Blount (1865-1940)
203	iv.	Elizabeth (1866-1949)
204	v.	Rebecca Rice (1870-1946)

118. Elizabeth Lewis "Betsy" Harris (Gideon[6], Lewis[5], David[4], William[3], William[2], Thomas[1]). Born on 21 Dec 1809 in Prince Edward County, VA. Elizabeth Lewis "Betsy" died in Marshall County, TN, on 23 Feb 1885; she was 75.

Information about the marriage is from Whitley, *Maury Co. Marriages*; information about the children is from Marshall Co., TN, Census 1850 and 1860.

On 23 Mar 1826 when Elizabeth Lewis "Betsy" was 16, she married John David Vincent, in Maury County, TN. Born on 24 Mar 1796 in North Carolina. John David died in Marshall County, TN, on 25 Nov 1853; he was 57.

They had the following children:

205	i.	Elizabeth (1830-1886)
206	ii.	Martha (1832-1857)
207	iii.	John H. (1835-1915)
208	iv.	Sarah J. (1838-1883)
209	v.	James Anderson (1840-1933)

210	vi.	Iowa Florida (1843-1913)
211	vii.	William H. (1846-1887)
212	viii.	Robert F. (1848-1915)
213	ix.	Emma V. (1853-1931)

119. James Gilliam Harris (Gideon[6], Lewis[5], David[4], William[3], William[2], Thomas[1]). Born on 13 Dec 1811 in Wilson County, TN. James Gilliam died in Marshall County, TN, on 22 Apr 1882; he was 70.

Information about the children is from LDS and Marshall Co. Census 1860. Information about the first and third marriages is from Whitley, *Marriages of Maury Co.* Information about the second marriage is from Porch, *Marriages Marshall Co.*

On 20 May 1832 when James Gilliam was 20, he first married Mary Ann Daughtery. Born on 27 Sep 1814 in Tennessee. Mary Ann died in Marshall County, TN, on 6 Feb 1845; she was 30.

They had the following children:

214	i.	Sarah Elizabeth (1832-?)
215	ii.	Mary J. (1834-1897)
216	iii.	Martha Jane (1835-1915)
217	iv.	Elizabeth Lindsey (1837-1838)

218	v.	Gideon Lewis (1839-1862)

219	vi.	John Hopkins (1840-1847)

220	vii.	Nancy Bennett (1841-1889)

221	viii.	Frances Caroline (1843-1919)

222	ix.	Aurelia Ann (1845-1919)

On 23 Jul 1845 when James Gilliam was 33, he second married Jane Melissa Lowrance, in Marshall County, TN. Born on 30 Dec 1813. Jane Melissa died in Marshall County, TN, on 21 Jul 1847; she was 33.

On 9 Dec 1847 when James Gilliam was 35, he third married Susan Angaline Hill, in Marshall County, TN. Born on 7 Feb 1818. Susan Angaline died in Marshall County, TN, on 27 May 1900; she was 82.

They had the following children:

223	i.	James Clanton (1848-?)
224	ii.	Unnamed (1851-1851)
225	iii.	Unnamed (1852-1852)
226	iv.	William Thomas (1853-1913)
227	v.	Robert Claiborne (1856-1916)

228	vi.	John Lindsey (1859-?)
229	vii.	David Tinsley (1860-?)

120. Gideon Lindsey Harris (Gideon[6], Lewis[5], David[4], William[3], William[2], Thomas[1]). Born on 12 Dec 1813 in Wilson County, TN. Gideon Lindsey died in McNairy County, TN, on 11 Mar 1896; he was 82.

Information about the first marriage is from Lucas, *Marriages from Early Tennessee Newspapers*; information about the second and third marriages is from W. Lee Harris. Information about the children is from LDS, Hardin Co., TN, Census 1850, and McNairy Co., TN, Census 1860 and 1900.

On 17 Dec 1831 when Gideon Lindsey was 18, he first married Lucy Elizabeth Ledbetter, in Maury County, TN. Born on 14 Dec 1814 in Chatham County, NC. Lucy Elizabeth died in McNairy County, TN, on 11 Apr 1856; she was 41.

They had the following children:

230	i.	James Lindsey (1833-1848)
231	ii.	Martha Elizabeth (1834-1926)
232	iii.	Giles Claiborne (1837-1881)
233	iv.	David Thomas (1839-1895)
234	v.	Mary Catherine "Cassie" (1840-1898)

235 vi. Gideon Lindsey (1843-1919)

236 vii. John Gardner (1845-1846)

237 viii. Sarah Francis "Frankie" (1847-1920)

238 ix. William Ashley (1849-1916)

239 x. Doctor Franklin "Docky" (1853-1915)

240 xi. Marion A. (1856-1873)

In Aug 1857 when Gideon Lindsey was 43, he second married Catherine McDaniel, in Tennessee. Born ca 1816 in North Carolina. Catherine died in McNairy County, TN, on 16 Dec 1893; she was 77.

In Feb 1894 when Gideon Lindsey was 80, he third married Margaret Gray Harrison, in McNairy County, TN. Born ca 1860. Margaret died ? .

They had one child:

241 i. Martha Jane "Mattie" (1895-1978)

121. Giles Claiborne Harris (Gideon[6], Lewis[5], David[4], William[3], William[2], Thomas[1]). Born on 15 Dec 1815 in Wilson County, TN. Giles Claiborne died in Macon County, TN, on 4 Mar 1889; he was 73. Buried in Harris Cemetery, Macon County, TN.

Information about the marriages is from Stinson and Spurlock, *Sumner Co. Marriages* and Whitley, *Marriages of Sumner Co.* Information about the children is from the Macon Co., TN, Census 1850-1880.

On 15 Feb 1837 when Giles Claiborne was 21, he first married Frances Catherine Meador, daughter of Thomas S. Meador & Frances Gilmore, in Sumner County, TN. Born in 1816 in Macon County, TN. Frances Catherine died in Macon County, TN, on 6 Jan 1844; she was 28.

They had the following children:

242	i.	Thomas Gideon (1839-1932)
243	ii.	William Tinsley (1841-1898)

On 14 Aug 1844 when Giles Claiborne was 28, he second married Sarah H. Hawkins, daughter of Robert Hawkins & Sarah Frances Gilliam, in Sumner County, TN. Born on 15 Jan 1821 in Sumner County, TN. Sarah H. died in Sumner County, TN, on 23 Oct 1847; she was 26.

They had the following children:

244	i.	Mary (ca1845-<1860)
245	ii.	Robert Wiseman (1847-1915)

On 9 Feb 1848 when Giles Claiborne was 32, he third married Elizabeth Catherine Wood Davis, in Sumner County, TN. Born ca 1822 in Tennessee. Elizabeth Catherine died in Macon County, TN, on 13 Mar 1889; she was 67.

They had the following children:

    246 i.   Martha Anna "Matt" (1849-1927)

    247 ii.   John Sumpter (1852-1927)

    248 iii.   James Lindsey (1855-1904)

    249 iv.   Giles Rice (1858-1882)

    250 v.   Malvina "Mallie" C. (1861-1894)

    251 vi.   David Baxter (1863-1951)

    252 vii.   Joseph Carrol (1866-1928)

122. John Gardner Harris (Gideon[6], Lewis[5], David[4], William[3], William[2], Thomas[1]). Born on 13 Oct 1817 in Wilson County, TN. John Gardner died in Hardin County, TN, in Nov 1892; he was 75.

Information about the marriage and daughter is from W. Lee Harris.

On 5 Apr 1838 when John Gardner was 20, he married Rosannah London, daughter of John London & Permelia Cheek, in Marshall County, TN. Born ca 1821 in Maury County, TN. Rosannah died in Hardin County, TN, in 1894; she was 73.

They had one child:

253 i. Margaret Elizabeth "Maggie" (1842-1916)

123. Mary Tinsley Harris (Gideon[6], Lewis[5], David[4], William[3], William[2], Thomas[1]). Born on 5 Sep 1819 in Maury County, TN. Mary Tinsley died in Marshall County, TN, on 1 Nov 1829; she was 10.

124. Sarah Giles Harris (Gideon[6], Lewis[5], David[4], William[3], William[2], Thomas[1]). Born on 3 Oct 1823 in Maury County, TN. Sarah Giles died in Marshall County, TN, on 24 Jan 1854; she was 30.

Information about the marriage is from Porch, *Marriage Records, Marshall Co.* Information about the daughter is from W. Lee Harris.

On 24 Apr 1840 when Sarah Giles was 16, she married William Fletcher Baxter, in Marshall County, TN. Born on 5 May 1820 in Maury County, TN. William Fletcher died in Marshall County, TN, on 28 Nov 1898; he was 78.

They had one child:

254 i. Amanda Jane (1847-1899)

125. Martha Jane Harris (Gideon[6], Lewis[5], David[4], William[3], William[2], Thomas[1]). Born on 11 May 1826 in Maury County, TN. Martha Jane died in Marshall County, TN, on 9 Dec 1914; she was 88.

Information about the marriage is from Porch, *Marriage Records, Marshall Co.* Information about the children is from Marshall Co., TN, Census 1880.

On 6 Jun 1854 when Martha Jane was 28, she married William Fletcher Baxter, in Marshall County, TN. Born on 5 May 1820 in Maury County, TN. William Fletcher died in Marshall County, TN, on 28 Nov 1898; he was 78.

They had the following children:

255	i.	William H. (1854-1930)
256	ii.	James N. (1857-1937)
257	iii.	Robert G. (1860-1931)
258	iv.	Montgomery H. (1863-1880)
259	v.	Edmond S. (1865-1955)
260	vi.	John F. (1868-1897)
261	vii.	Martha N. (1870-1935)

126. William Lindsey Harris (David[6], Lewis[5], David[4], William[3], William[2], Thomas[1]). Born on 18 Aug 1821 in Maury County, TN. William Lindsey died in Marshall County, TN, on 15 Jan 1897; he was 75.

Information about the marriage is from Porch, *Marriage Records, Marshall Co.* Information about the children is from Marshall Co. Census 1860.

On 18 Apr 1844 when William Lindsey was 22, he married
Mary Ann Patterson, daughter of James Patterson & Mary
Reed, in Marshall County, TN. Born on 29 Jun 1823 in
Maury County, TN. Mary Ann died in Marshall County, TN,
on 15 Jul 1905; she was 82.

They had the following children:

> **262**   i.   David Lawson (1845-1916)
>
> **263**   ii.   Sarah Jane (1846-1923)
>
> **264**   iii.   James Patterson (1848-1922)
>
> **265**   iv.   Mary Katherine (1850-1933)
>
> **266**   v.   Elizabeth Annie (1858-1939)

127. Lewis Tinsley Harris (David[6], Lewis[5], David[4],
William[3], William[2], Thomas[1]). Born on 10 Aug 1825 in
Marshall County, TN. Lewis Tinsley died in Marshall
County, TN, on 25 Mar 1858; he was 32.

128. John Brantley Prewitt (Elizabeth Harris[7], Edmond[6], Giles[5], David[4], William[3], William[2], Thomas[1]). Born on 22 Feb 1819 in Maury County, TN. John Brantley died in Monroe County, MS, on 10 Jun 1905; he was 86.

129. William Henderson Wilkes (Judith Harris[7], Edmond[6], Giles[5], David[4], William[3], William[2], Thomas[1]). Born on 7 May 1821 in Maury County, TN. William Henderson died in Maury County, TN, on 15 Oct 1895; he was 74.

130. Franklin C. Wilkes (Judith Harris[7], Edmond[6], Giles[5], David[4], William[3], William[2], Thomas[1]). Born on 3 Dec 1822 in Maury County, TN. Franklin C. died in Texas on 8 Dec 1881; he was 59.

131. Ann Eliza Wilkes (Judith Harris[7], Edmond[6], Giles[5], David[4], William[3], William[2], Thomas[1]). Born on 5 Sep 1825 in Maury County, TN. Ann Eliza died in Maury County, TN, on 14 Jul 1854; she was 28.

132. Martha Virginia Wilkes (Judith Harris[7], Edmond[6], Giles[5], David[4], William[3], William[2], Thomas[1]). Born on 17 Jan 1828 in Maury County, TN. Martha Virginia died on 5 May 1895; she was 67.

133. Richard Sparks Wilkes (Judith Harris[7], Edmond[6], Giles[5], David[4], William[3], William[2], Thomas[1]). Born on 27 Dec 1829 in Marshall County, TN. Richard Sparks died ? in Aberdeen, MS.

134. Benjamin Leroy Wilkes (Judith Harris[7], Edmond[6], Giles[5], David[4], William[3], William[2], Thomas[1]). Born on 14 Jan 1832 in Maury County, TN. Benjamin Leroy died in Maury County, TN, on 10 Mar 1862; he was 30.

135. George Washington Wilkes (Judith Harris[7], Edmond[6], Giles[5], David[4], William[3], William[2], Thomas[1]). Born on 22 Feb 1834 in Maury County, TN. George Washington died in Maury County, TN, on 24 Aug 1853; he was 19.

136. Josephine Castera Wilkes (Judith Harris[7], Edmond[6], Giles[5], David[4], William[3], William[2], Thomas[1]). Born on 17 Jun 1836 in Maury County, TN. Josephine Castera died in Maury County, TN, on 8 Sep 1912; she was 76.

137. James Horace Wilkes (Judith Harris[7], Edmond[6], Giles[5], David[4], William[3], William[2], Thomas[1]). Born on 7 Nov 1838 in Maury County, TN. James Horace died in Maury County, TN, on 22 Jul 1912; he was 73.

138. John Summerfield Wilkes (Judith Harris[7], Edmond[6], Giles[5], David[4], William[3], William[2], Thomas[1]). Born on 21 Mar 1841 in Maury County, TN. John Summerfield died in Giles County, TN, on 2 Feb 1908; he was 66.

139. William Harris (Giles Turner[7], Edmond[6], Giles[5], David[4], William[3], William[2], Thomas[1]). Born ca 1828 in Tennessee. William died ? .

140. Robert Giles Harris (Giles Turner[7], Edmond[6], Giles[5], David[4], William[3], William[2], Thomas[1]). Born on 17 Aug 1835. Robert Giles died on 27 Jun 1910; he was 74.

Information about the wife is from Maury Co. Cemetery Records (Website); information about the children is from Maury Co., TN, Census 1880.

Robert Giles married Martha R. Neeley, daughter of Lee Neeley & Hettie Smith. Born on 1 Dec 1840. Martha R. died on 9 Nov 1918; she was 77.

They had the following children:

267	i.	Robert (ca1863-?)
268	ii.	Edmund (ca1865-?)
269	iii.	Guy (ca1867-?)
270	iv.	Kate (ca1870-?)
271	v.	Hettie (ca1872-?)
272	vi.	Andrew Curran (1876-1958)
273	vii.	Clifford Frierson (1878-1933)
274	viii.	Joseph (ca1879-?)

141. Carlos C. Harris (Giles Turner[7], Edmond[6], Giles[5], David[4], William[3], William[2], Thomas[1]). Born on 24 May 1837 in Tennessee. Carlos C. died on 29 Jul 1903; he was 66.

Information about the wife is from Maury Co. Cemetery Records (Website). Carlos C. married Laura Tharue. Born ? . Laura died ? .

142. Rowena Harris (Giles Turner[7], Edmond[6], Giles[5], David[4], William[3], William[2], Thomas[1]). Born ca 1839 in Tennessee. Rowena died ? .

Information about the marriage and sons is from Maury Co. Cemetery Records (Website).

On 29 Apr 1858 when Rowena was 19, she married Robert N. Moore. Born ? . Robert N. died ? .

They had the following children:

> **275**   i.   James Giles (1859-1928)
>
> **276**   ii.   Robert Nathaniel (1861-1939)

143. Edmund Harris (Giles Turner[7], Edmond[6], Giles[5], David[4], William[3], William[2], Thomas[1]). Born ca 1839 in Tennessee. Edmund died ? .

144. Mary Harris (Giles Turner[7], Edmond[6], Giles[5], David[4], William[3], William[2], Thomas[1]). Born ca 1848 in Tennessee. Mary died ? .

145. Alice Harris (Giles Turner[7], Edmond[6], Giles[5], David[4], William[3], William[2], Thomas[1]). Born in 1850 in Tennessee. Alice died ? .

146. Thomas Woodson Harris (Giles[7], Claiborne[6], Giles[5], David[4], William[3], William[2], Thomas[1]). Born on 29 Apr 1833. Thomas Woodson died on 24 Jul 1851; he was 18.

147. William Bransford Harris (Giles[7], Claiborne[6], Giles[5], David[4], William[3], William[2], Thomas[1]). Born on 29 Jul 1835. William Bransford died on 14 Feb 1862; he was 26.

148. Lucy Hatcher Harris (Giles[7], Claiborne[6], Giles[5], David[4], William[3], William[2], Thomas[1]). Born on 25 Oct 1837. Lucy Hatcher died on 24 Feb 1860; she was 22.

149. Mary Robertson "Molly" Harris (Giles[7], Claiborne[6], Giles[5], David[4], William[3], William[2], Thomas[1]). Born on 18 Dec 1839. Mary Robertson "Molly" died in 1896; she was 56.

Information about the marriage and daughter is from WorldConnect.

On 15 Nov 1859 when Mary Robertson "Molly" was 19, she married Frank Binford. Born ? . Frank died ? .

They had one child:

        277   i.   Katherine

150. Sarah Catherine Harris (Giles[7], Claiborne[6], Giles[5], David[4], William[3], William[2], Thomas[1]). Born on 23 Nov 1841. Sarah Catherine died in 1918; she was 76.

Information about the marriage and children is from McLean Co., KY, Census 1870 and WorldConnect.

On 19 May 1863 when Sarah Catherine was 21, she married Thomas Hatcher Frayser, in Petersburg, VA. Born on 9 Feb 1837. Thomas Hatcher died on 8 Dec 1894; he was 57.

They had the following children:

        278   i.   Frederick Harris (1864-?)

279 ii. Judith Bransford (1866-?)

280 iii. Virginia (1867-<1870)

281 iv. Mary Susan (1869-?)

282 v. Thomas Hatcher (1870-?)

283 vi. Sarah Catherine (1872-?)

284 vii. Jessamine (1874-?)

285 viii. William (1876-?)

286 ix. Giles Harris (1878-?)

287 x. Martha Bransford (1880-?)

288 xi. Sidney Anderson (1883-?)

151. Frederick Giles Harris (Giles[7], Claiborne[6], Giles[5], David[4], William[3], William[2], Thomas[1]). Born on 5 Oct 1843. Frederick Giles died on 30 Aug 1862; he was 18.

152. Susan Elizabeth Harris (Giles[7], Claiborne[6], Giles[5], David[4], William[3], William[2], Thomas[1]). Born on 23 Mar 1846. Susan Elizabeth died in Jefferson County, TN, on 11 Feb 1925; she was 78.

Information about the marriage and children is from WorldConnect and Jefferson Co., TN, census 1910.

On 29 May 1867 when Susan Elizabeth was 21, she married Thomas Sidney Anderson, in Petersburg, VA. Born on 8 Jul 1842 in Daviess County, KY. Thomas Sidney died in Jefferson County, TN, on 10 Nov 1925; he was 83.

They had the following children:

> **289**   i.   Mary Ann (1868-1932)
>
> **290**   ii.   Patty Bransford (1871-1948)
>
> **291**   iii.   Sue Harris (1874-1922)

153. Martha Virginia Harris (Giles[7], Claiborne[6], Giles[5], David[4], William[3], William[2], Thomas[1]). Born on 23 Feb 1831. Martha Virginia died on 30 Oct 1856; she was 25.

154. William Moore Harris (John Claiborn[7], Claiborne[6], Giles[5], David[4], William[3], William[2], Thomas[1]). Born in 1842 in Virginia. William Moore died in 1870; he was 28.

155. Tandy Harris (John Claiborn[7], Claiborne[6], Giles[5], David[4], William[3], William[2], Thomas[1]). Born on 25 Oct 1844 in Virginia. Tandy died on 13 Jun 1927; he was 82.

Information about the marriage is from WorldConnect; information about the children is from Appomattox Co., VA, 1880, 1900, and 1910.

On 26 Dec 1877 when Tandy was 33, he married Roberta Alice Marks, daughter of Hudson Watkins Marks & Ellen Jane Ballard, in Virginia. Born on 4 Dec 1858 in Virginia. Roberta Alice died on 29 Jul 1912; she was 53.

They had the following children:

292	i.	Helen M. (1879-1960)
293	ii.	Roberta Lee (1880-?)
294	iii.	William B. (1882-

1972)

295	iv.	Tandy D. (1884-1962)
296	v.	Hattie L. (1887-?)
297	vi.	Walter E. (1890-1971)
298	vii.	Lillie M. (1890-?)
299	viii.	Susie L. (1896-?)
300	ix.	Esther R. (1898-?)
301	x.	Dille (1902-?)

156. Mary Elizabeth Harris (John Claiborn[7], Claiborne[6], Giles[5], David[4], William[3], William[2], Thomas[1]). Born in 1847 in Virginia. Mary Elizabeth died in 1913; she was 66.

Information about the marriage is from Jamerson, *Appomattox Co. Marriages.* I have not identified the Samuel Harris, John's father.

On 2 Jul 1871 when Mary Elizabeth was 24, she married John A. Harris, son of Samuel Harris & ?, in Appomattox County, VA. Born ca 1844. John A. died ? .

157. Mary Constance Harris (Edmond[7], Claiborne[6], Giles[5], David[4], William[3], William[2], Thomas[1]). Born ? . Mary Constance died ? .

Information about the husband and children is from Thomas Harris.

Mary Constance married John Archer Caldwell. Born ? . John Archer died ? .

They had the following children:

    302   i.   Caliborne

    303   ii.   Aurelia

    304   iii. Constance

    305   iv.   William Christopher

158. Virginia Harris (Edmond[7], Claiborne[6], Giles[5], David[4], William[3], William[2], Thomas[1]). Born ? . Virginia died ? .

159. Amanda Harris (Edmond[7], Claiborne[6], Giles[5], David[4], William[3], William[2], Thomas[1]). Born ? . Amanda died ? .

160. Nancy Harris (Edmond[7], Claiborne[6], Giles[5], David[4], William[3], William[2], Thomas[1]). Born ? . Nancy died ? .

161. Patsy Harris (Edmond[7], Claiborne[6], Giles[5], David[4], William[3], William[2], Thomas[1]). Born ? . Patsy died ? .

162. William Harris (Edmond[7], Claiborne[6], Giles[5], David[4], William[3], William[2], Thomas[1]). Born ? . William died ? .

163. Christopher Harris (Edmond[7], Claiborne[6], Giles[5], David[4], William[3], William[2], Thomas[1]). Born ? . Christopher died ? .

164. John Harris (Edmond[7], Claiborne[6], Giles[5], David[4], William[3], William[2], Thomas[1]). Born ? . John died ? .

165. Claiborne Harris (Edmond[7], Claiborne[6], Giles[5], David[4], William[3], William[2], Thomas[1]). Born ? . Claiborne died ? .

166. Giles Harris (Obediah[7], Obediah[6], Giles[5], David[4], William[3], William[2], Thomas[1]). Born ca 1841 in Virginia. Giles died ? .

167. Susanna Harris (Obediah[7], Obediah[6], Giles[5], David[4], William[3], William[2], Thomas[1]). Born ca 1843 in Virginia. Susanna died ? .

168. Mina Dora Harris (Obediah[7], Obediah[6], Giles[5], David[4], William[3], William[2], Thomas[1]). Born ca 1845 in Virginia. Mina Dora died ? .

169. Mary Harris (Obediah[7], Obediah[6], Giles[5], David[4], William[3], William[2], Thomas[1]). Born ca 1847 in Virginia. Mary died ? .

170. Emily Harris (Obediah[7], Obediah[6], Giles[5], David[4], William[3], William[2], Thomas[1]). Born ca 1849 in Virginia. Emily died ? .

171. Philip Watkins Harris (Ammon[7], Obediah[6], Giles[5], David[4], William[3], William[2], Thomas[1]). Born on 2 May 1842 in Prince Edward County, VA. Philip Watkins died in Saline County, MO, on 23 Oct 1906; he was 64.

Information about the first marriage is from WorldConnect; information about the second marriage is from LDS. Information about the children is from Saline Co., MO, Census 1880. Ammon is a member of the household in 1880.

On 13 May 1868 when Philip Watkins was 26, he first married Almeda Holmes, in Saline County, MO. Born ca 1844 in Virginia. Almeda died ? .

They had the following children:

> **306**   i.   E. C. (ca1871-?)

307	ii.	R. A. (ca1872-?)
308	iii.	P. H. (ca1874-?)
309	iv.	E. W. (ca1876-?)
310	v.	T. J. (ca1877-?)
311	vi.	L. W. (1880-?)

On 1 Jun 1893 when Philip Watkins was 51, he second married Pearl A. Williams, in Saline County, MO. Born ? . Pearl A. died ? .

172. Samuel Harris (Ammon[7], Obediah[6], Giles[5], David[4], William[3], William[2], Thomas[1]). Born on 4 Feb 1844 in Prince Edward County, VA. Samuel died bef 1860; he was 15.

173. Josephine Harris (Ammon[7], Obediah[6], Giles[5], David[4], William[3], William[2], Thomas[1]). Born on 19 Nov 1845 in Prince Edward County, VA. Josephine died in Clinton County, MO, on 4 May 1931; she was 85.

Information about the marriage is from Prince Edward Co., VA, Website; information about the children is from Saline Co., MO, Census 1900.

On 11 Jan 1872 when Josephine was 26, she married Robert James Erwin Jr., in Saline County, MO. Born ? . Robert James died bef 1900 in Missouri.

They had the following children:

| **312** | i. | John B. (1872-1957) |
| **313** | ii. | James R. (1874-1912) |

314	iii.	Susan V. (1877-1964)
315	iv.	Lena (1879-1956)
316	v.	Lillie (1882-1947)
317	vi.	Margaret V. (1884-1964)

174. Mary Elizabeth Harris (Ammon[7], Obediah[6], Giles[5], David[4], William[3], William[2], Thomas[1]). Born on 7 Aug 1847 in Prince Edward County, VA. Mary Elizabeth died in Kansas City, KS, on 22 May 1924; she was 76.

Information about the marriage is from WorldConnect; information about the children is from Knox Co., MO, Census 1880.

On 22 Nov 1868 when Mary Elizabeth was 21, she married Edmond Singleton, in Saline County, MO. Born ca 1842 in Kentucky. Edmond died ? .

They had the following children:

318	i.	Margaret L. (ca1869-?)
319	ii.	Elizabeth J. (ca1873-?)
320	iii.	Georgiana (ca1875-?)
321	iv.	Philip A. (ca1877-?)
322	v.	Edmond M. (ca1879-?)

175. Penelope Harris (Obadiah[7], Giles[6], Lewis[5], David[4], William[3], William[2], Thomas[1]). Born ca 1833 in Alabama. Penelope died ? .

176. William W. Harris (Obadiah[7], Giles[6], Lewis[5], David[4], William[3], William[2], Thomas[1]). Born ca 1834 in Alabama. William W. died ? .

177. Nancy Harris (Obadiah[7], Giles[6], Lewis[5], David[4], William[3], William[2], Thomas[1]). Born ca 1838 in Georgia. Nancy died ? .

178. Giles Ward Harris (Obadiah[7], Giles[6], Lewis[5], David[4], William[3], William[2], Thomas[1]). Born on 15 Oct 1839 in Walker County, GA. Giles Ward died in Sebastian County, AR, on 4 Aug 1877; he was 37.

Information about the marriage and Arthur is from WorldConnect; information about the first two children is from Rutherford Co., TN, Census 1870.

On 7 Oct 1859 when Giles Ward was 19, he married Minerva Ann Gilbert, in Catoosa County, GA. Born on 30 Nov 1842 in Walker County, GA. Minerva Ann died in Sebastian County, AR, on 17 Jan 1908; she was 65.

They had the following children:

323	i.	Jasper (ca1865-?)
324	ii.	Elizabeth (ca1867-?)
325	iii.	Arthur Giles (1869-1944)

179. Augustus G. Harris (Obadiah[7], Giles[6], Lewis[5], David[4], William[3], William[2], Thomas[1]). Born ca 1842 in Georgia. Augustus G. died ? .

180. Luvinia Harris (William Austin[7], Giles[6], Lewis[5], David[4], William[3], William[2], Thomas[1]). Born on 3 Feb 1831 in Pike Co., Georgia. Luvinia died on 15 Jun 1899; she was 68.

181. William Harris (William Austin[7], Giles[6], Lewis[5], David[4], William[3], William[2], Thomas[1]). Born on 30 Apr 1833 in Pike Co., Georgia. William died on 20 Sep 1863; he was 30.

Information about the marriage and daughter is from LDS.

Ca 1853 when William was 19, he married Julia Ann Dismuke, in Georgia. Born ca 1839 in Coffee Co., Alabama. Julia Ann died ? .

They had one child:

> **326** i. Emma Frances (1861-1951)

182. Austin Dabney Harris (William Austin[7], Giles[6], Lewis[5], David[4], William[3], William[2], Thomas[1]). Born in 1835 in Georgia. Austin Dabney died in Louisiana on 10 Aug 1881; he was 46.

Information about the marriage is from LDS; information about the children is from Claiborne Co., LA, Census 1880.

On 12 Dec 1854 when Austin Dabney was 19, he married Rebecca Milner, in Louisiana. Born ca 1837 in Georgia. Rebecca died ? .

They had the following children:

> **327** i. Dayton (ca1860-?)
>
> **328** ii. Charlie (ca1863-?)
>
> **329** iii. Austin (ca1867-?)

330	iv.	Lee (ca1869-?)
331	v.	Annie (ca1872-?)
332	vi.	Claude M. (1874-?)
333	vii.	Ralph (ca1877-?)

183. Mary J. Harris (Richard W.[7], John[6], Lewis[5], David[4], William[3], William[2], Thomas[1]). Born ? . Mary J. died ? .

Information about the husband is from Richard's will (Partlow, *Wilson Co., TN, Miscellaneous Records*).

Mary J. married ? Owen. Born ? . ? died ? .

184. Sarah B. Harris (Richard W.[7], John[6], Lewis[5], David[4], William[3], William[2], Thomas[1]). Born ? . Sarah B. died ? .

Information about the husband is from Richard's will; information about the children is from J.H. Allen, guardian record *(Partlow, Wilson Co., TN, Miscellaneous Records)*.

Sarah B. married Larkin G. Allen. Born ? . Larkin G. died ca 1863.

They had the following children:

334	i.	Angeline
335	ii.	Richard
336	iii.	William
337	iv.	Ann Elizabeth

185. Evaline N. Harris (Richard W.[7], John[6], Lewis[5], David[4], William[3], William[2], Thomas[1]). Born ? . Evaline N. died ? .

Information about the husband is from Richard's will (Partlow, *Wilson Co., TN, Miscellaneous Records*).

Evaline N. married ? Debow. Born ? . ? died ? .

186. Joseph B. Harris (Richard W.[7], John[6], Lewis[5], David[4], William[3], William[2], Thomas[1]). Born ? . Joseph B. died ? .

187. Harriett F. Harris (Richard W.[7], John[6], Lewis[5], David[4], William[3], William[2], Thomas[1]). Born ? . Harriett F. died ? .

188. Susan E. Harris (Richard W.[7], John[6], Lewis[5], David[4], William[3], William[2], Thomas[1]). Born ? . Susan E. died ? .

189. Andrew McDonald (Nancy Harris[7], John[6], Lewis[5], David[4], William[3], William[2], Thomas[1]). Born ? . Andrew died ? .

190. Elizabeth A. McDonald (Nancy Harris[7], John[6], Lewis[5], David[4], William[3], William[2], Thomas[1]). Born ca 1827 in Wilson County, TN. Elizabeth A. died ? .

191. Martha Elizabeth Steele (Francis Hopkins Harris[7], Gideon[6], Lewis[5], David[4], William[3], William[2], Thomas[1]). Born in Nov 1824 in Maury County, TN. Martha Elizabeth died in Maury County, TN, in Jun 1842; she was 17.

Information about the marriage is from W. Lee Harris.

On 7 Jun 1841 when Martha Elizabeth was 16, she married J. P. Smith, in Maury County, TN. Born ? . J. P. died ? .

192. Gideon Lindsey Moore (Francis Hopkins Harris[7], Gideon[6], Lewis[5], David[4], William[3], William[2], Thomas[1]). Born in 1842 in Marshall County, TN. Gideon Lindsey died ca 1862; he was 20.

193. Robert Hawkins Moore (Francis Hopkins Harris[7], Gideon[6], Lewis[5], David[4], William[3], William[2], Thomas[1]). Born on 3 Jan 1844 in Marshall County, TN. Robert Hawkins died on 3 Mar 1918; he was 74.

Information about the marriage is from W. Lee Harris.

On 17 Apr 1866 when Robert Hawkins was 22, he married Lavenia Laemon Bryant, in Marshall County, TN. Born on 25 Feb 1842. Lavenia Laemon died on 16 Aug 1931; she was 89.

194. Elisha Moore (Francis Hopkins Harris[7], Gideon[6], Lewis[5], David[4], William[3], William[2], Thomas[1]). Born ca 1847 in Tennessee. Elisha died ? .

195. John R. Harris (David Rice[7], Gideon[6], Lewis[5], David[4], William[3], William[2], Thomas[1]). Born ca 1833. John R. died in Perry County, TN, ca 1858; he was 25.

Information about the wife is from WorldConnect.

John R. married Sarah Dodson, daughter of Marshall Dodson & Emily Brown. Born ca 1834. Sarah died ? .

196. Gideon Lewis Harris (David Rice[7], Gideon[6], Lewis[5], David[4], William[3], William[2], Thomas[1]). Born on 17 Sep 1835. Gideon Lewis died on 25 Dec 1889; he was 54.

Information about the marriage is from WorldConnect; information about the children is from Perry Co., TN, Census 1870.

On 17 Sep 1861 when Gideon Lewis was 26, he married Clara Adalaide Kittrell. Born on 31 Dec 1837. Clara Adalaide died on 8 Sep 1912; she was 74.

They had the following children:

> **338** i. David Ashley (1862-1901)
>
> **339** ii. Sarah Martha "Mattie" (1869-?)

197. Sarah Harris (David Rice[7], Gideon[6], Lewis[5], David[4], William[3], William[2], Thomas[1]). Born ca 1837. Sarah died ca 1858; she was 21.

Information about the marriages is from WorldConnect; information about the daughter is from Perry Co., TN, Census 1860.

Ca 1857 when Sarah was 20, she married Phelin Journey. Born ? . Phelin died ? .

They had one child:

> **340** i. Frances Eugenia (1858-1901)

198. William Harris (David Rice[7], Gideon[6], Lewis[5], David[4], William[3], William[2], Thomas[1]). Born ca 1839. William died in Hardin County, TN, on 6 Apr 1862; he was 23.

William was killed during the Battle of Shiloh.

199. Martha Jane Harris (David Rice[7], Gideon[6], Lewis[5], David[4], William[3], William[2], Thomas[1]). Born on 27 Dec 1840. Martha Jane died on 28 Sep 1895; she was 54.

Information about the marriage is from WorldConnect; information about the children is from Perry Co., TN, Census 1870-1900.

On 4 Nov 1856 when Martha Jane was 15, she married James Monroe Dodson, son of Marshall Dodson & Emily Brown. Born on 19 Jun 1836. James Monroe died on 22 Jul 1892; he was 56.

They had the following children:

341	i.	Mary L. Magruder (1865-1950)
342	ii.	Addie Jane (1868-1893)
343	iii.	Martha Willie (1870-1933)
344	iv.	James Ashley (1875-1967)
345	v.	Flora Newstate (1878->1956)
346	vi.	Mary Byron (1880-?)
347	vii.	Augusta Cleveland (1883->1956)

200. Giles Tinsley Harris (David Rice[7], Gideon[6], Lewis[5], David[4], William[3], William[2], Thomas[1]). Born on 16 Nov 1861 in Tennessee. Giles Tinsley died in Tennessee in May 1950; he was 88.

Information about the marriage is from WorldConnect; information about the children is from Perry Co., TN, Census 1900.

On 7 Mar 1886 when Giles Tinsley was 24, he married Sarah Katherine Sewell, daughter of Hiram Shepherd Sewell & Martha J. ?, in Tennessee. Born on 4 May 1861 in Tennessee. Sarah Katherine died in Tennessee on 26 Jan 1942; she was 80.

They had the following children:

348	i.	Eura Magruder (1887-?)
349	ii.	Maude May (1888-?)
350	iii.	Cecil Rice (1890-1947)
351	iv.	David Shepherd (1893-?)
352	v.	Alice (1895-?)
353	vi.	Ruth (1898-?)

201. Margaret Safronia "Maggie" Harris (David Rice[7], Gideon[6], Lewis[5], David[4], William[3], William[2], Thomas[1]). Born on 27 Aug 1863. Margaret Safronia "Maggie" died on 29 Nov 1953; she was 90.

Information about the marriages is from WorldConnect.

On 9 Jan 1881 when Margaret Safronia "Maggie" was 17, she first married William Wiley Wilburn. Born in Apr 1858. William Wiley died on 14 Feb 1881; he was 22.

On 3 Mar 1885 when Margaret Safronia "Maggie" was 21, she second married Michael Byrd. Born in Feb 1861. Michael died on 15 Jul 1888; he was 27.

On 15 Sep 1889 when Margaret Safronia "Maggie" was 26, she third married Samuel Johnson. Born in Jun 1864. Samuel died in Sep 1891; he was 27.

On 1 Aug 1893 when Margaret Safronia "Maggie" was 29, she fourth married William Thomas Huff. Born on 29 Aug 1872. William Thomas died on 16 Aug 1945; he was 72.

202. Thomas Blount Harris (David Rice[7], Gideon[6], Lewis[5], David[4], William[3], William[2], Thomas[1]). Born on 18 Jan 1865. Thomas Blount died on 1 Jul 1940; he was 75.

Information about the marriage is from WorldConnect; information about the children is from Dyer Co., TN, Census 1900-1920.

On 2 Feb 1888 when Thomas Blount was 23, he married Rebecca Elizabeth King. Born on 28 Jan 1870. Rebecca Elizabeth died ? .

They had the following children:

354	i.	Clarence D. (1889-1938)
355	ii.	William Burl (1893-1927)
356	iii.	Giles Hunter (1895-?)
357	iv.	Robert Taylor (1897-?)
358	v.	Gideon Lewis (1900-?)

| **359** | vi. | Thomas Blount (1903-?) |

| **360** | vii. | Ryman Abner (1906-?) |

| **361** | viii. | Milam King (1910-?) |

203. Elizabeth Harris (David Rice[7], Gideon[6], Lewis[5], David[4], William[3], William[2], Thomas[1]). Born on 28 Aug 1866. Elizabeth died on 3 Jun 1949; she was 82.

Information about the marriages and is from WorldConnect; information about the children is from Perry Co., TN, Census 1900 and 1910.

On 20 Jan 1889 when Elizabeth was 22, she first married William Washington Nichols. Born on 30 Sep 1854. William Washington died on 6 Mar 1892; he was 37.

They had the following children:

| **362** | i. | Will Vivian (1890-?) |

| **363** | ii. | Joe Henry (1892-1913) |

On 10 Nov 1895 when Elizabeth was 29, she second married James Morgan Kittrell. Born on 1 Jul 1864. James Morgan died on 12 Oct 1907; he was 43.

They had the following children:

| **364** | i. | Blanche (1897-1990) |

| **365** | ii. | Harris David (1901-1966) |

| **366** | iii. | Jack Morgan (1902-1959) |

| | 367 | iv. | Ruth (1905-1960) |

367 iv. Ruth (1905-1960)

368 v. Elizabeth (1906-?)

204. Rebecca Rice Harris (David Rice[7], Gideon[6], Lewis[5], David[4], William[3], William[2], Thomas[1]). Born on 17 May 1870. Rebecca Rice died on 6 May 1946; she was 75.

Information about the marriage and is from WorldConnect; information about the children is from Perry Co., TN, Census 1900 and 1910.

On 16 May 1888 when Rebecca Rice was 17, she married Samuel Lee Bates. Born in Jan 1867. Samuel Lee died on 27 Dec 1954; he was 87.

They had the following children:

369 i. William Howard (1889-1955)

370 ii. Kittie Lucille (1893-1958)

371 iii. Giles Lee Blount (1904-1941)

372 iv. Eliza Amelia (1907-?)

205. Elizabeth Vincent (Elizabeth Lewis "Betsy" Harris[7], Gideon[6], Lewis[5], David[4], William[3], William[2], Thomas[1]). Born on 17 Jul 1830 in Marshall County, TN. Elizabeth died on 9 Aug 1886; she was 56.

206. Martha Vincent (Elizabeth Lewis "Betsy" Harris[7], Gideon[6], Lewis[5], David[4], William[3], William[2], Thomas[1]). Born on 18 Nov

1832 in Marshall County, TN. Martha died in Marshall County, TN, on 22 Sep 1857; she was 24.

207. John H. Vincent (Elizabeth Lewis "Betsy" Harris[7], Gideon[6], Lewis[5], David[4], William[3], William[2], Thomas[1]). Born on 19 Aug 1835 in Marshall County, TN. John H. died on 6 Apr 1915; he was 79.

208. Sarah J. Vincent (Elizabeth Lewis "Betsy" Harris[7], Gideon[6], Lewis[5], David[4], William[3], William[2], Thomas[1]). Born on 7 Jan 1838 in Marshall County, TN. Sarah J. died on 8 May 1883; she was 45.

209. James Anderson Vincent (Elizabeth Lewis "Betsy" Harris[7], Gideon[6], Lewis[5], David[4], William[3], William[2], Thomas[1]). Born on 17 Oct 1840 in Marshall County, TN. James Anderson died on 31 Jul 1933; he was 92.

210. Iowa Florida Vincent (Elizabeth Lewis "Betsy" Harris[7], Gideon[6], Lewis[5], David[4], William[3], William[2], Thomas[1]). Born on 18 Jun 1843 in Marshall County, TN. Iowa Florida died on 18 Jan 1913; she was 69.

211. William H. Vincent (Elizabeth Lewis "Betsy" Harris[7], Gideon[6], Lewis[5], David[4], William[3], William[2], Thomas[1]). Born on 22 Jul 1846 in Marshall County, TN. William H. died in Marshall County, TN, on 12 Nov 1887; he was 41.

212. Robert F. Vincent (Elizabeth Lewis "Betsy" Harris[7], Gideon[6], Lewis[5], David[4], William[3], William[2], Thomas[1]). Born on 16 Aug 1848 in Marshall County, TN. Robert F. died on 8 Sep 1915; he was 67.

213. Emma V. Vincent (Elizabeth Lewis "Betsy" Harris[7], Gideon[6], Lewis[5], David[4], William[3], William[2], Thomas[1]). Born on 17

Oct 1853 in Marshall County, TN. Emma V. died on 23 Mar 1931; she was 77.

214. Sarah Elizabeth Harris (James Gilliam[7], Gideon[6], Lewis[5], David[4], William[3], William[2], Thomas[1]). Born on 7 Sep 1832 in Maury County, TN. Sarah Elizabeth died ? .

Information about the first marriage is from Porch, *Marriage Records, Marshall Co.* Information about the second is from LDS.

On 11 Sep 1849 when Sarah Elizabeth was 17, she first married Joseph Lee Kerr, in Marshall County, TN. Born on 7 Apr 1829. Joseph Lee died on 28 Mar 1862; he was 32.

On 30 Nov 1865 when Sarah Elizabeth was 33, she second married Paddy Paul Graves. Born ? . Paddy Paul died ? .

215. Mary J. Harris (James Gilliam[7], Gideon[6], Lewis[5], David[4], William[3], William[2], Thomas[1]). Born on 24 Jan 1834 in Maury County, TN. Mary J. died on 15 Nov 1897; she was 63.

Information about the first marriage is from Whitley, *Marriages of Maury Co.* Information about the second marriage and daughter is from LDS.

On 12 Dec 1850 when Mary J. was 16, she first married John T. Dillehay. Born on 6 Oct 1824. John T. died on 3 Feb 1863; he was 38.

They had one child:

> **373** i. Sarah Reece (1851-1906)

On 16 Feb 1865 when Mary J. was 31, she second married Jefferson H. Brown. Born on 21 Nov 1809. Jefferson H. died on 7 Apr 1891; he was 81.

216. Martha Jane Harris (James Gilliam[7], Gideon[6], Lewis[5], David[4], William[3], William[2], Thomas[1]). Born on 9 Nov 1835 in Maury County, TN. Martha Jane died on 3 Nov 1915; she was 79.

Information about the marriages is from Porch, *Marriage Records, Marshall Co* On 25 Jan 1855 when Martha Jane was 19, she first married L. Crab Beaty, in Marshall County, TN. Born in 1827. L. Crab died in 1858; he was 31.

On 17 Jan 1861 when Martha Jane was 25, she second married Harris Dark. Born ? . Harris died ? .

217. Elizabeth Lindsey Harris (James Gilliam[7], Gideon[6], Lewis[5], David[4], William[3], William[2], Thomas[1]). Born on 21 Jul 1837 in Maury County, TN. Elizabeth Lindsey died in Marshall County, TN, on 20 Feb 1838; she was <1.

218. Gideon Lewis Harris (James Gilliam[7], Gideon[6], Lewis[5], David[4], William[3], William[2], Thomas[1]). Born on 11 Jan 1839 in Marshall County, TN. Gideon Lewis died in Perryville, KY, on 8 Oct 1862; he was 23.

219. John Hopkins Harris (James Gilliam[7], Gideon[6], Lewis[5], David[4], William[3], William[2], Thomas[1]). Born on 17 Jun 1840 in Marshall County, TN. John Hopkins died on 21 Jul 1847; he was 7.

220. Nancy Bennett Harris (James Gilliam[7], Gideon[6], Lewis[5], David[4], William[3], William[2], Thomas[1]). Born on 10 Dec 1841 in

Marshall County, TN. Nancy Bennett died in Marshall County, TN, on 26 Nov 1889; she was 47.

Information about the marriage is from Marshall Co. Website; information about the children is from Wayne Co., TN, Census 1880 and LDS.

On 7 Mar 1867 when Nancy Bennett was 25, she married Rufus Whitfield Kittrell, in Marshall County, TN. Born on 25 Sep 1841. Rufus Whitfield died on 7 Mar 1888; he was 46.

They had the following children:

374	i.	Mary Elizabeth (1868-1874)
375	ii.	George (1870-1888)
376	iii.	Katherine (1873-1947)
377	iv.	Addie M. (1875-1933)
378	v.	Frances Lillian (1885-1948)

221. Frances Caroline Harris (James Gilliam[7], Gideon[6], Lewis[5], David[4], William[3], William[2], Thomas[1]). Born on 18 Feb 1843 in Marshall County, TN. Frances Caroline died on 15 Mar 1919; she was 76.

Information about the marriage is from Porch, *Marriage Records, Marshall Co.*

On 3 Jun 1858 when Frances Caroline was 15, she married Calvin Dewit Ritchie, in Marshall County, TN. Born on 17 Sep 1836. Calvin Dewit died on 2 Dec 1921; he was 85.

222. Aurelia Ann Harris (James Gilliam[7], Gideon[6], Lewis[5], David[4], William[3], William[2], Thomas[1]). Born on 29 Jan 1845 in Marshall County, TN. Aurelia Ann died on 22 Mar 1919; she was 74.

Information about the marriage is from LDS.

On 12 Jun 1872 when Aurelia Ann was 27, she married Jasper Newton Peeler. Born on 14 Aug 1844. Jasper Newton died on 12 Jul 1920; he was 75.

223. James Clanton Harris (James Gilliam[7], Gideon[6], Lewis[5], David[4], William[3], William[2], Thomas[1]). Born on 12 Nov 1848 in Marshall County, TN. James Clanton died ? .

Information about the marriage is from WorldConnect; information about the sons is from Marshall Co., TN, Census 1880.

On 17 Dec 1873 when James Clanton was 25, he married Nancy Gibson. Born ca 1853 in Tennessee. Nancy died ? They had the following children:

379	i.	Edward Olley (1874-?)
380	ii.	James Virgil (1879-?)

224. Unnamed Harris (James Gilliam[7], Gideon[6], Lewis[5], David[4], William[3], William[2], Thomas[1]). Born on 14 May 1851 in Marshall County, TN. Unnamed died in Marshall County, TN, on 14 May 1851; she was <1.

225. Unnamed Harris (James Gilliam[7], Gideon[6], Lewis[5], David[4], William[3], William[2], Thomas[1]). Born on 4 May 1852 in Marshall County, TN. Unnamed died in Marshall County, TN, on 4 May 1852; she was <1.

226. William Thomas Harris (James Gilliam[7], Gideon[6], Lewis[5], David[4], William[3], William[2], Thomas[1]). Born on 2 Aug 1853 in Marshall County, TN. William Thomas died in Marshall County, TN, on 29 Aug 1913; he was 60.

Information about the marriages is from LDS; information about the children is from Marshall Co., TN, Census 1880 and 1910.

On 18 Nov 1874 when William Thomas was 21, he first married Martha Elizabeth Garrett, in Marshall County, TN. Born on 20 Apr 1854 in Marshall County, TN. Martha Elizabeth died in Marshall County, TN, on 21 Aug 1893; she was 39.

They had the following children:

> **381**   i.   William Lee (1875-1971)
>
> **382**   ii.   John Bryce (1880-1895)
>
> **383**   iii.   Gilliam Garrett (1885-1918)

On 15 May 1894 when William Thomas was 40, he second married Clarissa B. Hunter, in Marshall County, TN. Born on 15 Nov 1861 in Marshall County, TN. Clarissa B. died in Marshall County, TN, in Jul 1938; she was 76.

They had the following children:

> **384**   i.   Hunter Hill (1896-1981)

385	ii.	Thomas Earl (1898-1966)
386	iii.	Charley Robert (1900-1929)
387	iv.	Dovie Florene (1903-1982)

227. Robert Claiborne Harris (James Gilliam[7], Gideon[6], Lewis[5], David[4], William[3], William[2], Thomas[1]). Born on 24 Sep 1856 in Marshall County, TN. Robert Claiborne died on 17 Nov 1916; he was 60.

Information about the marriage is from LDS; information about the children is from Marshall Co., TN, Census 1900.

On 11 Oct 1880 when Robert Claiborne was 24, he married Mary Ann "Polly" Perry. Born on 20 Dec 1857. Mary Ann "Polly" died on 25 Feb 1929; she was 71.

They had the following children:

| **388** | i. | Lula May (1882-1931) |
| **389** | ii. | Homer T. (1885-1939) |

228. John Lindsey Harris (James Gilliam[7], Gideon[6], Lewis[5], David[4], William[3], William[2], Thomas[1]). Born on 16 Feb 1859 in Marshall County, TN. John Lindsey died ? .

Information about the marriage is from LDS; information about the children is from Maury Co., TN, Census 1910.

On 7 Mar 1886 when John Lindsey was 27, he married Roxanna Nora Phillips, in Tennessee. Born ca 1867 in Tennessee. Roxanna Nora died ? .

They had the following children:

       390   i.   James C. (ca1892-?)

       391   ii.   Thomas C. (ca1902-?)

       392   iii.   Joe Cletus (1906-1979)

229. David Tinsley Harris (James Gilliam[7], Gideon[6], Lewis[5], David[4], William[3], William[2], Thomas[1]). Born on 26 Dec 1860 in Marshall County, TN. David Tinsley died ? .

Information about the marriages is from LDS.

On 15 Oct 1889 when David Tinsley was 28, he first married Lula Lee Mayberry. Born ? . Lula Lee died ? .

On 11 Jun 1911 when David Tinsley was 50, he second married Zilla Ross Kirby. Born ? . Zilla Ross died ? .

230. James Lindsey Harris (Gideon Lindsey[7], Gideon[6], Lewis[5], David[4], William[3], William[2], Thomas[1]). Born on 5 Jan 1833 in McNairy County, TN. James Lindsey died on 17 Jun 1848; he was 15.

231. Martha Elizabeth Harris (Gideon Lindsey[7], Gideon[6], Lewis[5], David[4], William[3], William[2], Thomas[1]). Born on 3 Sep 1834 in McNairy County, TN. Martha Elizabeth died in Tennessee on 26 Jun 1926; she was 91.

Information about the marriage is from WorldConnect; information about the children is from McNairy Co., TN, Census 1870 and 1880.

Ca 1855 when Martha Elizabeth was 20, she married John Walker, in Tennessee. Born in 1827. John died on 1 May 1913; he was 86.

They had the following children:

 393   i.   James Thomas (1857-1912)

 394   ii.   Joseph Anthony (1859-1933)

 395   iii.   Mary Frances (1861-1933)

 396   iv.   John Gideon (1862-1894)

 397   v.   Mary F. (ca1865-?)

 398   vi.   Lucinda Catherine (1869-?)

 399   vii.   Mattie Ann Belle (1871-<1940)

232. Giles Claiborne Harris (Gideon Lindsey[7], Gideon[6], Lewis[5], David[4], William[3], William[2], Thomas[1]). Born on 1 Jul 1837 in McNairy County, TN. Giles Claiborne died in McNairy County, TN, on 25 Apr 1881; he was 43.

Information about the marriage and children is from the Sumner Co. website and McNairy Co., TN, Census 1870 and 1880.

On 8 Feb 1857 when Giles Claiborne was 19, he married Sarah Massengill, in McNairy County, TN. Born on 27 Oct 1841 in McNairy County, TN. Sarah died in Dunklin County, MO, on 26 Dec 1915; she was 74.

They had the following children:

400	i.	William Marion (1857-1941)
401	ii.	Gideon Simpson (1859-1919)
402	iii.	Mahalye Jane (1861-1943)
403	iv.	John Madison (1863-1951)
404	v.	Lucy Elizabeth (1865-1948)
405	vi.	Sarah Frances (1867-1963)
406	vii.	Amanda Catherine (1869-1944)
407	viii.	George Calvin (1872-1936)
408	ix.	Julia Kinnell (1877-1961)
409	x.	Jeptha Virgil (1879-1925)

233. David Thomas Harris (Gideon Lindsey[7], Gideon[6], Lewis[5], David[4], William[3], William[2], Thomas[1]). Born on 29 Jul 1839 in McNairy County, TN. David Thomas died in McNairy County, TN, on 9 Jul 1895; he was 55.

Information about the marriages and children is from LDS and McNairy Co., TN, Census 1880 and 1910.

On 9 Mar 1859 when David Thomas was 19, he first married Matilda Ann Parrish. Born on 3 Jan 1843 in McNairy County, TN. Matilda Ann died in McNairy County, TN, on 3 Mar 1873; she was 30.

They had the following children:

410   i.   Lucy Jane (1860-1959)

411   ii.   Florence Aurelia (1866-1866)

412   iii.   Consatie Frances (1868-1868)

413   iv.   James Marley (1870-1924)

On 2 Oct 1873 when David Thomas was 34, he second married Elizabeth Jane Lilly. Born on 12 May 1855. Elizabeth Jane died in McNairy County, TN, on 14 Sep 1949; she was 94.

They had the following children:

414   i.   Thomas Gideon (1874-?)

415   ii.   Clayborne Franklin (1876-1953)

416   iii.   William Tinsley (1877-1878)

417   iv.   Dorothy Lee (1880-1909)

418   v.   Bertie Lou (1883-1942)

419	vi.	Samuel Sneed (1886-1886)
420	vii.	Mittie Ophelia (1887-?)
421	viii.	Robert Andrew (1889-1954)
422	ix.	Ocie Bedford (1892-1967)
423	x.	John Blanchard (1893-?)

234. Mary Catherine "Cassie" Harris (Gideon Lindsey[7], Gideon[6], Lewis[5], David[4], William[3], William[2], Thomas[1]). Born on 31 Oct 1840 in McNairy County, TN. Mary Catherine "Cassie" died on 17 Feb 1898; she was 57.

Information about the marriage is from LDS; information about the children is from McNairy Co., TN, Census 1870 and 1880.

On 21 Mar 1859 when Mary Catherine "Cassie" was 18, she married Jesse Jordon Parrish, son of Jordon Parrish & Elizabeth ?, in McNairy County, TN. Born on 3 Jan 1839. Jesse Jordon died on 4 Aug 1887; he was 48.

They had the following children:

424	i.	James Clayborn (1859-?)
425	ii.	Cordie Crittenden (1861-1888)
426	iii.	Jordon Augustus (1863-1922)

427	iv.	Lucy Elizabeth (1865-1928)
428	v.	Cora Edna (1871-ca1958)
429	vi.	Willie Baxter (1873-1931)
430	vii.	Eber Nathaniel (1875-?)
431	viii.	Gilliam Harris (1878-1959)

235. Gideon Lindsey Harris Jr. (Gideon Lindsey[7], Gideon[6], Lewis[5], David[4], William[3], William[2], Thomas[1]). Born on 16 Mar 1843 in McNairy County, TN. Gideon Lindsey died in McNairy County, TN, on 5 May 1919; he was 76.

Information about the marriage is from WorldConnect; information about the children is from McNairy Co., TN, Census 1870-1900.

On 4 Apr 1867 when Gideon Lindsey was 24, he married Mary Jane Dallas, in McNairy County, TN. Born on 21 Mar 1847. Mary Jane died in McNairy County, TN, on 19 Mar 1910; she was 62.

They had the following children:

| **432** | i. | Lucy Almedia (1868-1950) |
| **433** | ii. | Lewis Gideon (1870-1961) |

434	iii.	Rebecca Elizabeth (1872-1955)
435	iv.	George Madison (1874-1887)
436	v.	Giles Furman (1885-1969)
437	vi.	May Augustus (1888-1965)

236. John Gardner Harris (Gideon Lindsey[7], Gideon[6], Lewis[5], David[4], William[3], William[2], Thomas[1]). Born on 10 Apr 1845 in McNairy County, TN. John Gardner died in McNairy County, TN, on 9 Feb 1846; he was <1.

237. Sarah Francis "Frankie" Harris (Gideon Lindsey[7], Gideon[6], Lewis[5], David[4], William[3], William[2], Thomas[1]). Born on 22 Mar 1847 in McNairy County, TN. Sarah Francis "Frankie" died in McNairy County, TN, on 4 Mar 1920; she was 72.

Information about the marriage is from WorldConnect; information about the children is from Clay Co., AR, Census 1880 and McNairy Co., TN, Census 1930.

On 18 Nov 1868 when Sarah Francis "Frankie" was 21, she married John Riley Pyron, in McNairy County, TN. Born on 12 Aug 1847 in McNairy County, TN. John Riley died in McNairy County, TN, on 21 Mar 1932; he was 84.

They had the following children:

438	i.	Gideon Lindsey (1869-1963)

439 ii. Sidney Augustus (1877-1918)

440 iii. Aurelia Aquilla (1879-1898)

441 iv. James Clayborne (1881-?)

238. William Ashley Harris (Gideon Lindsey[7], Gideon[6], Lewis[5], David[4], William[3], William[2], Thomas[1]). Born on 19 May 1849 in McNairy County, TN. William Ashley died in McNairy County, TN, on 12 Mar 1916; he was 66.

Information about the marriage is from LDS; information about the children is from McNairy Co., TN, Census 1870-1910.

On 18 Oct 1868 when William Ashley was 19, he married Sarah Agatha Littlefield, in McNairy County, TN. Born on 28 Oct 1849 in Tippah County, MS. Sarah Agatha died in McNairy County, TN, on 7 Feb 1940; she was 90.

They had the following children:

442 i. Lucy Artimus (1869-1965)

443 ii. James David (1871-1938)

444 iii. William Franklin (1873-1968)

445 iv. John Lindon (1875-1940)

446 v. Isam Gilliam (1879-1880)

447 vi. Albert Royal (1882-1949)

448 vii. Julius Andrew (1884-1974)

449 viii. Mary Percilla (1886-1972)

450 ix. Thurman Lindsey (1888-1982)

451 x. Bunyan Stephens (1890-1954)

239. Doctor Franklin "Docky" Harris (Gideon Lindsey[7], Gideon[6], Lewis[5], David[4], William[3], William[2], Thomas[1]). Born on 12 Dec 1853 in McNairy County, TN. Doctor Franklin "Docky" died in McNairy County, TN, on 7 Aug 1915; he was 61.

Information about the marriage is from WorldConnect; information about the children is from McNairy Co., TN, Census 1900 and 1910.

On 9 Jul 1874 when Doctor Franklin "Docky" was 20, he married Sarah Jane Duren, in McNairy County, TN. Born on 11 Feb 1859 in Tennessee. Sarah Jane died in McNairy County, TN, on 13 Nov 1934; she was 75.

They had the following children:

452	i.	Mannon Lindsey (1878-1962)
453	ii.	Robert Lee (1878-1956)
454	iii.	Tolbert Dalton (1880-1960)
455	iv.	Artemas Duren (1884-1902)
456	v.	Hubert Vernon (1886-1927)
457	vi.	Sarah Myrtle (1889-1979)
458	vii.	Arthur Cleatus (1892-?)

240. Marion A. Harris (Gideon Lindsey[7], Gideon[6], Lewis[5], David[4], William[3], William[2], Thomas[1]). Born on 22 Feb 1856 in McNairy County, TN. Marion A. died in McNairy County, TN, in 1873; she was 16.

241. Martha Jane "Mattie" Harris (Gideon Lindsey[7], Gideon[6], Lewis[5], David[4], William[3], William[2], Thomas[1]). Born on 10 Nov 1895 in McNairy County, TN. Martha Jane "Mattie" died in Fayette County, TN, in Jan 1978; she was 82.

Information about the husband is from WorldConnect; information about the children is from Hardeman Co., TN, Census 1920.

On 2 Oct 1910 when Martha Jane "Mattie" was 14, she married Joseph Oscar Houston, in Tennessee. Born on 19

Apr 1884 in Tennessee. Joseph Oscar died on 22 Sep 1956; he was 72.

They had the following children:

> **459**   i.   Lessie (ca1910-?)
>
> **460**   ii.   Talmage Ray (1912-1999)

242. Thomas Gideon Harris (Giles Claiborne[7], Gideon[6], Lewis[5], David[4], William[3], William[2], Thomas[1]). Born on 21 Apr 1839 in Sumner County, TN. Thomas Gideon died in Tennessee on 12 Aug 1932; he was 93. Buried in Pleasant Grove Methodist Cemetery, Sumner Co., TN.

Information about the first marriage is from WorldConnect; information about the second marriage is from LDS; information about the daughter is from Trousdale Co., TN, Census 1880. Apparently, Thomas and Naomi didn't live together very long. He is listed as a member of his father's household in Macon Co., TN, Census 1860, but she is not listed with this household. In 1880 she is a member of her mother's household in Trousdale Co.

In 1930 Thomas is an inmate of the Confederate Veterns' Home and Hospital (Davidson Co., TN, Census 1930).

On 16 Mar 1859 when Thomas Gideon was 19, he first married Naomi Carr. Born in 1839. Naomi died in Aug 1897; she was 58.

They had one child:

> **461**   i.   Alice (1860-1942)

Ca 1899 when Thomas Gideon was 59, he second married Mallie J. ?. Born on 22 Sep 1850. Mallie J. died on 21 Oct 1925; she was 75.

243. William Tinsley Harris (Giles Claiborne[7], Gideon[6], Lewis[5], David[4], William[3], William[2], Thomas[1]). Born on 21 Sep 1841 in Sumner County, TN. William Tinsley died in Sumner County, TN, on 20 Sep 1898; he was 56. Buried in Pleasant Grove Methodist Cemetery, Sumner Co., TN.

William T. moved with his parents to Macon Co., TN; then he moved to Robertson Co., TN, and eventually to Allen Co., KY (Sumner Co. Website). Information about the first marriage and daughters also from Sumner Co. Website. Information about the second marriage is from Allen Co., KY, Website.

On 25 Feb 1869 when William Tinsley was 27, he first married Amanda J. Jenkins, in Tennessee. Born ca 1842 in Tennessee. Amanda J. died on 15 Sep 1885; she was 43.

They had the following children:

> **462** i. Dolly Lucy Catherine (1874-?)
>
> **463** ii. Minnie Jane (1877-1971)

On 12 Feb 1888 when William Tinsley was 46, he second married Henrietta Ann Thomas, in Tennessee. Born on 18 Aug 1852. Henrietta Ann died ? .

244. Mary Harris (Giles Claiborne[7], Gideon[6], Lewis[5], David[4], William[3], William[2], Thomas[1]). Born ca 1845 in Sumner County, TN. Mary died bef 1860; she was 15.

Mary does not appear in the 1860 Census with Giles
Claiborne.

245. Robert Wiseman Harris (Giles Claiborne[7], Gideon[6],
Lewis[5], David[4], William[3], William[2], Thomas[1]). Born on 27
May 1847 in Sumner County, TN. Robert Wiseman died in
Macon County, TN, on 9 Sep 1915; he was 68. Buried in
Pleasant Grove Methodist Cemetery, Sumner Co., TN.

Information about the wife and children is from Sumner Co.,
TN, Census 1880-1900.

Robert Wiseman married Susan Elizabeth "Betty"
Robertson. Born on 27 Apr 1850 in Tennessee. Susan
Elizabeth "Betty" died on 17 Jan 1937; she was 86.

They had the following children:

464	i.	William T. (1871-1896)
465	ii.	Giles Bledsoe (1872-1951)
466	iii.	Sarah Tennie (1874-1915)
467	iv.	Mary C. (1877-1937)
468	v.	Mallie E. (1879-1959)
469	vi.	Mattie Anna (1881-1957)
470	vii.	Rice Odell (1883-1965)
471	viii.	Bessie N. (1885-?)

472	ix.	Maggie L. (1887-1960)
473	x.	James R. (1889-1900)
474	xi.	I. Effie (1891-?)

246. Martha Anna "Matt" Harris (Giles Claiborne[7], Gideon[6], Lewis[5], David[4], William[3], William[2], Thomas[1]). Born on 26 Feb 1849 in Macon County, TN. Martha Anna "Matt" died on 6 Jan 1927; she was 77. Buried in Old Union Cemetery, Warren County, KY.

Information about the marriages is from *Macon County History*; information about the children is from Allen Co., KY, Census 1880 and Warren Co., KY, Census 1900.

On 19 Feb 1871 when Martha Anna "Matt" was 21, she first married Charlie Lewis Pike, son of James Pike & Elizabeth Tooley. Born on 29 Jan 1851 in Tennessee. Charlie Lewis died in Kentucky on 26 Feb 1893; he was 42.

They had the following children:

475	i.	Clayborn (ca1872-?)
476	ii.	Mallie C. (ca1877-?)
477	iii.	Dary (ca1883-?)
478	iv.	Ally (ca1887-?)

On 24 Dec 1894 when Martha Anna "Matt" was 45, she second married William W. Pike, son of James Pike & Elizabeth Tooley, in Warren County, KY. Born on 3 Sep 1844. William W. died on 22 Dec 1898; he was 54.

On 15 Mar 1905 when Martha Anna "Matt" was 56, she third married Henry Martin Simmons. Born on 14 Oct 1840. Henry Martin died on 18 Apr 1922; he was 81.

247. John Sumpter Harris (Giles Claiborne[7], Gideon[6], Lewis[5], David[4], William[3], William[2], Thomas[1]). Born on 7 Jul 1852 in Macon County, TN. John Sumpter died on 27 Apr 1927; he was 74. Buried in Rocky Mound Cemetery, Macon Co., TN.

Information about the marriage and sons is from Macon Co. Census 1880 and 1900.

Ca 1877 when John Sumpter was 24, he married Jane Vibert. Born in Feb 1854 in Tennessee. Jane died on 20 Sep 1924; she was 70.

They had the following children:

479	i.	Henry H. (1878-1944)
480	ii.	Charlie W. (1880-1947)
481	iii.	James R. (1884-?)
482	iv.	Giles S. (1887-1955)

248. James Lindsey Harris (Giles Claiborne[7], Gideon[6], Lewis[5], David[4], William[3], William[2], Thomas[1]). Born on 6 Mar 1855 in Macon County, TN. James Lindsey died on 17 Mar 1904; he was 49.

Information about the marriage is from WorldConnect; information about the children is from Marshall Co., TN, Census 1900.

On 15 Nov 1885 when James Lindsey was 30, he married Martha Amanda Hill. Born on 20 Apr 1863. Martha Amanda died on 18 Jun 1899; she was 36.

They had the following children:

483	i.	Ethel C. (1887-?)
484	ii.	James C. (1888-?)
485	iii.	Fletch (1890-?)
486	iv.	Lonzy (1891-?)
487	v.	Charley (1893-?)

249. Giles Rice Harris (Giles Claiborne[7], Gideon[6], Lewis[5], David[4], William[3], William[2], Thomas[1]). Born on 28 Dec 1858 in Macon County, TN. Giles Rice died in Sumner County, TN, on 8 Jul 1882; he was 23.

250. Malvina "Mallie" C. Harris (Giles Claiborne[7], Gideon[6], Lewis[5], David[4], William[3], William[2], Thomas[1]). Born on 28 May 1861 in Sumner County, TN. Malvina "Mallie" C. died in Macon County, TN, on 24 Jan 1894; she was 32.

251. David Baxter Harris (Giles Claiborne[7], Gideon[6], Lewis[5], David[4], William[3], William[2], Thomas[1]). Born on 28 Jun 1863 in Macon County, TN. David Baxter died on 23 Jul 1951; he was 88.

Information about the marriages and children of the first wife is from WorldConnect; information about the children of the second wife is from Lawrence Co., TN, Census 1910.

In Sep 1880 when David Baxter was 17, he first married Addie May Gammon. Born in 1859. Addie May died on 13 Oct 1888; she was 29.

They had the following children:

488	i.	Honor Delpha
489	ii.	William Carnath
490	iii.	Glennon Porter

In Jun 1890 when David Baxter was 26, he second married Nannie Tennison Weaver. Born on 16 Apr 1873. Nannie Tennison died on 8 Mar 1916; she was 42.

They had the following children:

491	i.	Carl O. (ca1891-?)
492	ii.	Lillie N. (ca1894-?)
493	iii.	Dennie L. (ca1898-?)
494	iv.	Claudia M. (ca1904-?)

On 8 Jan 1917 when David Baxter was 53, he third married Ella Hines. Born on 2 Dec 1874. Ella died ? .

252. Joseph Carrol Harris (Giles Claiborne[7], Gideon[6], Lewis[5], David[4], William[3], William[2], Thomas[1]). Born on 12 Sep 1866 in Tennessee. Joseph Carrol died on 2 Jan 1928; he was 61. Buried in Pleasant Grove Methodist Cemetery, Sumner Co., TN.

Information about the marriage is from WorldConnect; information about the daughter is from Sumner Co., TN, Census 1910. Maggie's father, Mark Perry, is a member of the household in 1910.

On 28 Dec 1893 when Joseph Carrol was 27, he married Maggie May Perry. Born on 12 Feb 1878. Maggie May died on 4 Nov 1951; she was 73.

They had one child:

> **495**   i.   Minnie A. (ca1904-?)

253. Margaret Elizabeth "Maggie" Harris (John Gardner[7], Gideon[6], Lewis[5], David[4], William[3], William[2], Thomas[1]). Born on 14 Sep 1842 in Marshall County, TN. Margaret Elizabeth "Maggie" died in Lawrence County, TN, on 26 Dec 1916; she was 74.

Information about the marriage is from W. Lee Harris; information about the children is from Lewis Co., TN, Census 1880.

On 11 Jan 1866 when Margaret Elizabeth "Maggie" was 23, she married William Henry Rone, in Marshall County, TN. Born on 16 Jun 1842. William Henry died in Lawrence County, TN, on 30 Dec 1872; he was 30.

They had the following children:

> **496**   i.   Martha J. (1866-1939)
>
> **497**   ii.   George R. (1868-1935)
>
> **498**   iii.   John H. (1870-1925)
>
> **499**   iv.   William H. (1872-1957)

254. Amanda Jane Baxter (Sarah Giles Harris[7], Gideon[6], Lewis[5], David[4], William[3], William[2], Thomas[1]). Born on 12 Jul 1847 in

Marshall County, TN. Amanda Jane died on 9 May 1899; she was 51.

Information about the husband is from W. Lee Harris.

In Mar 1863 when Amanda Jane was 15, she married John Rambo, son of Francis K. Rambo & Mary B. Hardin, in Marshall County, TN. Born in 1842 in Marshall County, TN. John died in 1911; he was 69.

255. William H. Baxter (Martha Jane Harris[7], Gideon[6], Lewis[5], David[4], William[3], William[2], Thomas[1]). Born on 6 Jun 1854 in Marshall County, TN. William H. died on 21 Jun 1930; he was 76.

256. James N. Baxter (Martha Jane Harris[7], Gideon[6], Lewis[5], David[4], William[3], William[2], Thomas[1]). Born on 22 Dec 1857 in Marshall County, TN. James N. died on 14 Apr 1937; he was 79.

257. Robert G. Baxter (Martha Jane Harris[7], Gideon[6], Lewis[5], David[4], William[3], William[2], Thomas[1]). Born on 25 Oct 1860 in Marshall County, TN. Robert G. died on 3 Nov 1931; he was 71.

258. Montgomery H. Baxter (Martha Jane Harris[7], Gideon[6], Lewis[5], David[4], William[3], William[2], Thomas[1]). Born on 24 May 1863 in Marshall County, TN. Montgomery H. died in Marshall County, TN, on 19 Sep 1880; he was 17.

259. Edmond S. Baxter (Martha Jane Harris[7], Gideon[6], Lewis[5], David[4], William[3], William[2], Thomas[1]). Born on 22 Dec 1865 in Marshall County, TN. Edmond S. died on 10 Nov 1955; he was 89.

260. John F. Baxter (Martha Jane Harris[7], Gideon[6], Lewis[5], David[4], William[3], William[2], Thomas[1]). Born on 9 Dec 1868 in Marshall County, TN. John F. died on 31 Jul 1897; he was 28.

261. Martha N. Baxter (Martha Jane Harris[7], Gideon[6], Lewis[5], David[4], William[3], William[2], Thomas[1]). Born on 29 Sep 1870 in Marshall County, TN. Martha N. died on 31 Jul 1935; she was 64

262. David Lawson Harris (William Lindsey[7], David[6], Lewis[5], David[4], William[3], William[2], Thomas[1]). Born on 21 Jan 1845 in Marshall County, TN. David Lawson died in Tennessee on 13 Feb 1916; he was 71.

Information about the marriage is from WorldConnect; information about the children is from Marshall Co., TN, Census 1880 and 1900.

On 5 Oct 1871 when David Lawson was 26, he married Mildred Nancy Tidwell, in Marshall County, TN. Born on 14 Jan 1852. Mildred Nancy died on 18 Oct 1934; she was 82.

They had the following children:

500	i.	Wiley A. (1872-1921)
501	ii.	Gertrude V. (1874-1949)
502	iii.	Riggs Tidwell (1876-1936)
503	iv.	Jesse Reed (1883-1953)

263. Sarah Jane Harris (William Lindsey[7], David[6], Lewis[5], David[4], William[3], William[2], Thomas[1]). Born in 1846 in Marshall County, TN. Sarah Jane died in 1923; she was 77.

Information about the marriage and children is from Porch, *Marriage Records, Marshall Co.*

On 4 May 1864 when Sarah Jane was 18, she married Murdock McKenzie Malone, in Marshall County, TN. Born on 24 Oct 1840 in Marshall County, TN. Murdock McKenzie died on 14 Jun 1903; he was 62.

They had the following children:

> **504** i. Martha Ann "Mattie" (1865-1923)
>
> **505** ii. Edgar Bruce (1874-1944)

264. James Patterson Harris (William Lindsey[7], David[6], Lewis[5], David[4], William[3], William[2], Thomas[1]). Born on 17 May 1848 in Marshall County, TN. James Patterson died on 13 Apr 1922; he was 73.

Information about the marriage is from LDS; information about the sons is from Marshall Co., TN, Census 1900. Lewis's wife is also a member of the household in 1900.

On 22 Nov 1871 when James Patterson was 23, he married Sarah Reece Dillehay (373), daughter of John T. Dillehay & Mary J. Harris (215), in Marshall County, TN. Born on 28 Sep 1851 in Marshall County, TN. Sarah Reece died on 22 Jun 1906; she was 54.

They had the following children:

| 506 | i. | Lewis J. (1873-1967) |
| 507 | ii. | J. Fount (1883-1948) |

265. Mary Katherine Harris (William Lindsey[7], David[6], Lewis[5], David[4], William[3], William[2], Thomas[1]). Born on 26 Apr 1850 in Marshall County, TN. Mary Katherine died on 17 Nov 1933; she was 83.

Information about the marriage is from LDS; information about the children is from Marshall Co., TN, Census 1880 and 1920. James and Mary Katherine apparently divorced before 1900 (Marshall Co., TN, Census 1900).

On 25 Oct 1871 when Mary Katherine was 21, she married James Theodore Cheatham, in Marshall County, TN. Born on 11 Jul 1849 in Marshall County, TN. James Theodore died on 27 Nov 1924; he was 75.

They had the following children:

508	i.	Annes Edith (1872-1936)
509	ii.	William Thomas (1874-1935)
510	iii.	Luther M. (1878-1958)
511	iv.	Mary Ora (1886-1956)

266. Elizabeth Annie Harris (William Lindsey[7], David[6], Lewis[5], David[4], William[3], William[2], Thomas[1]). Born on 19 Oct 1858 in Marshall County, TN. Elizabeth Annie died on 17 Mar 1939; she was 80.

Information about the marriage and children is from
WorldConnect and Marshall Co., TN, Census 1910.

On 8 Nov 1881 when Elizabeth Annie was 23, she married
Hampton Humphrey Liggett, son of John C. Liggett & Sarah
E. ?. Born on 11 Jun 1856 in Marshall County, TN. Hampton
Humphrey died on 18 Oct 1888; he was 32.

They had the following children:

512   i.   Lelia Mai (1882-1967)

513   ii.   Sarah Vashti (1883-
1967)

514   iii.   Harris Claiborn (1885-
1981)

515   iv.   Mary Ethel (1886-
1892)

516   v.   Ivey Hampton (1888-
1978)

---

267. Robert Harris (Robert Giles[8], Giles Turner[7], Edmond[6], Giles[5], David[4], William[3], William[2], Thomas[1]). Born ca 1863 in Tennessee. Robert died ? .

268. Edmund Harris (Robert Giles[8], Giles Turner[7], Edmond[6], Giles[5], David[4], William[3], William[2], Thomas[1]). Born ca 1865 in Tennessee. Edmund died ? .

269. Guy Harris (Robert Giles[8], Giles Turner[7], Edmond[6], Giles[5], David[4], William[3], William[2], Thomas[1]). Born ca 1867 in Tennessee. Guy died ? .

270. Kate Harris (Robert Giles[8], Giles Turner[7], Edmond[6], Giles[5], David[4], William[3], William[2], Thomas[1]). Born ca 1870 in Tennessee. Kate died ? .

271. Hettie Harris (Robert Giles[8], Giles Turner[7], Edmond[6], Giles[5], David[4], William[3], William[2], Thomas[1]). Born ca 1872 in Tennessee. Hettie died ? .

272. Andrew Curran Harris (Robert Giles[8], Giles Turner[7], Edmond[6], Giles[5], David[4], William[3], William[2], Thomas[1]). Born on 7 Sep 1876. Andrew Curran died on 7 Aug 1958; he was 81.

Information about the wife and son is from Maury Co. Cemetery Records (Website).

Andrew Curran married Pearl Joyce, daughter of John Stammer Joyce & Frances Ezell. Born on 17 Aug 1892. Pearl died on 17 May 1981; she was 88.

They had one child:

        517   i.   John Joyce (1915-1981)

273. Clifford Frierson Harris (Robert Giles[8], Giles Turner[7], Edmond[6], Giles[5], David[4], William[3], William[2], Thomas[1]). Born on 16 Jul 1878. Clifford Frierson died on 31 Mar 1933; he was 54.

Information about the wife is from Maury Co. Cemetery Records (Website).

Clifford Frierson married Leia Hight. Born on 19 Apr 1879. Leia died ? .

274. Joseph Harris (Robert Giles[8], Giles Turner[7], Edmond[6], Giles[5], David[4], William[3], William[2], Thomas[1]). Born ca 1879. Joseph died ? .

275. James Giles Moore (Rowena Harris[8], Giles Turner[7], Edmond[6], Giles[5], David[4], William[3], William[2], Thomas[1]). Born on 13 Feb 1859. James Giles died on 24 May 1928; he was 69.

276. Robert Nathaniel Moore (Rowena Harris[8], Giles Turner[7], Edmond[6], Giles[5], David[4], William[3], William[2], Thomas[1]). Born on 1 Oct 1861. Robert Nathaniel died on 12 Jul 1939; he was 77.

277. Katherine Binford (Mary Robertson "Molly" Harris[8], Giles[7], Claiborne[6], Giles[5], David[4], William[3], William[2], Thomas[1]). Born ? . Katherine died ? .

278. Frederick Harris Frayser (Sarah Catherine Harris[8], Giles[7], Claiborne[6], Giles[5], David[4], William[3], William[2], Thomas[1]). Born on 2 Jun 1864 in Virginia. Frederick Harris died ? .

279. Judith Bransford Frayser (Sarah Catherine Harris[8], Giles[7], Claiborne[6], Giles[5], David[4], William[3], William[2], Thomas[1]). Born on 9 Feb 1866 in Virginia. Judith Bransford died ? .

280. Virginia Frayser (Sarah Catherine Harris[8], Giles[7], Claiborne[6], Giles[5], David[4], William[3], William[2], Thomas[1]). Born on 3 May 1867. Virginia died bef 1870; she was 2.

Virginia is not listed in the 1870 Census.

281. Mary Susan Frayser (Sarah Catherine Harris[8], Giles[7], Claiborne[6], Giles[5], David[4], William[3], William[2], Thomas[1]). Born on 24 Feb 1869 in Kentucky. Mary Susan died ? .

282. Thomas Hatcher Frayser Jr. (Sarah Catherine Harris[8], Giles[7], Claiborne[6], Giles[5], David[4], William[3], William[2], Thomas[1]). Born on 10 Nov 1870. Thomas Hatcher died ? .

283. Sarah Catherine Frayser (Sarah Catherine Harris[8], Giles[7], Claiborne[6], Giles[5], David[4], William[3], William[2], Thomas[1]). Born on 19 Nov 1872. Sarah Catherine died ? .

284. Jessamine Frayser (Sarah Catherine Harris[8], Giles[7], Claiborne[6], Giles[5], David[4], William[3], William[2], Thomas[1]). Born on 29 Sep 1874. Jessamine died ? .

285. William Frayser (Sarah Catherine Harris[8], Giles[7], Claiborne[6], Giles[5], David[4], William[3], William[2], Thomas[1]). Born on 3 Oct 1876. William died ? .

286. Giles Harris Frayser (Sarah Catherine Harris[8], Giles[7], Claiborne[6], Giles[5], David[4], William[3], William[2], Thomas[1]). Born on 28 Feb 1878. Giles Harris died ? .

287. Martha Bransford Frayser (Sarah Catherine Harris[8], Giles[7], Claiborne[6], Giles[5], David[4], William[3], William[2], Thomas[1]). Born on 12 Apr 1880. Martha Bransford died ? .

288. Sidney Anderson Frayser (Sarah Catherine Harris[8], Giles[7], Claiborne[6], Giles[5], David[4], William[3], William[2], Thomas[1]). Born on 11 Mar 1883. Sidney Anderson died ? .

289. Mary Ann Anderson (Susan Elizabeth Harris[8], Giles[7], Claiborne[6], Giles[5], David[4], William[3], William[2], Thomas[1]). Born on 11 Feb 1868. Mary Ann died on 16 Sep 1932; she was 64.

290. Patty Bransford Anderson (Susan Elizabeth Harris[8], Giles[7], Claiborne[6], Giles[5], David[4], William[3], William[2], Thomas[1]). Born on 30 Sep 1871. Patty Bransford died in Washington, DC, on 9 Mar 1948; she was 76.

291. Sue Harris Anderson (Susan Elizabeth Harris[8], Giles[7], Claiborne[6], Giles[5], David[4], William[3], William[2], Thomas[1]). Born on 28 Feb 1874. Sue Harris died in May 1922; she was 48.

292. Helen M. Harris (Tandy[8], John Claiborn[7], Claiborne[6], Giles[5], David[4], William[3], William[2], Thomas[1]). Born on 22 Feb 1879 in Virginia. Helen M. died on 8 Feb 1960; she was 80.

Information about the marriage is from WorldConnect; information about the children is from Alleghania Co., VA, Census 1920.

On 19 Feb 1899 when Helen M. was 19, she married Lewis Mason Kern, in Virginia. Born on 8 Dec 1870 in Virginia. Lewis Mason died on 13 Sep 1947; he was 76.

They had the following children:

> **518**   i.   Albert L. (1900-1963)

519	ii.	William M. (1903-1963)
520	iii.	Marvin H. (1906-1978)
521	iv.	Fara E. (1911-?)
522	v.	Verna A. (1915-1988)
523	vi.	John T. (1919-?)

293. Roberta Lee Harris (Tandy[8], John Claiborn[7], Claiborne[6], Giles[5], David[4], William[3], William[2], Thomas[1]). Born on 17 Nov 1880 in Virginia. Roberta Lee died ? .

Information about the marriage is from WorldConnect.

In 1901 when Roberta Lee was 20, she married James W. Burge, son of William Fletcher Burge & Emily F. Coleman, in Virginia. Born in 1881 in Appomattox County, VA. James W. died in 1937; he was 56.

294. William B. Harris (Tandy[8], John Claiborn[7], Claiborne[6], Giles[5], David[4], William[3], William[2], Thomas[1]). Born on 26 Jan 1882 in Virginia. William B. died in Lynchburg, VA, in May 1972; he was 90.

Information about the wife is from WorldConnect.

William B. married Ruby Smith. Born ? in Virginia. Ruby died ? .

295. Tandy D. Harris (Tandy[8], John Claiborn[7], Claiborne[6], Giles[5], David[4], William[3], William[2], Thomas[1]). Born on 31 May 1884 in Virginia. Tandy D. died on 23 Sep 1962; he was 78.

Information about the marriage and second wife is from WorldConnect.

In 1929 when Tandy D. was 44, he first married Anna Louise Ferguson, daughter of Allan Blanchard Ferguson & Mattie Ann Coleman, in Virginia. Born on 7 Jun 1905 in Virginia. Anna Louise died ? .

Tandy D. second married Edna Burge. Born ? . Edna died ? .

296. Hattie L. Harris (Tandy[8], John Claiborn[7], Claiborne[6], Giles[5], David[4], William[3], William[2], Thomas[1]). Born on 6 Oct 1887 in Virginia. Hattie L. died ? .

Information about the husband is from WorldConnect.

Hattie L. married Jacob Kern. Born ? in Virginia. Jacob died ? .

297. Walter E. Harris (Tandy[8], John Claiborn[7], Claiborne[6], Giles[5], David[4], William[3], William[2], Thomas[1]). Born on 1 Nov 1890 in Virginia. Walter E. died in Clifton Forge, VA, in Mar 1971; he was 80.

Information about the wife is from WorldConnect.

Walter E. married Etta Gooding. Born ? . Etta died ? .

298. Lillie M. Harris (Tandy[8], John Claiborn[7], Claiborne[6], Giles[5], David[4], William[3], William[2], Thomas[1]). Born on 1 Nov 1890 in Virginia. Lillie M. died ? .

Information about the marriage is from WorldConnect.

In 1911 when Lillie M. was 20, she married Charles Mays, in Virginia. Born ca 1886 in Virginia. Charles died ? .

299. Susie L. Harris (Tandy[8], John Claiborn[7], Claiborne[6], Giles[5], David[4], William[3], William[2], Thomas[1]). Born on 25 Jan 1896 in Virginia. Susie L. died ? .

Information about the husband is from WorldConnect.

Susie L. married Burleigh Chenault. Born ? in Virginia. Burleigh died ? .

300. Esther R. Harris (Tandy[8], John Claiborn[7], Claiborne[6], Giles[5], David[4], William[3], William[2], Thomas[1]). Born on 10 Nov 1898 in Virginia. Esther R. died ? .

301. Dille Harris (Tandy[8], John Claiborn[7], Claiborne[6], Giles[5], David[4], William[3], William[2], Thomas[1]). Born on 25 Apr 1902 in Virginia. Dille died ? .

302. Caliborne Caldwell (Mary Constance Harris[8], Edmond[7], Claiborne[6], Giles[5], David[4], William[3], William[2], Thomas[1]). Born ? . Caliborne died ? .

303. Aurelia Caldwell (Mary Constance Harris[8], Edmond[7], Claiborne[6], Giles[5], David[4], William[3], William[2], Thomas[1]). Born ? . Aurelia died ? .

304. Constance Caldwell (Mary Constance Harris[8], Edmond[7], Claiborne[6], Giles[5], David[4], William[3], William[2], Thomas[1]). Born ? . Constance died ? .

305. William Christopher Caldwell (Mary Constance Harris[8], Edmond[7], Claiborne[6], Giles[5], David[4], William[3], William[2], Thomas[1]). Born ? . William Christopher died ? .

306. E. C. Harris (Philip Watkins[8], Ammon[7], Obediah[6], Giles[5], David[4], William[3], William[2], Thomas[1]). Born ca 1871 in Saline County, MO. E. C. died ? .

307. R. A. Harris (Philip Watkins[8], Ammon[7], Obediah[6], Giles[5], David[4], William[3], William[2], Thomas[1]). Born ca 1872 in Saline County, MO. R. A. died ? .

308. P. H. Harris (Philip Watkins[8], Ammon[7], Obediah[6], Giles[5], David[4], William[3], William[2], Thomas[1]). Born ca 1874 in Saline County, MO. P. H. died ? .

309. E. W. Harris (Philip Watkins[8], Ammon[7], Obediah[6], Giles[5], David[4], William[3], William[2], Thomas[1]). Born ca 1876 in Saline County, MO. E. W. died ? .

310. T. J. Harris (Philip Watkins[8], Ammon[7], Obediah[6], Giles[5], David[4], William[3], William[2], Thomas[1]). Born ca 1877 in Saline County, MO. T. J. died ? .

311. L. W. Harris (Philip Watkins[8], Ammon[7], Obediah[6], Giles[5], David[4], William[3], William[2], Thomas[1]). Born in 1880 in Saline County, MO. L. W. died ? .

312. John B. Erwin (Josephine Harris[8], Ammon[7], Obediah[6], Giles[5], David[4], William[3], William[2], Thomas[1]). Born on 31 Dec 1872 in Saline County, MO. John B. died in Clinton County, MO, on 10 May 1957; he was 84.

313. James R. Erwin (Josephine Harris[8], Ammon[7], Obediah[6], Giles[5], David[4], William[3], William[2], Thomas[1]). Born on 28 Oct 1874 in Saline County, MO. James R. died in Saline County, MO, on 19 Dec 1912; he was 38.

314. Susan V. Erwin (Josephine Harris[8], Ammon[7], Obediah[6], Giles[5], David[4], William[3], William[2], Thomas[1]). Born on 2 Aug 1877 in Saline County, MO. Susan V. died in Clinton County, MO, on 30 Apr 1964; she was 86.

315. Lena Erwin (Josephine Harris[8], Ammon[7], Obediah[6], Giles[5], David[4], William[3], William[2], Thomas[1]). Born on 3 Oct 1879 in Saline County, MO. Lena died in Clinton County, MO, on 22 Aug 1956; she was 76.

316. Lillie Erwin (Josephine Harris[8], Ammon[7], Obediah[6], Giles[5], David[4], William[3], William[2], Thomas[1]). Born on 24 Mar 1882 in Saline County, MO. Lillie died in Clinton County, MO, on 27 Oct 1947; she was 65.

317. Margaret V. Erwin (Josephine Harris[8], Ammon[7], Obediah[6], Giles[5], David[4], William[3], William[2], Thomas[1]). Born on 19 Sep 1884 in Saline County, MO. Margaret V. died in Jackson County, MO, on 23 Mar 1964; she was 79.

318. Margaret L. Singleton (Mary Elizabeth Harris[8], Ammon[7], Obediah[6], Giles[5], David[4], William[3], William[2], Thomas[1]). Born ca 1869 in Saline County, MO. Margaret L. died ? .

319. Elizabeth J. Singleton (Mary Elizabeth Harris[8], Ammon[7], Obediah[6], Giles[5], David[4], William[3], William[2], Thomas[1]). Born ca 1873 in Missouri. Elizabeth J. died ? .

320. Georgiana Singleton (Mary Elizabeth Harris[8], Ammon[7], Obediah[6], Giles[5], David[4], William[3], William[2], Thomas[1]). Born ca 1875 in Missouri. Georgiana died ? .

321. Philip A. Singleton (Mary Elizabeth Harris[8], Ammon[7], Obediah[6], Giles[5], David[4], William[3], William[2], Thomas[1]). Born ca 1877 in Missouri. Philip A. died ? .

322. Edmond M. Singleton (Mary Elizabeth Harris[8], Ammon[7], Obediah[6], Giles[5], David[4], William[3], William[2], Thomas[1]). Born ca 1879 in Missouri. Edmond M. died ? .

323. Jasper Harris (Giles Ward[8], Obadiah[7], Giles[6], Lewis[5], David[4], William[3], William[2], Thomas[1]). Born ca 1865 in Georgia. Jasper died ? .

324. Elizabeth Harris (Giles Ward[8], Obadiah[7], Giles[6], Lewis[5], David[4], William[3], William[2], Thomas[1]). Born ca 1867 in Georgia. Elizabeth died ? .

325. Arthur Giles Harris (Giles Ward[8], Obadiah[7], Giles[6], Lewis[5], David[4], William[3], William[2], Thomas[1]). Born on 22 Nov 1869 in Rutherford County, TN. Arthur Giles died in Stephens County, TX, on 21 Jul 1944; he was 74.

Information about the marriage is from WorldConnect.

On 12 May 1901 when Arthur Giles was 31, he married Nora Gertrude Pack, in Robertson County, TN. Born ? in Marion County, TN. Nora Gertrude died on 9 Mar 1971 in Stephens County, TX.

326. Emma Frances Harris (William[8], William Austin[7], Giles[6], Lewis[5], David[4], William[3], William[2], Thomas[1]). Born in 1861 in Alabama. Emma Frances died in Alabama in 1951; she was 90.

327. Dayton Harris (Austin Dabney[8], William Austin[7], Giles[6], Lewis[5], David[4], William[3], William[2], Thomas[1]). Born ca 1860 in Louisiana. Dayton died ? .

328. Charlie Harris (Austin Dabney[8], William Austin[7], Giles[6], Lewis[5], David[4], William[3], William[2], Thomas[1]). Born ca 1863 in Louisiana. Charlie died ? .

329. Austin Harris (Austin Dabney[8], William Austin[7], Giles[6], Lewis[5], David[4], William[3], William[2], Thomas[1]). Born ca 1867 in Louisiana. Austin died ? .

330. Lee Harris (Austin Dabney[8], William Austin[7], Giles[6], Lewis[5], David[4], William[3], William[2], Thomas[1]). Born ca 1869 in Louisiana. Lee died ? .

331. Annie Harris (Austin Dabney[8], William Austin[7], Giles[6], Lewis[5], David[4], William[3], William[2], Thomas[1]). Born ca 1872 in Louisiana. Annie died ? .

332. Claude M. Harris (Austin Dabney[8], William Austin[7], Giles[6], Lewis[5], David[4], William[3], William[2], Thomas[1]). Born in 1874 in Louisiana. Claude M. died ? .

Information about the marriage is from LDS; information about the children is from Grant Co., LA, Census 1910. Claude's sister, Bettie, is a member of the household in 1910.

On 10 Mar 1900 when Claude M. was 26, he married Daisy Dean Wilson, in Louisiana. Born ca 1881 in Louisiana. Daisy Dean died ? .

They had the following children:

524	i.	Claude M. (ca1908-?)
525	ii.	Reginald W. (ca1901-?)
526	iii.	Aubyn (ca1905-?)

333. Ralph Harris (Austin Dabney[8], William Austin[7], Giles[6], Lewis[5], David[4], William[3], William[2], Thomas[1]). Born ca 1877 in Louisiana. Ralph died ? .

334. Angeline Allen (Sarah B. Harris[8], Richard W.[7], John[6], Lewis[5], David[4], William[3], William[2], Thomas[1]). Born ? . Angeline died ? .

335. Richard Allen (Sarah B. Harris[8], Richard W.[7], John[6], Lewis[5], David[4], William[3], William[2], Thomas[1]). Born ? . Richard died ? .

336. William Allen (Sarah B. Harris[8], Richard W.[7], John[6], Lewis[5], David[4], William[3], William[2], Thomas[1]). Born ? . William died ? .

337. Ann Elizabeth Allen (Sarah B. Harris[8], Richard W.[7], John[6], Lewis[5], David[4], William[3], William[2], Thomas[1]). Born ? . Ann Elizabeth died ? .

338. David Ashley Harris (Gideon Lewis[8], David Rice[7], Gideon[6], Lewis[5], David[4], William[3], William[2], Thomas[1]). Born on 30 Dec 1862. David Ashley died on 26 Oct 1901; he was 38.

339. Sarah Martha "Mattie" Harris (Gideon Lewis[8], David Rice[7], Gideon[6], Lewis[5], David[4], William[3], William[2], Thomas[1]). Born in 1869 in Tennessee. Sarah Martha "Mattie" died ? .

Information about the marriage is from WorldConnect; information about the children is from Marion Co., FL, Census 1900. Mattie's mother is a member of the household in 1900.

On 4 Mar 1886 when Sarah Martha "Mattie" was 17, she married John Sullivan McFall. Born on 3 Nov 1855 in Florida. John Sullivan died on 4 Dec 1936; he was 81.

They had the following children:

> **527**   i.   Janie Clara (1887-1950)

528   ii.   John Harold (1890-?)

529   iii.   Andrew Norris (1892-
1928)

530   iv.   Robert Trice (1896-?)

340. Frances Eugenia Journey (Sarah Harris[8], David Rice[7], Gideon[6], Lewis[5], David[4], William[3], William[2], Thomas[1]). Born on 19 May 1858. Frances Eugenia died on 29 Jul 1901; she was 43.

Information about the husbands is from WorldConnect.

Frances Eugenia first married Thomas Clinton Kelly. Born in 1857. Thomas Clinton died on 15 Apr 1877; he was 20.

On 11 Sep 1879 when Frances Eugenia was 21, she second married Daniel Starbuck. Born on 26 Jul 1850. Daniel died on 12 May 1906; he was 55.

341. Mary L. Magruder Dodson (Martha Jane Harris[8], David Rice[7], Gideon[6], Lewis[5], David[4], William[3], William[2], Thomas[1]). Born on 11 Nov 1865 in Perry County, TN. Mary L. Magruder died in Nashville, TN, on 20 Aug 1950; she was 84.

Information about the marriage is from WorldConnect.

On 18 Feb 1883 when Mary L. Magruder was 17, she married George Smith Britt. Born on 8 Oct 1863. George Smith died on 2 Sep 1952; he was 88.

342. Addie Jane Dodson (Martha Jane Harris[8], David Rice[7], Gideon[6], Lewis[5], David[4], William[3], William[2], Thomas[1]). Born on 1 May 1868 in Perry County, TN. Addie Jane died on 27 Sep 1893; she was 25.

Information about the marriage is from WorldConnect.

On 8 Aug 1886 when Addie Jane was 18, she married James Morgan Kittrell. Born on 1 Jul 1864. James Morgan died on 12 Oct 1907; he was 43.

343. Martha Willie Dodson (Martha Jane Harris[8], David Rice[7], Gideon[6], Lewis[5], David[4], William[3], William[2], Thomas[1]). Born on 29 Dec 1870. Martha Willie died on 30 Apr 1933; she was 62.

Information about the marriage is from WorldConnect.

On 12 Mar 1892 when Martha Willie was 21, she married John Thomas Sheffield. Born on 3 Feb 1871. John Thomas died on 31 Jan 1909; he was 37.

344. James Ashley Dodson (Martha Jane Harris[8], David Rice[7], Gideon[6], Lewis[5], David[4], William[3], William[2], Thomas[1]). Born on 18 Oct 1875. James Ashley died on 3 Feb 1967; he was 91.

Information about the marriage is from WorldConnect.

On 14 Jul 1898 when James Ashley was 22, he married Eugenia Malenia Beard. Born on 21 Mar 1874. Eugenia Malenia died on 25 Apr 1944; she was 70.

345. Flora Newstate Dodson (Martha Jane Harris[8], David Rice[7], Gideon[6], Lewis[5], David[4], William[3], William[2], Thomas[1]). Born on 1 May 1878. Flora Newstate died aft 1956; she was 77.

Information about the marriage is from WorldConnect.

On 16 Nov 1899 when Flora Newstate was 21, she married Pleas L. Richardson. Born on 14 Jul 1876. Pleas L. died ? .

346. Mary Byron Dodson (Martha Jane Harris[8], David Rice[7], Gideon[6], Lewis[5], David[4], William[3], William[2], Thomas[1]). Born on 19 Dec 1880. Mary Byron died ? .

Information about the marriage is from WorldConnect.

On 6 Aug 1899 when Mary Byron was 18, she married Fritz Becker Emmerling. Born on 16 Mar 1875. Fritz Becker died on 30 Jul 1903; he was 28.

347. Augusta Cleveland Dodson (Martha Jane Harris[8], David Rice[7], Gideon[6], Lewis[5], David[4], William[3], William[2], Thomas[1]). Born on 24 Dec 1883. Augusta Cleveland died aft 1956; she was 72.

Information about the husband is from WorldConnect.

Augusta Cleveland married Frank Wallace Cox. Born on 2 Apr 1885. Frank Wallace died on 14 Jun 1931; he was 46.

348. Eura Magruder Harris (Giles Tinsley[8], David Rice[7], Gideon[6], Lewis[5], David[4], William[3], William[2], Thomas[1]). Born on 21 Feb 1887. Eura Magruder died ? .

349. Maude May Harris (Giles Tinsley[8], David Rice[7], Gideon[6], Lewis[5], David[4], William[3], William[2], Thomas[1]). Born on 14 Jul 1888. Maude May died ? .

Information about the marriage is from WorldConnect; information about the children is from Perry Co., TN, Census 1920.

On 20 May 1909 when Maude May was 20, she married Larimore Webb. Born on 25 Apr 1885. Larimore died ? .

They had the following children:

> **531** i. Ned Harris (1912-1936)
>
> **532** ii. William Carey (1917-)

350. Cecil Rice Harris (Giles Tinsley[8], David Rice[7], Gideon[6], Lewis[5], David[4], William[3], William[2], Thomas[1]). Born on 30 Jun 1890. Cecil Rice died on 12 May 1947; he was 56.

Information about the marriage is from WorldConnect; information about the children is from Perry Co., TN, Census 1920.

On 3 Nov 1914 when Cecil Rice was 24, he married Ada Pearl Twoney. Born on 14 Aug 1892. Ada Pearl died ? .

They had the following children:

533	i.	Ralph T. (1916-?)
534	ii.	Sarah C. (1920-)

351. David Shepherd Harris (Giles Tinsley[8], David Rice[7], Gideon[6], Lewis[5], David[4], William[3], William[2], Thomas[1]). Born on 7 Oct 1893. David Shepherd died ? .

Information about the marriage is from WorldConnect.

On 21 Feb 1926 when David Shepherd was 32, he married Annie Lucille Duncan. Born on 25 May 1908. Annie Lucille died ? .

352. Alice Harris (Giles Tinsley[8], David Rice[7], Gideon[6], Lewis[5], David[4], William[3], William[2], Thomas[1]). Born on 27 Jun 1895. Alice died ? .

Information about the marriage is from WorldConnect.

On 13 Jun 1925 when Alice was 29, she married Fred Allen Goodwin. Born on 25 Aug 1894. Fred Allen died ? .

353. Ruth Harris (Giles Tinsley[8], David Rice[7], Gideon[6], Lewis[5], David[4], William[3], William[2], Thomas[1]). Born on 3 Jul 1898. Ruth died ? .

Information about the marriage is from WorldConnect.

On 17 Oct 1928 when Ruth was 30, she married Carl Phillip Persons. Born on 21 May 1895. Carl Phillip died ? .

354. Clarence D. Harris (Thomas Blount[8], David Rice[7], Gideon[6], Lewis[5], David[4], William[3], William[2], Thomas[1]). Born on 25 Jan 1889. Clarence D. died on 15 Nov 1938; he was 49.

Information about the marriage is from WorldConnect.

On 26 Nov 1925 when Clarence D. was 36, he married Jetta Beatrice Harris. Born on 19 Apr 1894. Jetta Beatrice died ? .

355. William Burl Harris (Thomas Blount[8], David Rice[7], Gideon[6], Lewis[5], David[4], William[3], William[2], Thomas[1]). Born on 19 Dec 1893. William Burl died on 23 Jan 1927; he was 33.

356. Giles Hunter Harris (Thomas Blount[8], David Rice[7], Gideon[6], Lewis[5], David[4], William[3], William[2], Thomas[1]). Born on 23 Jan 1895. Giles Hunter died ? .

357. Robert Taylor Harris (Thomas Blount[8], David Rice[7], Gideon[6], Lewis[5], David[4], William[3], William[2], Thomas[1]). Born on 19 Jan 1897. Robert Taylor died ? .

Information about the marriage is from McNairy Co., TN, Website.

On 18 Oct 1925 when Robert Taylor was 28, he married Myrtle Jane Brasher. Born on 7 Oct 1905. Myrtle Jane died on 15 Nov 1987; she was 82.

358. Gideon Lewis Harris (Thomas Blount[8], David Rice[7], Gideon[6], Lewis[5], David[4], William[3], William[2], Thomas[1]). Born on 10 Sep 1900. Gideon Lewis died ? .

Information about the marriage is from WorldConnect.

On 21 Nov 1925 when Gideon Lewis was 25, he married Nancy Olive Hughey. Born on 28 Aug 1908. Nancy Olive died ? .

359. Thomas Blount Harris Jr. (Thomas Blount[8], David Rice[7], Gideon[6], Lewis[5], David[4], William[3], William[2], Thomas[1]). Born on 28 Feb 1903. Thomas Blount died ? .

Information about the marriage is from WorldConnect.

On 24 Dec 1927 when Thomas Blount was 24, he married Sammil Nolan. Born ? . Sammil died ? .

360. Ryman Abner Harris (Thomas Blount[8], David Rice[7], Gideon[6], Lewis[5], David[4], William[3], William[2], Thomas[1]). Born on 24 Dec 1906. Ryman Abner died ? .

Information about the marriage is from WorldConnect.

On 4 Dec 1931 when Ryman Abner was 24, he married Vannale Belle Skruggs. Born on 5 Feb 1905. Vannale Belle died ? .

361. Milam King Harris (Thomas Blount[8], David Rice[7], Gideon[6], Lewis[5], David[4], William[3], William[2], Thomas[1]). Born on 29 Oct 1910. Milam King died ? .

Information about the marriage is from WorldConnect.

On 3 Jan 1935 when Milam King was 24, he married Annabell Williams. Born on 3 Mar 1906. Annabell died ? .

362. Will Vivian Nichols (Elizabeth Harris[8], David Rice[7], Gideon[6], Lewis[5], David[4], William[3], William[2], Thomas[1]). Born on 1 Jan 1890. Will Vivian died ? .

Information about the wife is from WorldConnect.

Will Vivian married Pearl Ledbetter. Born on 20 Feb 1894. Pearl died on 12 Jul 1968; she was 74.

363. Joe Henry Nichols (Elizabeth Harris[8], David Rice[7], Gideon[6], Lewis[5], David[4], William[3], William[2], Thomas[1]). Born on 15 Apr 1892. Joe Henry died on 18 Feb 1913; he was 20.

364. Blanche Kittrell (Elizabeth Harris[8], David Rice[7], Gideon[6], Lewis[5], David[4], William[3], William[2], Thomas[1]). Born on 14 Aug 1897. Blanche died in Williamson County, TN, on 16 Sep 1990; she was 93.

Information about the marriage is from WorldConnect.

On 30 Jul 1921 when Blanche was 23, she married Cecil Haywood Cude, in Tennessee. Born on 17 Apr 1886. Cecil Haywood died on 22 Oct 1960; he was 74.

365. Harris David Kittrell (Elizabeth Harris[8], David Rice[7], Gideon[6], Lewis[5], David[4], William[3], William[2], Thomas[1]). Born on 23 Jun 1901. Harris David died on 12 Oct 1966; he was 65.

Information about the marriage is from WorldConnect.

On 18 Sep 1921 when Harris David was 20, he married Lila Lucille Land. Born on 27 Jun 1901. Lila Lucille died on 1 Feb 1958; she was 56.

366. Jack Morgan Kittrell (Elizabeth Harris[8], David Rice[7], Gideon[6], Lewis[5], David[4], William[3], William[2], Thomas[1]). Born on 28 Nov 1902. Jack Morgan died on 31 Jul 1959; he was 56.

Information about the marriage is from WorldConnect.

On 31 Dec 1940 when Jack Morgan was 38, he married Ita Webb. Born on 22 Mar 1910. Ita died ? .

367. Ruth Kittrell (Elizabeth Harris[8], David Rice[7], Gideon[6], Lewis[5], David[4], William[3], William[2], Thomas[1]). Born on 2 Feb 1905. Ruth died on 5 Dec 1960; she was 55.

Information about the marriage is from WorldConnect.

On 28 Feb 1930 when Ruth was 25, she married Roy Edwards Hunt. Born on 9 Nov 1903. Roy Edwards died ? .

368. Elizabeth Kittrell (Elizabeth Harris[8], David Rice[7], Gideon[6], Lewis[5], David[4], William[3], William[2], Thomas[1]). Born on 31 Jul 1906. Elizabeth died ? .

Information about the marriage is from WorldConnect.

On 31 Dec 1930 when Elizabeth was 24, she married Malcolm Patterson Burn. Born on 25 Dec 1908. Malcolm Patterson died ? .

369. William Howard Bates (Rebecca Rice Harris[8], David Rice[7], Gideon[6], Lewis[5], David[4], William[3], William[2], Thomas[1]). Born on 20 Mar 1889. William Howard died on 8 Feb 1955; he was 65.

Information about the marriage is from WorldConnect.

On 10 Nov 1907 when William Howard was 18, he married Hallie Josephine Peters. Born on 30 Mar 1888. Hallie Josephine died ? .

370. Kittie Lucille Bates (Rebecca Rice Harris[8], David Rice[7], Gideon[6], Lewis[5], David[4], William[3], William[2], Thomas[1]). Born on 29 May 1893. Kittie Lucille died on 22 Jan 1958; she was 64.

Information about the marriage is from WorldConnect.

Ca 1911 when Kittie Lucille was 17, she married John William Vaughn. Born on 26 Jul 1886. John William died on 20 Feb 1946; he was 59.

371. Giles Lee Blount Bates (Rebecca Rice Harris[8], David Rice[7], Gideon[6], Lewis[5], David[4], William[3], William[2], Thomas[1]). Born on 10 Jan 1904. Giles Lee Blount died on 22 Nov 1941; he was 37.

Information about the marriage is from WorldConnect.

On 1 Jul 1923 when Giles Lee Blount was 19, he married Clara Dell Dudley. Born on 21 Apr 1903. Clara Dell died ? .

372. Eliza Amelia Bates (Rebecca Rice Harris[8], David Rice[7], Gideon[6], Lewis[5], David[4], William[3], William[2], Thomas[1]). Born on 12 Jan 1907. Eliza Amelia died ? .

373. Sarah Reece Dillehay (Mary J. Harris[8], James Gilliam[7], Gideon[6], Lewis[5], David[4], William[3], William[2], Thomas[1]). Born on 28 Sep 1851 in Marshall County, TN. Sarah Reece died on 22 Jun 1906; she was 54.

On 22 Nov 1871 when Sarah Reece was 20, she married James Patterson Harris (264) , son of William Lindsey Harris (126) & Mary Ann Patterson, in Marshall County, TN. Born on 17 May 1848 in Marshall County, TN. James Patterson died on 13 Apr 1922; he was 73.

They had the following children:

<blockquote>

506   i.   Lewis J. (1873-1967)

507   ii.   J. Fount (1883-1948)

</blockquote>

374. Mary Elizabeth Kittrell (Nancy Bennett Harris[8], James Gilliam[7], Gideon[6], Lewis[5], David[4], William[3], William[2], Thomas[1]). Born on 23 Sep 1868. Mary Elizabeth died on 18 Aug 1874; she was 5.

375. George Kittrell (Nancy Bennett Harris[8], James Gilliam[7], Gideon[6], Lewis[5], David[4], William[3], William[2], Thomas[1]). Born on 18 May 1870. George died on 8 Mar 1888; he was 17.

376. Katherine Kittrell (Nancy Bennett Harris[8], James Gilliam[7], Gideon[6], Lewis[5], David[4], William[3], William[2], Thomas[1]). Born on 15 Jan 1873. Katherine died on 26 Dec 1947; she was 74.

377. Addie M. Kittrell (Nancy Bennett Harris[8], James Gilliam[7], Gideon[6], Lewis[5], David[4], William[3], William[2], Thomas[1]). Born on 11 May 1875. Addie M. died on 24 Nov 1933; she was 58.

378. Frances Lillian Kittrell (Nancy Bennett Harris[8], James Gilliam[7], Gideon[6], Lewis[5], David[4], William[3], William[2], Thomas[1]). Born on 5 Jun 1885. Frances Lillian died on 16 May 1948; she was 62.

379. Edward Olley Harris (James Clanton[8], James Gilliam[7], Gideon[6], Lewis[5], David[4], William[3], William[2], Thomas[1]). Born on 5 Sep 1874. Edward Olley died ? .

380. James Virgil Harris (James Clanton[8], James Gilliam[7], Gideon[6], Lewis[5], David[4], William[3], William[2], Thomas[1]). Born on 9 Dec 1879. James Virgil died ? .

381. William Lee Harris (William Thomas[8], James Gilliam[7], Gideon[6], Lewis[5], David[4], William[3], William[2], Thomas[1]). Born on 14 Dec 1875 in Marshall County, TN. William Lee died in Wilson County, TN, in Nov 1971; he was 95.

Information about the marriage is from LDS; information about the children is from Wilson Co., TN, Census 1920.

On 8 Feb 1906 when William Lee was 30, he married Nell Dale Ferrell, in Wilson County, TN. Born ca 1885 in Wilson County, TN. Nell Dale died ? .

They had the following children:

> **535**   i.   Elizabeth Lee (ca1908-?)
>
> **536**   ii.   Thomas Ferrell (ca1911-?)
>
> **537**   iii.   Waller B. (ca1914-)

382. John Bryce Harris (William Thomas[8], James Gilliam[7], Gideon[6], Lewis[5], David[4], William[3], William[2], Thomas[1]). Born on 16 Feb 1880 in Marshall County, TN. John Bryce died in Marshall County, TN, on 7 Apr 1895; he was 15.

383. Gilliam Garrett Harris (William Thomas[8], James Gilliam[7], Gideon[6], Lewis[5], David[4], William[3], William[2], Thomas[1]). Born on 14 Sep 1885 in Marshall County, TN. Gilliam Garrett died in Maury County, TN, on 19 Oct 1918; he was 33.

Information about the marriage is from LDS

On 20 Jun 1917 when Gilliam Garrett was 31, he married Beula Holman, in Lincoln County, TN. Born ca 1896 in Lincoln County, TN. Beula died ? .

384. Hunter Hill Harris (William Thomas[8], James Gilliam[7], Gideon[6], Lewis[5], David[4], William[3], William[2], Thomas[1]). Born on 16 Oct 1896 in Marshall County, TN. Hunter Hill died in Maury County, TN, in Jun 1981; he was 84.

Information about the marriage is from LDS.

On 15 Jan 1928 when Hunter Hill was 31, he married Kimmie Johnson, in Nashville, TN. Born ? . Kimmie died ? .

385. Thomas Earl Harris (William Thomas[8], James Gilliam[7], Gideon[6], Lewis[5], David[4], William[3], William[2], Thomas[1]). Born on 21 Sep 1898 in Marshall County, TN. Thomas Earl died in Marshall County, TN, in Oct 1966; he was 68.

Information about the marriage is from WorldConnect.

On 21 Dec 1929 when Thomas Earl was 31, he married Martha Elizabeth Reaves, in Maury County, TN. Born ? . Martha Elizabeth died ? .

386. Charley Robert Harris (William Thomas[8], James Gilliam[7], Gideon[6], Lewis[5], David[4], William[3], William[2], Thomas[1]). Born on 20 Dec 1900 in Marshall County, TN. Charley Robert died in Marshall County, TN, on 9 Feb 1929; he was 28.

387. Dovie Florene Harris (William Thomas[8], James Gilliam[7], Gideon[6], Lewis[5], David[4], William[3], William[2], Thomas[1]). Born on 27 Nov 1903 in Marshall County, TN. Dovie Florene died in Maury County, TN, in Mar 1982; she was 78.

Information about the marriage is from LDS.

On 3 Apr 1924 when Dovie Florene was 20, she married Walter Ewing Pinkston, in Maury County, TN. Born in 1899 in Maury County, TN. Walter Ewing died ? .

388. Lula May Harris (Robert Claiborne[8], James Gilliam[7], Gideon[6], Lewis[5], David[4], William[3], William[2], Thomas[1]). Born on 31 Jul 1882 in Tennessee. Lula May died on 5 Jul 1931; she was 48.

389. Homer T. Harris (Robert Claiborne[8], James Gilliam[7], Gideon[6], Lewis[5], David[4], William[3], William[2], Thomas[1]). Born on 22 May 1885 in Tennessee. Homer T. died on 28 Nov 1939; he was 54.

390. James C. Harris (John Lindsey[8], James Gilliam[7], Gideon[6], Lewis[5], David[4], William[3], William[2], Thomas[1]). Born ca 1892 in Tennessee. James C. died ? .

391. Thomas C. Harris (John Lindsey[8], James Gilliam[7], Gideon[6], Lewis[5], David[4], William[3], William[2], Thomas[1]). Born ca 1902 in Tennessee. Thomas C. died ? .

392. Joe Cletus Harris (John Lindsey[8], James Gilliam[7], Gideon[6], Lewis[5], David[4], William[3], William[2], Thomas[1]). Born on 2 Jun 1906 in Giles County, TN. Joe Cletus died in Lauderdale County, AL, on 28 Jun 1979; he was 73. Buried in Marshall County, TN.

Information about the marriage is from LDS.

Joe Cletus married Olive Strohmeyer, daughter of Charles Frederick Strohmeyer & Lydia May Glenn. Born on 7 Mar 1912 in Maricopa County, AZ. Olive died in Madison County, AL, on 10 Aug 1997; she was 85.

393. James Thomas Walker (Martha Elizabeth Harris[8], Gideon Lindsey[7], Gideon[6], Lewis[5], David[4], William[3], William[2], Thomas[1]). Born on 15 Nov 1857. James Thomas died in McNairy County, TN, on 18 Oct 1912; he was 54.

On 1 Jan 1886 when James Thomas was 28, he married Lucy Almedia Harris (432), daughter of Gideon Lindsey Harris Jr. (235) & Mary Jane Dallas, in McNairy County, TN. Born on

13 Oct 1868 in McNairy County, TN. Lucy Almedia died in McNairy County, TN, on 13 Oct 1950; she was 82.

They had the following children:

> **538**   i.   Grover Cisco (1886-1970)
>
> **539**   ii.   Manson Rupert (1888-1948)
>
> **540**   iii.   Duel Rastus (1890-1975)
>
> **541**   iv.   Everette Cecil (1894-1987)

394. Joseph Anthony Walker (Martha Elizabeth Harris[8], Gideon Lindsey[7], Gideon[6], Lewis[5], David[4], William[3], William[2], Thomas[1]). Born on 25 Oct 1859. Joseph Anthony died on 2 Feb 1933; he was 73.

Information about the marriage is from Worldconnect information about the daughter is from McNairy Co., TN, Census 1910.

On 17 Jul 1901 when Joseph Anthony was 41, he married Cornelia Brooder. Born on 12 Feb 1879. Cornelia died on 9 Nov 1923; she was 44.

They had one child:

> **542**   i.   Irma (ca1905-?)

395. Mary Frances Walker (Martha Elizabeth Harris[8], Gideon Lindsey[7], Gideon[6], Lewis[5], David[4], William[3], William[2], Thomas[1]).

Born on 24 Aug 1861. Mary Frances died on 29 Oct 1933; she was 72.

Information about the marriages is from WorldConnect (Gohr).

On 10 Sep 1885 when Mary Frances was 24, she first married Samuel D. Cobb. Born ca 1858. Samuel D. died on 15 Sep 1885; he was 27.

On 13 Jan 1889 when Mary Frances was 27, she second married William Hodges DeVault. Born on 17 Jul 1866. William Hodges died on 2 Jun 1938; he was 71.

396. John Gideon Walker (Martha Elizabeth Harris[8], Gideon Lindsey[7], Gideon[6], Lewis[5], David[4], William[3], William[2], Thomas[1]). Born on 29 Nov 1862 in Tennessee. John Gideon died in Texas in Nov 1894; he was 31.

397. Mary F. Walker (Martha Elizabeth Harris[8], Gideon Lindsey[7], Gideon[6], Lewis[5], David[4], William[3], William[2], Thomas[1]). Born ca 1865 in McNairy County, TN. Mary F. died ? .

398. Lucinda Catherine Walker (Martha Elizabeth Harris[8], Gideon Lindsey[7], Gideon[6], Lewis[5], David[4], William[3], William[2], Thomas[1]). Born on 15 Aug 1869. Lucinda Catherine died ? .

Information about the marriage is from WorldConnect.

On 11 Oct 1888 when Lucinda Catherine was 19, she married Hezekiah Simpson Brooks. Born on 6 Mar 1868. Hezekiah Simpson died ? .

399. Mattie Ann Belle Walker (Martha Elizabeth Harris[8], Gideon Lindsey[7], Gideon[6], Lewis[5], David[4], William[3], William[2],

Thomas[1]). Born in 1871 in McNairy County, TN. Mattie Ann Belle died in Indianapolis, IN, bef 1940; she was 69.

Information about the husband is from WorldConnect.

Mattie Ann Belle married Emmett Baldridge. Born ? . Emmett died ? .

400. William Marion Harris (Giles Claiborne[8], Gideon Lindsey[7], Gideon[6], Lewis[5], David[4], William[3], William[2], Thomas[1]). Born on 11 Nov 1857 in McNairy County, TN. William Marion died in Clay County, AR, on 20 Nov 1941; he was 84.

Information about the marriage is from WorldConnect; information about the daughter is from McNairy Co., TN, Census 1900.

On 17 Mar 1881 when William Marion was 23, he married America Virginia Sewell, in Jackson, TN. Born on 27 Dec 1863 in McNairy County, TN. America Virginia died in Clay County, AR, in Apr 1940; she was 76.

They had one child:

> **543** i. Ella May (1886-1967)

401. Gideon Simpson Harris (Giles Claiborne[8], Gideon Lindsey[7], Gideon[6], Lewis[5], David[4], William[3], William[2], Thomas[1]). Born on 1 Aug 1859 in McNairy County, TN. Gideon Simpson died in Dunklin County, MO, on 23 Apr 1919; he was 59.

Information about the marriages is from WorldConnect; information about the children is from McNairy Co., TN, Census 1900 and Dunklin Co., MO, Census 1910.

On 12 Feb 1882 when Gideon Simpson was 22, he first married Maude Holman, in McNairy County, TN. Born on 14 Jun 1862. Maude died in McNairy County, TN, on 9 Mar 1882; she was 19.

On 3 Jan 1886 when Gideon Simpson was 26, he second married Mary Margaret Jackson, in McNairy County, TN. Born on 7 Jan 1863. Mary Margaret died in Dunklin County, MO, on 13 Jun 1905; she was 42.

They had the following children:

544 i. Dulber Odell (1886-1929)

545 ii. Nolus Guy (1887-1941)

546 iii. Cordia Licurgus (1889-1961)

547 iv. Vander Eason (1892-1962)

548 v. William Goss (1894-1968)

549 vi. Sallie Gladys (1895-1966)

550 vii. Robert Taylor (1898-1972)

551 viii. Alfred Taylor (1898-1980)

552 ix. Ervin Lafayette (1900-1964)

553	x.	Jewel Thedus (1902-1974)

402. Mahalye Jane Harris (Giles Claiborne[8], Gideon Lindsey[7], Gideon[6], Lewis[5], David[4], William[3], William[2], Thomas[1]). Born on 20 May 1861 in McNairy County, TN. Mahalye Jane died in McNairy County, TN, on 29 Mar 1943; she was 81.

Information about the marriage is from WorldConnect; information about the children is from McNairy Co., TN, Census 1900 and 1910.

On 26 Apr 1884 when Mahalye Jane was 22, she married George Washington English, in McNairy County, TN. Born on 20 Aug 1860. George Washington died in McNairy County, TN, on 24 Jun 1933; he was 72.

They had the following children:

554	i.	Claude Pascal (1886-1954)
555	ii.	Ernest Buster (1887-1953)
556	iii.	Ova Agatha (1889-1978)
557	iv.	Doran J. (1891-1960)
558	v.	Eva M. (1893-1923)
559	vi.	George Harter (1896-1986)
560	vii.	Sally M. (1898-1998)
561	viii.	Mary (1900-1974)

403. John Madison Harris (Giles Claiborne[8], Gideon Lindsey[7], Gideon[6], Lewis[5], David[4], William[3], William[2], Thomas[1]). Born on 22 Nov 1863 in McNairy County, TN. John Madison died in Flint, MI, on 25 Nov 1951; he was 88.

Information about the marriage is from WorldConnect; information about the children is from Dunklin Co., MO, Census 1910 and 1920.

On 27 Dec 1888 when John Madison was 25, he married Selena Palestine Wallace, in McNairy County, TN. Born on 4 Sep 1872 in McNairy County, TN. Selena Palestine died in Flint, MI, on 9 Jul 1959; she was 86.

They had the following children:

562	i.	Columbus Gavin (1889-1977)
563	ii.	Willie Ilah (1904-1964)
564	iii.	Clyde Pascal (1910-1997)
565	iv.	F. L. (1913-)

404. Lucy Elizabeth Harris (Giles Claiborne[8], Gideon Lindsey[7], Gideon[6], Lewis[5], David[4], William[3], William[2], Thomas[1]). Born on 15 Sep 1865 in McNairy County, TN. Lucy Elizabeth died in Tishomingo County, MS, on 20 Sep 1948; she was 83.

Information about the marriage is from LDS; information about the children is from Johnson Co., IL, Census 1900.

On 25 Dec 1884 when Lucy Elizabeth was 19, she married Marion Patrick George Anderson Nagle, in McNairy County, TN. Born on 21 Feb 1863 in Mississippi. Marion Patrick

George Anderson died in Tishomingo County, MS, on 20 Mar 1936; he was 73.

They had the following children:

566	i.	Minnie (1885-1947)
567	ii.	Millard (1887-1977)
568	iii.	Fayette (1890-1988)
569	iv.	Maudie (1895-?)

405. Sarah Frances Harris (Giles Claiborne[8], Gideon Lindsey[7], Gideon[6], Lewis[5], David[4], William[3], William[2], Thomas[1]). Born on 25 Jan 1867 in McNairy County, TN. Sarah Frances died in Jonesboro, AR, on 28 Oct 1963; she was 96.

Information about the marriage is from WorldConnect; information about the sons is from McNairy Co., TN, Census 1900.

On 13 Feb 1887 when Sarah Frances was 20, she married George Harrison Riggs, in McNairy County, TN. Born on 3 Jun 1858. George Harrison died in McNairy County, TN, on 2 Jan 1894; he was 35.

They had the following children:

570	i.	William V. (1888-1936)
571	ii.	Eber H. (1890-1904)

406. Amanda Catherine Harris (Giles Claiborne[8], Gideon Lindsey[7], Gideon[6], Lewis[5], David[4], William[3], William[2], Thomas[1]). Born on 16 Jan 1869 in McNairy County, TN. Amanda Catherine died in Corinth, MS, in 1944; she was 74.

Information about the marriage is from WorldConnect; information about the children is from McNairy Co., TN, Census 1900.

On 2 Mar 1890 when Amanda Catherine was 21, she married William Calvin Butler, son of William Bennett Butler & Louisa Sewell, in McNairy County, TN. Born on 1 Sep 1865 in McNairy County, TN. William Calvin died in Corinth, MS, in 1947; he was 81.

They had the following children:

> **572** i. William C. (1891-1969)
>
> **573** ii. Zula M. (1893-1981)
>
> **574** iii. Plaught (1895-1972)
>
> **575** iv. Sally I. (1899-1980)

407. George Calvin Harris (Giles Claiborne[8], Gideon Lindsey[7], Gideon[6], Lewis[5], David[4], William[3], William[2], Thomas[1]). Born on 27 Aug 1872 in McNairy County, TN. George Calvin died in Dunklin County, MO, on 17 Mar 1936; he was 63.

Information about the marriage is from WorldConnect; information about the children is from Dunklin Co., MO, Census 1910 and 1930.

On 4 Jan 1894 when George Calvin was 21, he married Rosa Lee Wallace, in McNairy County, TN. Born on 28 Jun 1877 in McNairy County, TN. Rosa Lee died in Dunklin County, MO, on 26 Dec 1971; she was 94.

They had the following children:

> **576** i. Eura (1894-1994)

577	ii.	Straudy (1896-1997)
578	iii.	Bessie (1900-1996)
579	iv.	Joseph (1902-1992)
580	v.	Verna L. (1909-1997)
581	vi.	Nina M. (1911-?)
582	vii.	Edwin R. (1914-1987)
583	viii.	Paul C. (1916-1975)
584	ix.	G. C. (ca1925-)

408. Julia Kinnell Harris (Giles Claiborne[8], Gideon Lindsey[7], Gideon[6], Lewis[5], David[4], William[3], William[2], Thomas[1]). Born on 15 May 1877 in McNairy County, TN. Julia Kinnell died in Nashville, TN, on 27 Oct 1961; she was 84.

Information about the marriages is from WorldConnect; information about the children is from Trousdale Co., TN, Census 1910 and 1920.

On 25 Aug 1892 when Julia Kinnell was 15, she first married William Perry Smith, in McNairy County, TN. Born on 30 Sep 1868 in McNairy County, TN. William Perry died in Parker County, TX, on 27 Feb 1900; he was 31.

They had the following children:

585	i.	Rosa (1893-1958)
586	ii.	Roxia (1896-1982)

On 2 Oct 1904 when Julia Kinnell was 27, she second married Bailey Peyton McClanahan, in McNairy County, TN. Born on 6 Jan 1856 in Trousdale County, TN. Bailey

Peyton died in Trousdale County, TN, on 25 Mar 1926; he was 70.

They had the following children:

587	i.	Donald (1905-1988)
588	ii.	Gladys (1908-1993)
589	iii.	Mamie (1910-1928)
590	iv.	Eugene (1912-1986)
591	v.	Talmage (1916-1924)

409. Jeptha Virgil Harris (Giles Claiborne^8, Gideon Lindsey^7, Gideon^6, Lewis^5, David^4, William^3, William^2, Thomas^1). Born on 1 Oct 1879 in McNairy County, TN. Jeptha Virgil died in Clay County, AR, on 30 Sep 1925; he was 45.

Information about the marriage is from WorldConnect; information about the children is from Clay Co., ARK, Census 1920.

On 11 Dec 1902 when Jeptha Virgil was 23, he married Lula Jane Rogers. Born on 16 Mar 1877 in Hardeman County, TN. Lula Jane died in Ripley County, MS, on 4 Jan 1945; she was 67.

They had the following children:

592	i.	Viola (1908-1961)
593	ii.	J. R. (1913-1923)
594	iii.	Thelma Nadine (1917-)

410. Lucy Jane Harris (David Thomas^8, Gideon Lindsey^7, Gideon^6, Lewis^5, David^4, William^3, William^2, Thomas^1). Born on 26

Jun 1860 in McNairy County, TN. Lucy Jane died in McNairy County, TN, in Nov 1959; she was 99.

Information about the marriage is from Ancestry; information about the children is from McNairy Co., TN, Census 1900 and 1910.

In Oct 1883 when Lucy Jane was 23, she married William Penn Littlefield, in McNairy County, TN. Born on 1 Dec 1857 in McNairy County, TN. William Penn died in McNairy County, TN, on 29 Apr 1942; he was 84.

They had the following children:

595	i.	James O. (1888-1909)
596	ii.	Aryte M. (1890-1954)
597	iii.	Luther R. (1893-1909)
598	iv.	Altha M. (1896-1923)
599	v.	William P. (1899-1979)
600	vi.	Lizzie E. (1902-1995)

411. Florence Aurelia Harris (David Thomas[8], Gideon Lindsey[7], Gideon[6], Lewis[5], David[4], William[3], William[2], Thomas[1]). Born on 20 Sep 1866 in McNairy County, TN. Florence Aurelia died in McNairy County, TN, on 28 Sep 1866; she was <1.

412. Consatie Frances Harris (David Thomas[8], Gideon Lindsey[7], Gideon[6], Lewis[5], David[4], William[3], William[2], Thomas[1]). Born in 1868 in McNairy County, TN. Consatie Frances died in McNairy County, TN, in 1868; she was <1.

413. James Marley Harris (David Thomas[8], Gideon Lindsey[7], Gideon[6], Lewis[5], David[4], William[3], William[2], Thomas[1]). Born on 8

Sep 1870 in McNairy County, TN. James Marley died on 24 Feb 1924; he was 53.

Information about the marriage is from WorldConnect; information about the daughter is from Hawkins Co., TN, Census 1900.

In Dec 1889 when James Marley was 19, he married Lenny English, in McNairy County, TN. Born ca 1870. Lenny died in 1902; she was 32.

They had one child:

> **601**   i.   Mable (1890-?)

414. Thomas Gideon Harris (David Thomas[8], Gideon Lindsey[7], Gideon[6], Lewis[5], David[4], William[3], William[2], Thomas[1]). Born on 13 Aug 1874 in McNairy County, TN. Thomas Gideon died ? .

415. Clayborne Franklin Harris (David Thomas[8], Gideon Lindsey[7], Gideon[6], Lewis[5], David[4], William[3], William[2], Thomas[1]). Born on 22 May 1876 in McNairy County, TN. Clayborne Franklin died on 17 Apr 1953; he was 76.

Information about the marriage is from Ancestry; information about the son is from McClennan Co., TX, Census 1910. Clayborne's brother Robert is a member of the household in 1910.

On 29 Mar 1900 when Clayborne Franklin was 23, he married Aggie Willolue Hurst, in McNairy County, TN. Born on 18 Feb 1874. Aggie Willolue died on 20 Jan 1945; she was 70.

They had one child:

	602	i.	Leonard Erskin (1901->1950)

416. William Tinsley Harris (David Thomas[8], Gideon Lindsey[7], Gideon[6], Lewis[5], David[4], William[3], William[2], Thomas[1]). Born on 21 Dec 1877 in McNairy County, TN. William Tinsley died in McNairy County, TN, on 24 Dec 1878; he was 1.

417. Dorothy Lee Harris (David Thomas[8], Gideon Lindsey[7], Gideon[6], Lewis[5], David[4], William[3], William[2], Thomas[1]). Born on 4 Jan 1880 in McNairy County, TN. Dorothy Lee died on 24 Mar 1909; she was 29.

Information about the marriage is from WorldConnect; information about the children is from McNairy Co., TN, Census 1920.

On 12 Sep 1895 when Dorothy Lee was 15, she married James Warren Barron, in McNairy County, TN. Born on 23 Dec 1876 in McNairy County, TN. James Warren died on 7 Oct 1918; he was 41.

They had the following children:

	603	i.	Herschell Warren (1903-1942)
	604	ii.	Thelma Lee (1905-1998)
	605	iii.	Alma Elizabeth (1909-1928)

418. Bertie Lou Harris (David Thomas[8], Gideon Lindsey[7], Gideon[6], Lewis[5], David[4], William[3], William[2], Thomas[1]). Born on 11

Apr 1883 in McNairy County, TN. Bertie Lou died on 6 Feb 1942; she was 58.

419. Samuel Sneed Harris (David Thomas[8], Gideon Lindsey[7], Gideon[6], Lewis[5], David[4], William[3], William[2], Thomas[1]). Born on 15 Mar 1886 in McNairy County, TN. Samuel Sneed died in McNairy County, TN, on 21 Dec 1886; he was <1.

420. Mittie Ophelia Harris (David Thomas[8], Gideon Lindsey[7], Gideon[6], Lewis[5], David[4], William[3], William[2], Thomas[1]). Born on 25 Sep 1887 in McNairy County, TN. Mittie Ophelia died ? .

Information about the marriage is from McNairy Co., TN, Website; information about the daughter is from McNairy Co., TN, Census 1920.

On 10 Sep 1916 when Mittie Ophelia was 28, she married Manual L. Wright, in McNairy County, TN. Born ca 1886 in Tennessee. Manual L. died ? .

They had one child:

<blockquote>

606   i.   Pauline (ca1917-?)

</blockquote>

421. Robert Andrew Harris (David Thomas[8], Gideon Lindsey[7], Gideon[6], Lewis[5], David[4], William[3], William[2], Thomas[1]). Born on 15 Jan 1889 in McNairy County, TN. Robert Andrew died on 7 Sep 1954; he was 65.

Information about the first marriage is from McNairy Co., TN, website; information about the second marriage is from WorldConnect.

In Feb 1916 when Robert Andrew was 27, he first married Rena Barnes, in McNairy County, TN. Born ? . Rena died ? .

On 26 Jul 1919 when Robert Andrew was 30, he second married Mary Elizabeth McBride. Born on 2 Jan 1897. Mary Elizabeth died ? .

422. Ocie Bedford Harris (David Thomas[8], Gideon Lindsey[7], Gideon[6], Lewis[5], David[4], William[3], William[2], Thomas[1]). Born on 12 Jan 1892 in McNairy County, TN. Ocie Bedford died on 20 Jul 1967; he was 75.

Information about the marriage is from McNairy Co., TN, Website; information about the children is from McNairy Co., TN, Census 1930. Ocie's mother, Elizabeth Jane, is a member of this household in 1930.

On 28 Dec 1913 when Ocie Bedford was 21, he married Letha Jewel "Dee" Newell, in McNairy County, TN. Born on 14 Sep 1893 in McNairy County, TN. Letha Jewel "Dee" died ? .

They had the following children:

> **607**   i.   Artis Glenn (1915-?)
>
> **608**   ii.   Cleyta (ca1920-)

423. John Blanchard Harris (David Thomas[8], Gideon Lindsey[7], Gideon[6], Lewis[5], David[4], William[3], William[2], Thomas[1]). Born on 21 Sep 1893 in McNairy County, TN. John Blanchard died ? .

Information about the marriage is from WorldConnect.

On 28 Nov 1923 when John Blanchard was 30, he married Emma Ruth Martyn. Born on 11 Jul 1896. Emma Ruth died ? .

424. James Clayborn Parrish (Mary Catherine "Cassie" Harris[8], Gideon Lindsey[7], Gideon[6], Lewis[5], David[4], William[3], William[2],

Thomas[1]). Born on 31 Dec 1859 in McNairy County, TN. James Clayborn died ? .

425. Cordie Crittenden Parrish (Mary Catherine "Cassie" Harris[8], Gideon Lindsey[7], Gideon[6], Lewis[5], David[4], William[3], William[2], Thomas[1]). Born on 22 Sep 1861. Cordie Crittenden died on 18 May 1888; he was 26.

426. Jordon Augustus Parrish (Mary Catherine "Cassie" Harris[8], Gideon Lindsey[7], Gideon[6], Lewis[5], David[4], William[3], William[2], Thomas[1]). Born on 29 Jul 1863. Jordon Augustus died in 1922; he was 58.

427. Lucy Elizabeth Parrish (Mary Catherine "Cassie" Harris[8], Gideon Lindsey[7], Gideon[6], Lewis[5], David[4], William[3], William[2], Thomas[1]). Born on 12 Oct 1865. Lucy Elizabeth died on 14 Jan 1928; she was 62.

428. Cora Edna Parrish (Mary Catherine "Cassie" Harris[8], Gideon Lindsey[7], Gideon[6], Lewis[5], David[4], William[3], William[2], Thomas[1]). Born on 25 May 1871. Cora Edna died ca 1958; she was 86.

429. Willie Baxter Parrish (Mary Catherine "Cassie" Harris[8], Gideon Lindsey[7], Gideon[6], Lewis[5], David[4], William[3], William[2], Thomas[1]). Born on 31 Mar 1873. Willie Baxter died on 18 Oct 1931; he was 58.

430. Eber Nathaniel Parrish (Mary Catherine "Cassie" Harris[8], Gideon Lindsey[7], Gideon[6], Lewis[5], David[4], William[3], William[2], Thomas[1]). Born on 18 Apr 1875. Eber Nathaniel died ? .

431. Gilliam Harris Parrish (Mary Catherine "Cassie" Harris[8], Gideon Lindsey[7], Gideon[6], Lewis[5], David[4], William[3], William[2],

Thomas[1]). Born on 11 Jan 1878. Gilliam Harris died on 17 Jun 1959; he was 81.

432. Lucy Almedia Harris (Gideon Lindsey[8], Gideon Lindsey[7], Gideon[6], Lewis[5], David[4], William[3], William[2], Thomas[1]). Born on 13 Oct 1868 in McNairy County, TN. Lucy Almedia died in McNairy County, TN, on 13 Oct 1950; she was 82.

Information about the marriage is from LDS; information about the children is from McNairy Co., TN, Census 1900.

On 1 Jan 1886 when Lucy Almedia was 17, she married James Thomas Walker (393) , son of John Walker & Martha Elizabeth Harris (231), in McNairy County, TN. Born on 15 Nov 1857. James Thomas died in McNairy County, TN, on 18 Oct 1912; he was 54.

They had the following children:

538	i.	Grover Cisco (1886-1970)
539	ii.	Manson Rupert (1888-1948)
540	iii.	Duel Rastus (1890-1975)
541	iv.	Everette Cecil (1894-1987)

433. Lewis Gideon Harris (Gideon Lindsey[8], Gideon Lindsey[7], Gideon[6], Lewis[5], David[4], William[3], William[2], Thomas[1]). Born on 9 Jan 1870 in McNairy County, TN. Lewis Gideon died on 13 May 1961; he was 91.

Information about the wife is from LDS; information about the sons is from McNairy Co., TN, Census 1910.

Lewis Gideon married Mollie Mary McBride. Born on 12 Aug 1874. Mollie Mary died on 2 Jun 1961; she was 86.

They had the following children:

    609   i.   Harold Augustus (1894-?)

    610   ii.   Furman (ca1894-?)

434. Rebecca Elizabeth Harris (Gideon Lindsey[8], Gideon Lindsey[7], Gideon[6], Lewis[5], David[4], William[3], William[2], Thomas[1]). Born on 17 Feb 1872 in McNairy County, TN. Rebecca Elizabeth died on 25 Oct 1955; she was 83.

Information about the marriage is from LDS; information about the children is from McNairy Co., TN, Census 1900-1920.

On 19 Aug 1888 when Rebecca Elizabeth was 16, she married William Thomas Landreth, son of James C. Landreth & Mary J. ?, in McNairy County, TN. Born on 21 Dec 1868 in Tennessee. William Thomas died on 25 May 1944; he was 75.

They had the following children:

    611   i.   James Gideon (1890-1903)

    612   ii.   Otto Levan (1893-?)

    613   iii.   Thomas Odell (1897-?)

    614   iv.   Paul Gipson (1916-?)

435. George Madison Harris (Gideon Lindsey[8], Gideon Lindsey[7], Gideon[6], Lewis[5], David[4], William[3], William[2], Thomas[1]). Born on 19 Aug 1874 in McNairy County, TN. George Madison died in McNairy County, TN, on 14 Aug 1887; he was 12.

436. Giles Furman Harris (Gideon Lindsey[8], Gideon Lindsey[7], Gideon[6], Lewis[5], David[4], William[3], William[2], Thomas[1]). Born on 14 Feb 1885 in McNairy County, TN. Giles Furman died in Denton County, TX, on 15 Jul 1969; he was 84.

Information about the marriages is from WorldConnect. Information about the first son is from McNairy Co., TN, Census 1910; Annice Belle is in the household of her father, George W. Smith. Information about the second son is from Wise Co., TX, Census 1920.

On 27 Nov 1904 when Giles Furman was 19, he first married Annice Belle Smith. Born on 8 Dec 1889. Annice Belle died aft 1910; she was 20.

They had one child:

> **615** i. Archie Herschell (1907-1953)

On 15 Jun 1918 when Giles Furman was 33, he second married Ruth Lurinda Reynolds. Born on 5 Jul 1891. Ruth Lurinda died on 5 May 1937; she was 45.

They had one child:

> **616** i. J. W. (1920-)

437. May Augustus Harris (Gideon Lindsey[8], Gideon Lindsey[7], Gideon[6], Lewis[5], David[4], William[3], William[2], Thomas[1]). Born on 8

Jan 1888 in McNairy County, TN. May Augustus died on 18
May 1965; he was 77.

Information about the marriage is from LDS; information
about the children is from McNairy Co., TN, Census 1910-
1930.

In 1906 when May Augustus was 17, he married Ida Leona
Plunk, in McNairy County, TN. Born on 5 Jul 1889 in
McNairy County, TN. Ida Leona died in McNairy County,
TN, on 15 Apr 1980; she was 90.

They had the following children:

617	i.	Effie Jane (1907-1942)
618	ii.	Ruby Demova (1908-?)
619	iii.	Malcolm Hobert (1909-1934)
620	iv.	Urbane Eustace (1912-1980)
621	v.	Eva Inez (1915-)
622	vi.	Ruth (ca1921-)
623	vii.	Lewis (ca1923-)
624	viii.	Roy (ca1924-)
625	ix.	Ray (ca1925-)

438. Gideon Lindsey Pyron (Sarah Francis "Frankie" Harris[8],
Gideon Lindsey[7], Gideon[6], Lewis[5], David[4], William[3], William[2],
Thomas[1]). Born on 10 Dec 1869 in McNairy County, TN.
Gideon Lindsey died on 4 Aug 1963; he was 93.

439. Sidney Augustus Pyron (Sarah Francis "Frankie" Harris[8], Gideon Lindsey[7], Gideon[6], Lewis[5], David[4], William[3], William[2], Thomas[1]). Born on 1 Dec 1877 in McNairy County, TN. Sidney Augustus died on 14 Aug 1918; he was 40.

Information about the wife and children is from McNairy Co., TN, Census 1910.

Sidney Augustus married Gusta ?. Born ca 1875 in Tennessee. Gusta died ? .

They had the following children:

626	i.	Hassie B. (ca1897-?)
627	ii.	DeWitt (ca1899-?)
628	iii.	Ory O. (ca1901-?)
629	iv.	William C. (ca1905-?)
630	v.	Effie M. (ca1908-?)

440. Aurelia Aquilla Pyron (Sarah Francis "Frankie" Harris[8], Gideon Lindsey[7], Gideon[6], Lewis[5], David[4], William[3], William[2], Thomas[1]). Born on 1 Mar 1879 in McNairy County, TN. Aurelia Aquilla died in McNairy County, TN, on 18 Sep 1898; she was 19.

441. James Clayborne Pyron (Sarah Francis "Frankie" Harris[8], Gideon Lindsey[7], Gideon[6], Lewis[5], David[4], William[3], William[2], Thomas[1]). Born on 21 Mar 1881 in McNairy County, TN. James Clayborne died ? .

Information about the wife is from McNairy Co., TN, Census 1930.

James Clayborne married Della ?. Born ca 1887. Della died
?.

442. Lucy Artimus Harris (William Ashley[8], Gideon Lindsey[7], Gideon[6], Lewis[5], David[4], William[3], William[2], Thomas[1]). Born on 31 Jul 1869 in McNairy County, TN. Lucy Artimus died in Tarrant County, TX, on 10 Mar 1965; she was 95.

Information about the marriage is from LDS; information about the children is from Parker Co., TX, Census 1910.

On 26 Nov 1889 when Lucy Artimus was 20, she married Siras Bell Hardin, in McNairy County, TN. Born on 13 Dec 1872 in McNairy County, TN. Siras Bell died in Jack County, TX, on 29 Jun 1934; he was 61.

They had the following children:

> **631** i. Fred Edward (1890-1967)
>
> **632** ii. William Inloe (1892-1968)
>
> **633** iii. Della Frances (1893-1971)
>
> **634** iv. Versie Aldora (1898-1977)
>
> **635** v. Reta Belle (1899-?)
>
> **636** vi. Ethel Mae (1901-1976)
>
> **637** vii. Luther Joseph (1903-?)
>
> **638** viii. Fant George (1905-1984)

639   ix.   Herbert Doyle (1908-1975)

443. James David Harris (William Ashley[8], Gideon Lindsey[7], Gideon[6], Lewis[5], David[4], William[3], William[2], Thomas[1]). Born on 9 Jan 1871 in McNairy County, TN. James David died in Stephens County, OK, on 22 Sep 1938; he was 67.

Information about the marriage is from LDS; information about the children is from Wise Co., TX, Census 1910 and Clay Co., TX, Census 1920.

On 28 Oct 1894 when James David was 23, he married Docia Bell Pyron, in McNairy County, TN. Born on 5 Oct 1872 in McNairy County, TN. Docia Bell died in Willacy County, TX, on 1 Sep 1944; she was 71.

They had the following children:

      640   i.   William Earl (1895-1967)

      641   ii.   Alvin Luther (1897-1969)

      642   iii.   Retie Ceulia (1898-1989)

      643   iv.   Margie Patie (1900-1974)

      644   v.   Ollin Littlefield (1903-1985)

      645   vi.   Avie Elizabeth (1906-1979)

646	vii.	Nona Agatha (1908-1984)
647	viii.	Leta May (1910-2004)
648	ix.	James Leland (1912-1999)
649	x.	Theola Pyron (1916-)

444. William Franklin Harris (William Ashley[8], Gideon Lindsey[7], Gideon[6], Lewis[5], David[4], William[3], William[2], Thomas[1]). Born on 16 Aug 1873 in McNairy County, TN. William Franklin died in Tulare County, CA, on 9 Apr 1968; he was 94.

Information about the first marriage and child is from McNairy Co., TN, Website. Information about the second marriage is from LDS; information about the children from the second marriage is from McNairy Co., TN, Census 1910, 1920, and LDS

William Franklin first married Minnie Claunch. Born on 28 May 1876 in Tennessee. Minnie died in Gibson County, TN, on 16 Jan 1952; she was 75.

They had one child:

650	i.	Jewel (1896-1992)

On 23 Dec 1903 when William Franklin was 30, he second married Maggie Doshie Norwood, in McNairy County, TN. Born on 13 Apr 1885. Maggie Doshie died ? .

They had the following children:

651	i.	Louis Gilbert (1904-1986)

652	ii.	Russell Elbert (1906-1991)
653	iii.	Reba Iola (1909-1984)
654	iv.	Ruby Viola (1911-2005)
655	v.	Lillie Pearl (1914-1984)
656	vi.	William Nelton (1917-1992)
657	vii.	Haskel Garwin (1919-1921)

445. John Lindon Harris (William Ashley[8], Gideon Lindsey[7], Gideon[6], Lewis[5], David[4], William[3], William[2], Thomas[1]). Born on 23 Jun 1875 in McNairy County, TN. John Lindon died in McNairy County, TN, on 6 Jul 1940; he was 65.

Information about the marriage is from LDS; information about the children is from McNairy Co. Census 1920 and LDS.

On 20 Apr 1902 when John Lindon was 26, he married Calista Ann Pyron, in McNairy County, TN. Born on 23 Jan 1875 in McNairy County, TN. Calista Ann died in McNairy County, TN, on 14 Nov 1942; she was 67.

They had the following children:

| 658 | i. | Vivian Milborn (1907-1907) |
| 659 | ii. | Bivian Lafayette (1908-1908) |

660　iii.　Raymond Garland (1910-1987)

446. Isam Gilliam Harris (William Ashley[8], Gideon Lindsey[7], Gideon[6], Lewis[5], David[4], William[3], William[2], Thomas[1]). Born on 21 Jul 1879 in McNairy County, TN. Isam Gilliam died in McNairy County, TN, on 12 Aug 1880; he was 1.

447. Albert Royal Harris (William Ashley[8], Gideon Lindsey[7], Gideon[6], Lewis[5], David[4], William[3], William[2], Thomas[1]). Born on 10 Apr 1882 in McNairy County, TN. Albert Royal died in Texas on 13 Jul 1949; he was 67.

Information about the marriage is from LDS; information about the children is from McNairy Co., TN, Census 1910 and Clay Co., TX, Census 1920.

In 1903 when Albert Royal was 20, he married Mary Lena Stout, in McNairy County, TN. Born on 27 May 1889 in Clay County, TX. Mary Lena died in Grobard, TX, on 20 Aug 1965; she was 76.

They had the following children:

661　i.　Dan (1906-1987)

662　ii.　William (ca1908-?)

663　iii.　Beatrice (1910-?)

664　iv.　Walter (1911-?)

665　v.　Price Edward (1914-1989)

666　vi.　Tenner M. (ca1919-)

667　vii.　Mary G. (1920-)

448. Julius Andrew Harris (William Ashley[8], Gideon Lindsey[7], Gideon[6], Lewis[5], David[4], William[3], William[2], Thomas[1]). Born on 8 Apr 1884 in McNairy County, TN. Julius Andrew died in McNairy County, TN, on 13 Dec 1974; he was 90.

Information about the marriage is from LDS; information about the children is from McNairy Co., TN, Census 1920, 1930, and LDS.

On 1 Nov 1906 when Julius Andrew was 22, he married Etta Jane Plunk, in McNairy County, TN. Born on 25 Apr 1887 in McNairy County, TN. Etta Jane died in McNairy County, TN, in Mar 1981; she was 93.

They had the following children:

668	i.	Mary Florence (1907-1999)
669	ii.	Everett Sylvan (1911-1990)
670	iii.	Edward Bunyan (1913-1987)
671	iv.	Lillie Faye (ca1914-1919)
672	v.	Troy (1916-1919)
673	vi.	Theatus (1919-1972)
674	vii.	Exie (ca1922-)
675	viii.	Millard (ca1929-1997)

449. Mary Percilla Harris (William Ashley[8], Gideon Lindsey[7], Gideon[6], Lewis[5], David[4], William[3], William[2], Thomas[1]). Born on 21

Feb 1886 in McNairy County, TN. Mary Percilla died in McNairy County, TN, on 15 May 1972; she was 86.

Information about the marriage is from LDS; information about the children is from McNairy Co., TN, Census 1910-1930 and LDS.

On 8 Dec 1903 when Mary Percilla was 17, she married Luther Albert Walker, in McNairy County, TN. Born on 27 Feb 1885 in McNairy County, TN. Luther Albert died in McNairy County, TN, on 30 Aug 1951; he was 66.

They had the following children:

676	i.	Roxie Theola (1905-1906)
677	ii.	Scleeta Aldonia (1908-1997)
678	iii.	Everett Virdell (1911-1991)
679	iv.	Hardy Odell (1913-1992)
680	v.	Luther Wilburn (1914-1986)
681	vi.	John Virgle (1916-1988)
682	vii.	Mary U. (ca1920-)
683	viii.	Rayburn (ca1922-)
684	ix.	Larance L. (ca1924-)

450. Thurman Lindsey Harris (William Ashley[8], Gideon Lindsey[7], Gideon[6], Lewis[5], David[4], William[3], William[2], Thomas[1]). Born on 15 Jul 1888 in McNairy County, TN. Thurman Lindsey died in McNairy County, TN, in May 1982; he was 93.

Information about the marriage is from McNairy Co., TN, Website; information about the children is from McNairy Co., TN, Census 1930.

On 26 Jul 1914 when Thurman Lindsey was 26, he married Bonnie Esther Carothers, in McNairy County, TN. Born on 26 Jun 1895 in McNairy County, TN. Bonnie Esther died in McNairy County, TN, on 4 Aug 1987; she was 92.

They had the following children:

> **685**   i.   Merlin Flynn (1915-1976)
>
> **686**   ii.   Thomas Clifford (1917-1996)
>
> **687**   iii.   Norris (ca1926-)

451. Bunyan Stephens Harris (William Ashley[8], Gideon Lindsey[7], Gideon[6], Lewis[5], David[4], William[3], William[2], Thomas[1]). Born on 28 May 1890 in McNairy County, TN. Bunyan Stephens died in McNairy County, TN, in 1954; he was 63.

Information about the first marriage is from LDS; information about the second marriage is from McNairy Co., TN, Website. Information about the children is from McNairy Co., TN, Census 1930.

Ca 1911 when Bunyan Stephens was 20, he first married Minnie Meek, in McNairy County, TN. Born on 23 Jul 1891 in McNairy County, TN. Minnie died in McNairy County, TN, on 26 Aug 1919; she was 28.

They had the following children:

>   **688**   i.   Audra Evelyn (1913-1995)
>
>   **689**   ii.   William Harlin (1917-?)

On 23 Oct 1919 when Bunyan Stephens was 29, he second married Fallie Alexander, in McNairy County, TN. Born on 21 Sep 1896 in McNairy County, TN. Fallie died in McNairy County, TN, on 1 Jun 1928; she was 31.

452. Mannon Lindsey Harris (Doctor Franklin "Docky"[8], Gideon Lindsey[7], Gideon[6], Lewis[5], David[4], William[3], William[2], Thomas[1]). Born on 26 May 1878 in McNairy County, TN. Mannon Lindsey died in 1962; he was 83.

Information about the first marriage is from WorldConnect; information about the second marriage is from McNairy Co., TN, Website. Information about the daughter is from McNairy Co., TN, Census 1910. The daughter Alva is in the household of Sarah, Mannon's mother, in 1920, and he is listed as head of a separate household with his wife Ophelia (McNairy Co., TN, Census 1920).

On 8 Apr 1900 when Mannon Lindsey was 21, he first married Lula Pearl Vinson, in McNairy County, TN. Born on 28 Jun 1882. Lula Pearl died ? .

They had one child:

$$690 \quad \text{i.} \qquad \text{Alva Zela (1901-} \\ \text{<1930)}$$

On 10 Feb 1918 when Mannon Lindsey was 39, he second married Ophelia Inman, in McNairy County, TN. Born ca 1888 in Tennessee. Ophelia died ? .

453. Robert Lee Harris (Doctor Franklin "Docky"[8], Gideon Lindsey[7], Gideon[6], Lewis[5], David[4], William[3], William[2], Thomas[1]). Born on 22 Nov 1878 in McNairy County, TN. Robert Lee died on 22 Oct 1956; he was 77.

In 1930 Lee is a head of household with his brother Cleatus, sister-in-law Eva, Mannon's daughter Alva, and Sarah his mother as members (McNairy Co., TN, Census 1930).

454. Tolbert Dalton Harris (Doctor Franklin "Docky"[8], Gideon Lindsey[7], Gideon[6], Lewis[5], David[4], William[3], William[2], Thomas[1]). Born on 24 Sep 1880 in McNairy County, TN. Tolbert Dalton died in Clay County, TX, on 8 Mar 1960; he was 79.

Information about the marriage is from WorldConnect; information about the daughter is from Clay Co., TX, Census 1930.

On 3 Aug 1913 when Tolbert Dalton was 32, he married Lillie Mae Henderson, in McNairy County, TN. Born on 26 Feb 1897. Lillie Mae died in Clay County, TX, on 28 May 1995; she was 98.

They had one child:

$$691 \quad \text{i.} \qquad \text{Doris (ca1925-)}$$

455. Artemas Duren Harris (Doctor Franklin "Docky"[8], Gideon Lindsey[7], Gideon[6], Lewis[5], David[4], William[3], William[2], Thomas[1]).

Born on 21 Mar 1884 in McNairy County, TN. Artemas
Duren died in McNairy County, TN, on 15 Jan 1902; he was
17.

456. Hubert Vernon Harris (Doctor Franklin "Docky"[8], Gideon
Lindsey[7], Gideon[6], Lewis[5], David[4], William[3], William[2], Thomas[1]).
Born on 11 Aug 1886 in McNairy County, TN. Hubert
Vernon died in McNairy County, TN, on 4 Mar 1927; he was
40.

Information about the marriage is from McNairy Co., TN,
Website; information about the children is from Caldwell
Co., LA, Census 1920 and 1930.

On 7 Sep 1914 when Hubert Vernon was 28, he married
Zella Carothers, in McNairy County, TN. Born on 22 Feb
1892 in McNairy County, TN. Zella died on 24 Jan 1945;
she was 52.

They had the following children:

692	i.	Wilma Sue (1917-)
693	ii.	Vera G. (ca1923-)
694	iii.	Hubert V. (ca1927-)

457. Sarah Myrtle Harris (Doctor Franklin "Docky"[8], Gideon
Lindsey[7], Gideon[6], Lewis[5], David[4], William[3], William[2], Thomas[1]).
Born on 1 Oct 1889 in McNairy County, TN. Sarah Myrtle
died in McNairy County, TN, on 25 Aug 1979; she was 89.

Information about the marriage is from WorldConnect;
information about the children is from McNairy Co., TN.
Census 1930.

On 6 Nov 1910 when Sarah Myrtle was 21, she married John Robert Walker, son of John Walker & Mary E. ?, in McNairy County, TN. Born on 12 Dec 1876 in McNairy County, TN. John Robert died in McNairy County, TN, on 5 Jun 1957; he was 80.

They had the following children:

695	i.	Raybun N. (ca1920-)
696	ii.	Varnie M. (ca1922-)
697	iii.	Nellie C. (ca1926-)

458. Arthur Cleatus Harris (Doctor Franklin "Docky"[8], Gideon Lindsey[7], Gideon[6], Lewis[5], David[4], William[3], William[2], Thomas[1]). Born on 16 Apr 1892 in McNairy County, TN. Arthur Cleatus died ?

Information about the marriage is from WorldConnect.

On 1 Apr 1928 when Arthur Cleatus was 35, he married Sarah Eva Crowell, in McNairy County, TN. Born on 27 Nov 1901 in Alabama. Sarah Eva died ? .

459. Lessie Houston (Martha Jane "Mattie" Harris[8], Gideon Lindsey[7], Gideon[6], Lewis[5], David[4], William[3], William[2], Thomas[1]). Born ca 1910 in Tennessee. Lessie died ? .

460. Talmage Ray Houston (Martha Jane "Mattie" Harris[8], Gideon Lindsey[7], Gideon[6], Lewis[5], David[4], William[3], William[2], Thomas[1]). Born on 3 Oct 1912 in Tennessee. Talmage Ray died in Fayette County, TN, on 13 Oct 1999; he was 87.

461. Alice Harris (Thomas Gideon[8], Giles Claiborne[7], Gideon[6], Lewis[5], David[4], William[3], William[2], Thomas[1]). Born on 28 Jun 1860. Alice died in 1942; she was 81.

Information about the husband is from WorldConnect; information about the children is from Graves Co., KY, Census 1900.

Alice married Joseph Robert Dalton, son of Shelton Dalton & Leonora J. ?. Born on 6 Jan 1852. Joseph Robert died on 24 Feb 1900; he was 48.

They had the following children:

698	i.	A. Doral (1881-?)
699	ii.	J. Suler (1883-?)
700	iii.	B. Sela (1883-?)
701	iv.	B. Irah (1885-?)
702	v.	L. Elzie (1886-?)
703	vi.	M. Hertie (1888-?)
704	vii.	M. Ivy (1889-?)
705	viii.	A. Bertha (1891-?)

462. Dolly Lucy Catherine Harris (William Tinsley[8], Giles Claiborne[7], Gideon[6], Lewis[5], David[4], William[3], William[2], Thomas[1]). Born on 8 Mar 1874. Dolly Lucy Catherine died ?.

Information about the marriage is from WorldConnect; information about the children is from Simpson Co., KY, Census 1910.

On 12 Oct 1893 when Dolly Lucy Catherine was 19, she married Claude Butts. Born on 28 Aug 1872. Claude died in Sep 1954; he was 82.

They had the following children:

> **706** i.   William Conrad (1895-?)
>
> **707** ii.   Denver Bertrand (1897-?)
>
> **708** iii.   Ima Elizabeth (1900-?)
>
> **709** iv.   Pauline (1904-?)
>
> **710** v.   Minnie Noreen (1906-?)

463. Minnie Jane Harris (William Tinsley[8], Giles Claiborne[7], Gideon[6], Lewis[5], David[4], William[3], William[2], Thomas[1]). Born on 14 Dec 1877 in Kentucky. Minnie Jane died on 9 Nov 1971; she was 93.

Information about the marriage is from WorldConnect; information about the children is from Lawrance Co., AL, Census 1910 and 1920.

On 10 Jan 1895 when Minnie Jane was 17, she married Bluit Pruit Gibson. Born on 6 Dec 1876 in Alabama. Bluit Pruit died on 12 Apr 1940; he was 63.

They had the following children:

> **711** i.   Willie D. (ca1898-?)
>
> **712** ii.   Dee O. (ca1903-?)

713	iii.	Katie M. (ca1907-?)
714	iv.	Bettie C. (ca1911-?)
715	v.	Joe C. (ca1914-?)
716	vi.	Minnie Annie (1917-)

464. William T. Harris (Robert Wiseman[8], Giles Claiborne[7], Gideon[6], Lewis[5], David[4], William[3], William[2], Thomas[1]). Born in 1871 in Sumner County, TN. William T. died in Macon County, TN, on 7 Aug 1896; he was 25. Buried in Pleasant Grove Methodist Cemetery, Sumner Co., TN.

Information about the wife and daughters is from family records.

William T. married Carrie Belle Doss. Born on 19 Nov 1871 in Macon County, TN. Carrie Belle died on 24 Jan 1952; she was 80.

They had the following children:

| **717** | i. | Nellie M. (1893-1990) |
| **718** | ii. | Willie W. (1896-1988) |

465. Giles Bledsoe Harris (Robert Wiseman[8], Giles Claiborne[7], Gideon[6], Lewis[5], David[4], William[3], William[2], Thomas[1]). Born in Aug 1872 in Sumner County, TN. Giles Bledsoe died in 1951; he was 78. Buried in Pleasant Grove Methodist Cemetery, Sumner Co., TN.

Information about the marriage and sons is from Macon Co., TN, Census 1900 and Sumner Co., TN, Website.

In 1898 when Giles Bledsoe was 25, he married Nellie Nimmo, daughter of Grau Nimmo & ?. Born in Mar 1874 in

Tennessee. Nellie died in Macon County, TN, on 22 Apr 1925; she was 51.

They had the following children:

> **719**   i.   Paul Nimmo (1899-1948)
>
> **720**   ii.   James Blanton (1903-1986)

466. Sarah Tennie Harris (Robert Wiseman[8], Giles Claiborne[7], Gideon[6], Lewis[5], David[4], William[3], William[2], Thomas[1]). Born on 3 Aug 1874 in Sumner County, TN. Sarah Tennie died in Sumner County, TN, on 28 Mar 1915; she was 40.

Information about the marriage is from WorldConnect; information about the children is from Sumner Co., TN, Census 1910 and 1920.

In 1902 when Sarah Tennie was 27, she married Robert Yancy Weatherford, son of Hilery J. Weatherford & Elizabeth J. ?, in Sumner County, TN. Born on 15 Jun 1863 in Sumner County, TN. Robert Yancy died in Sumner County, TN, on 2 Jul 1930; he was 67.

They had the following children:

> **721**   i.   Selma (ca1907-?)
>
> **722**   ii.   Willie (ca1908-<1920)
>
> **723**   iii.   Hilery Harris (1910-2000)
>
> **724**   iv.   Cordell (ca1913-?)

467. Mary C. Harris (Robert Wiseman[8], Giles Claiborne[7], Gideon[6], Lewis[5], David[4], William[3], William[2], Thomas[1]). Born in 1877 in Sumner County, TN. Mary C. died on 27 Aug 1937; she was 60.

468. Mallie E. Harris (Robert Wiseman[8], Giles Claiborne[7], Gideon[6], Lewis[5], David[4], William[3], William[2], Thomas[1]). Born in 1879 in Sumner County, TN. Mallie E. died on 17 Jan 1959; she was 80.

469. Mattie Anna Harris (Robert Wiseman[8], Giles Claiborne[7], Gideon[6], Lewis[5], David[4], William[3], William[2], Thomas[1]). Born on 12 Mar 1881 in Sumner County, TN. Mattie Anna died on 28 Aug 1957; she was 76.

Information about the first husband is from Macon Co., TN, Census 1900; information about the second husband is from Sumner Co., TN, Website. Information about the children is from Sumner Co., TN, Census 1910.

Mattie Anna first married Herschell Gilliam. Born in 1878 in Tennessee. Herschell died bef 1905; he was 27.

They had one child:

       725   i.   Annie L. (ca1904-?)

Mattie Anna second married Gideon Paul Moncrief. Born in 1874. Gideon Paul died in 1936; he was 62.

They had the following children:

       726   i.   Orby (ca1905-?)

       727   ii.   Caminet (1898-?)

       728   iii.   Venlist (ca1909-?)

470. Rice Odell Harris (Robert Wiseman[8], Giles Claiborne[7], Gideon[6], Lewis[5], David[4], William[3], William[2], Thomas[1]). Born on 3 Apr 1883. Rice Odell died on 6 Jun 1965; he was 82.

Information about the wife and daughters is from Sumner Co., TN, Census 1910 and 1920.

Rice Odell married Eunice ?. Born ca 1887 in Tennessee. Eunice died ? .

They had the following children:

> **729**   i.   Mary E. (ca1907-?)
>
> **730**   ii.   Bettie Lou (ca1912-?)

471. Bessie N. Harris (Robert Wiseman[8], Giles Claiborne[7], Gideon[6], Lewis[5], David[4], William[3], William[2], Thomas[1]). Born in 1885 in Tennessee. Bessie N. died ? .

Information about the husband and sons is from Macon Co., TN, Census 1910 and 1930.

Bessie N. married Idell L. Roark. Born ca 1874 in Tennessee. Idell L. died ? .

They had the following children:

> **731**   i.   Edna (ca1901-?)
>
> **732**   ii.   William F. (ca1912-?)
>
> **733**   iii.   Robert D. (ca1915-?)

472. Maggie L. Harris (Robert Wiseman[8], Giles Claiborne[7], Gideon[6], Lewis[5], David[4], William[3], William[2], Thomas[1]). Born in 1887 in Tennessee. Maggie L. died on 20 Jan 1960; she was 73.

473. James R. Harris (Robert Wiseman[8], Giles Claiborne[7], Gideon[6], Lewis[5], David[4], William[3], William[2], Thomas[1]). Born on 31 Jan 1889 in Sumner County, TN. James R. died on 16 Aug 1900; he was 11. Buried in Pleasant Grove Methodist Cemetery, Sumner Co., TN.

474. I. Effie Harris (Robert Wiseman[8], Giles Claiborne[7], Gideon[6], Lewis[5], David[4], William[3], William[2], Thomas[1]). Born in 1891 in Tennessee. I. Effie died ? .

475. Clayborn Pike (Martha Anna "Matt" Harris[8], Giles Claiborne[7], Gideon[6], Lewis[5], David[4], William[3], William[2], Thomas[1]). Born ca 1872 in Tennessee. Clayborn died ? .

476. Mallie C. Pike (Martha Anna "Matt" Harris[8], Giles Claiborne[7], Gideon[6], Lewis[5], David[4], William[3], William[2], Thomas[1]). Born ca 1877 in Tennessee. Mallie C. died ? .

477. Dary Pike (Martha Anna "Matt" Harris[8], Giles Claiborne[7], Gideon[6], Lewis[5], David[4], William[3], William[2], Thomas[1]). Born ca 1883 in Kentucky. Dary died ? .

478. Ally Pike (Martha Anna "Matt" Harris[8], Giles Claiborne[7], Gideon[6], Lewis[5], David[4], William[3], William[2], Thomas[1]). Born ca 1887 in Kentucky. Ally died ? .

479. Henry H. Harris (John Sumpter[8], Giles Claiborne[7], Gideon[6], Lewis[5], David[4], William[3], William[2], Thomas[1]). Born on 23 Mar 1878 in Macon County, TN. Henry H. died on 4 Mar 1944; he was 65. Buried in Rocky Mound Cemetery, Macon Co., TN.

Information about the marriage and children is from Macon Co. Census 1900 and 1910 and *Macon Co. Cemetery Book*, v. 1.

Ca 1898 when Henry H. was 19, he married Ella B. Sloan. Born on 1 Oct 1877 in Tennessee. Ella B. died on 8 Jun 1954; she was 76.

They had the following children:

734	i.	William I. (1899-1965)
735	ii.	Elisha O. (1902-1983)
736	iii.	Lillie Pearl (ca1905-?)
737	iv.	Vercil Claudie (1908-1976)

480. Charlie W. Harris (John Sumpter[8], Giles Claiborne[7], Gideon[6], Lewis[5], David[4], William[3], William[2], Thomas[1]). Born on 8 Dec 1880 in Macon County, TN. Charlie W. died on 23 Nov 1947; he was 66. Buried in Pleasant Grove Methodist Cemetery, Sumner Co., TN.

481. James R. Harris (John Sumpter[8], Giles Claiborne[7], Gideon[6], Lewis[5], David[4], William[3], William[2], Thomas[1]). Born in Apr 1884 in Macon County, TN. James R. died ? .

Information about the marriage is from Bronner, *Macon Co. Marriages*, v. 1.

On 1 Oct 1906 when James R. was 22, he married Emmer L. Miles, in Macon County, TN. Born ? . Emmer L. died ? .

482. Giles S. Harris (John Sumpter[8], Giles Claiborne[7], Gideon[6], Lewis[5], David[4], William[3], William[2], Thomas[1]). Born on 12 Sep 1887 in Macon County, TN. Giles S. died on 31 Dec 1955; he was 68. Buried in Pleasant Grove Methodist Cemetery, Sumner Co., TN.

Information about the wife and son is from Macon County Census 1920.

Giles S. married Ova Mattie ?. Born on 28 Aug 1889 in Tennessee. Ova Mattie died on 11 Oct 1964; she was 75.

They had one child:

> **738**   i.   Cordell (1913-1976)

483. Ethel C. Harris (James Lindsey[8], Giles Claiborne[7], Gideon[6], Lewis[5], David[4], William[3], William[2], Thomas[1]). Born in Apr 1887 in Tennessee. Ethel C. died ? .

484. James C. Harris (James Lindsey[8], Giles Claiborne[7], Gideon[6], Lewis[5], David[4], William[3], William[2], Thomas[1]). Born in Sep 1888 in Tennessee. James C. died ? .

485. Fletch Harris (James Lindsey[8], Giles Claiborne[7], Gideon[6], Lewis[5], David[4], William[3], William[2], Thomas[1]). Born in May 1890 in Tennessee. Fletch died ? .

486. Lonzy Harris (James Lindsey[8], Giles Claiborne[7], Gideon[6], Lewis[5], David[4], William[3], William[2], Thomas[1]). Born in Nov 1891 in Tennessee. Lonzy died ? .

487. Charley Harris (James Lindsey[8], Giles Claiborne[7], Gideon[6], Lewis[5], David[4], William[3], William[2], Thomas[1]). Born in Dec 1893 in Tennessee. Charley died ? .

488. Honor Delpha Harris (David Baxter[8], Giles Claiborne[7], Gideon[6], Lewis[5], David[4], William[3], William[2], Thomas[1]). Born ? . Honor Delpha died ? .

489. William Carnath Harris (David Baxter[8], Giles Claiborne[7], Gideon[6], Lewis[5], David[4], William[3], William[2], Thomas[1]). Born ? . William Carnath died ? .

490. Glennon Porter Harris (David Baxter[8], Giles Claiborne[7], Gideon[6], Lewis[5], David[4], William[3], William[2], Thomas[1]). Born ? . Glennon Porter died ? .

491. Carl O. Harris (David Baxter[8], Giles Claiborne[7], Gideon[6], Lewis[5], David[4], William[3], William[2], Thomas[1]). Born ca 1891 in Tennessee. Carl O. died ? .

492. Lillie N. Harris (David Baxter[8], Giles Claiborne[7], Gideon[6], Lewis[5], David[4], William[3], William[2], Thomas[1]). Born ca 1894 in Tennessee. Lillie N. died ? .

493. Dennie L. Harris (David Baxter[8], Giles Claiborne[7], Gideon[6], Lewis[5], David[4], William[3], William[2], Thomas[1]). Born ca 1898 in Tennessee. Dennie L. died ? .

494. Claudia M. Harris (David Baxter[8], Giles Claiborne[7], Gideon[6], Lewis[5], David[4], William[3], William[2], Thomas[1]). Born ca 1904 in Tennessee. Claudia M. died ? .

495. Minnie A. Harris (Joseph Carrol[8], Giles Claiborne[7], Gideon[6], Lewis[5], David[4], William[3], William[2], Thomas[1]). Born ca 1904 in Tennessee. Minnie A. died ? .

496. Martha J. Rone (Margaret Elizabeth "Maggie" Harris[8], John Gardner[7], Gideon[6], Lewis[5], David[4], William[3], William[2], Thomas[1]). Born on 27 Nov 1866 in Marshall County, TN. Martha J. died on 7 Apr 1939; she was 72.

497. George R. Rone (Margaret Elizabeth "Maggie" Harris[8], John Gardner[7], Gideon[6], Lewis[5], David[4], William[3], William[2], Thomas[1]).

Born on 16 Feb 1868 in Marshall County, TN. George R. died on 16 Jul 1935; he was 67.

498. John H. Rone (Margaret Elizabeth "Maggie" Harris[8], John Gardner[7], Gideon[6], Lewis[5], David[4], William[3], William[2], Thomas[1]). Born on 15 Mar 1870 in Lewis County, TN. John H. died on 29 Mar 1925; he was 55.

499. William H. Rone (Margaret Elizabeth "Maggie" Harris[8], John Gardner[7], Gideon[6], Lewis[5], David[4], William[3], William[2], Thomas[1]). Born on 3 Apr 1872 in Lewis County, TN. William H. died on 22 Jan 1957; he was 84.

500. Wiley A. Harris (David Lawson[8], William Lindsey[7], David[6], Lewis[5], David[4], William[3], William[2], Thomas[1]). Born on 22 Jul 1872. Wiley A. died on 20 Feb 1921; he was 48.

Information about the marriage is from WorldConnect; information about the children is from Marshall Co., TN, Census 1910.

On 18 Aug 1898 when Wiley A. was 26, he married Myrtle Ada Andrews. Born on 11 Sep 1878. Myrtle Ada died on 23 Apr 1952; she was 73.

They had the following children:

739	i.	Elgie Irwin (1900-1981)
740	ii.	Hazel (1904-1993)
741	iii.	David (1907-1974)

501. Gertrude V. Harris (David Lawson[8], William Lindsey[7], David[6], Lewis[5], David[4], William[3], William[2], Thomas[1]). Born on 31 Jan 1874. Gertrude V. died on 20 Sep 1949; she was 75.

502. Riggs Tidwell Harris (David Lawson[8], William Lindsey[7], David[6], Lewis[5], David[4], William[3], William[2], Thomas[1]). Born on 3 Apr 1876 in Tennessee. Riggs Tidwell died on 20 Jun 1936; he was 60.

Information about the marriage is from WorldConnect; information about the sons is from Wayne Co., IL, Census 1920.

On 18 Nov 1903 when Riggs Tidwell was 27, he married Sarah Jane Fox. Born on 18 Mar 1878 in Illinois. Sarah Jane died on 13 Aug 1947; she was 69.

They had the following children:

> **742**   i.   William Lawson (1905-1954)
>
> **743**   ii.   Joseph Linn (1906-?)

503. Jesse Reed Harris (David Lawson[8], William Lindsey[7], David[6], Lewis[5], David[4], William[3], William[2], Thomas[1]). Born on 26 Mar 1883 in Tennessee. Jesse Reed died on 8 Nov 1953; she was 70.

Information about the marriage is from WorldConnect; information about the children is from Marshall Co., TN, Census 1910.

On 12 Jun 1901 when Jesse Reed was 18, she married G. Frank Hardison, son of Thomas R. Hardison. Born on 21 Sep 1877 in Tennessee. G. Frank died in Marshall County, TN, on 2 Mar 1970; he was 92.

They had the following children:

> **744**   i.   Goodrum (1903-?)

745 ii.   Magneus (1905-?)

746 iii.   Cecil (1907-1983)

504. Martha Ann "Mattie" Malone (Sarah Jane Harris[8], William Lindsey[7], David[6], Lewis[5], David[4], William[3], William[2], Thomas[1]). Born on 30 Mar 1865. Martha Ann "Mattie" died on 1 Aug 1923; she was 58.

Information about the marriage is from WorldConnect.

On 16 Feb 1888 when Martha Ann "Mattie" was 22, she married Columbus Worth Hobby, son of Green Hobby & Sarah ?. Born in Sep 1860 in Tennessee. Columbus Worth died on 10 Mar 1917; he was 56.

505. Edgar Bruce Malone (Sarah Jane Harris[8], William Lindsey[7], David[6], Lewis[5], David[4], William[3], William[2], Thomas[1]). Born on 15 Jun 1874. Edgar Bruce died on 7 Sep 1944; he was 70.

Information about the marriage is from WorldConnect.

On 18 Mar 1897 when Edgar Bruce was 22, he married Ella Fount Rambo. Born on 31 Mar 1876. Ella Fount died on 7 Aug 1968; she was 92.

506. Lewis J. Harris (James Patterson[8], William Lindsey[7], David[6], Lewis[5], David[4], William[3], William[2], Thomas[1]). Born on 19 Sep 1873 in Tennessee. Lewis J. died on 7 Jun 1967; he was 93.

Information about the marriage is from WorldConnect; information about the son is from Marshall Co., TN, Census 1920. Lewis's father is a member of the household in 1920.

On 26 Dec 1899 when Lewis J. was 26, he married Sammie Gideon Ewing. Born on 9 Jun 1876. Sammie Gideon died on 7 Feb 1964; she was 87.

They had one child:

        747   i.   James E. (1911-1976)

507. J. Fount Harris (James Patterson[8], William Lindsey[7], David[6], Lewis[5], David[4], William[3], William[2], Thomas[1]). Born in Feb 1883 in Tennessee. J. Fount died on 31 Dec 1948; he was 65.

Information about the marriage is from WorldConnect; information about the daughter is from Marshall Co., TN, Census 1920.

On 27 Apr 1913 when J. Fount was 30, he married Zillah Emma Whitesell. Born on 22 Dec 1891 in Tennessee. Zillah Emma died on 9 Nov 1956; she was 64.

They had one child:

        748   i.   Christine (1915-)

508. Annes Edith Cheatham (Mary Katherine Harris[8], William Lindsey[7], David[6], Lewis[5], David[4], William[3], William[2], Thomas[1]). Born on 31 Oct 1872 in Tennessee. Annes Edith died on 14 Apr 1936; she was 63.

Information about the marriage is from Marshall Co., TN, Census 1910. Annes' father is a member of the household in 1910.

Ca 1898 when Annes Edith was 25, she married Thomas F. Higgs. Born on 1 Apr 1868 in Tennessee. Thomas F. died on 5 Jun 1930; he was 62.

509. William Thomas Cheatham (Mary Katherine Harris[8], William Lindsey[7], David[6], Lewis[5], David[4], William[3], William[2], Thomas[1]). Born on 17 May 1874 in Tennessee. William Thomas died on 7 Jun 1935; he was 61.

Information about the marriage is from WorldConnect.

On 11 Nov 1918 when William Thomas was 44, he married Mary Catherine Wheatly. Born in 1879. Mary Catherine died ?.

510. Luther M. Cheatham (Mary Katherine Harris[8], William Lindsey[7], David[6], Lewis[5], David[4], William[3], William[2], Thomas[1]). Born on 27 Jan 1878 in Tennessee. Luther M. died on 29 Jan 1958; he was 80.

Information about the wife is from Ancestry (Draft Registration Card).

Luther M. married Bessie Sue Baxter. Born on 12 Jul 1884. Bessie Sue died on 18 May 1962; she was 77.

511. Mary Ora Cheatham (Mary Katherine Harris[8], William Lindsey[7], David[6], Lewis[5], David[4], William[3], William[2], Thomas[1]). Born on 10 Feb 1886. Mary Ora died on 20 Dec 1956; she was 70.

Information about the marriage is from WorldConnect.

On 6 Jun 1918 when Mary Ora was 32, she married Elmo Bond. Born on 10 Jan 1886. Elmo died on 8 Feb 1963; he was 77.

512. Lelia Mai Liggett (Elizabeth Annie Harris[8], William Lindsey[7], David[6], Lewis[5], David[4], William[3], William[2], Thomas[1]). Born on 3 Sep 1882 in Marshall County, TN. Lelia Mai died in Marshall County, TN, in Feb 1967; she was 84.

Information about the marriage is from WorldConnect.

On 27 Nov 1907 when Lelia Mai was 25, she married Jessie Sewell Woodward, in Marshall County, TN. Born on 15 Aug

1877 in Marshall County, TN. Jessie Sewell died in Marshall County, TN, in Mar 1975; he was 97.

513. Sarah Vashti Liggett (Elizabeth Annie Harris[8], William Lindsey[7], David[6], Lewis[5], David[4], William[3], William[2], Thomas[1]). Born on 7 Dec 1883 in Marshall County, TN. Sarah Vashti died on 18 May 1967; she was 83.

Information about the marriage is from WorldConnect.

On 29 Dec 1910 when Sarah Vashti was 27, she married Robert Andrew Mount, in Marshall County, TN. Born on 17 Jul 1877. Robert Andrew died on 19 Jul 1938; he was 61.

514. Harris Claiborn Liggett (Elizabeth Annie Harris[8], William Lindsey[7], David[6], Lewis[5], David[4], William[3], William[2], Thomas[1]). Born on 17 Feb 1885 in Marshall County, TN. Harris Claiborn died in Bradley County, TN, in Nov 1981; he was 96.

Information about the Marriage is from WorldConnect.

On 20 Oct 1920 when Harris Claiborn was 35, he married Florence Annis Neeley, in Tennessee. Born on 20 Aug 1885. Florence Annis died in Bradley County, TN, in Dec 1979; she was 94.

515. Mary Ethel Liggett (Elizabeth Annie Harris[8], William Lindsey[7], David[6], Lewis[5], David[4], William[3], William[2], Thomas[1]). Born on 12 Sep 1886 in Marshall County, TN. Mary Ethel died in Marshall County, TN, on 13 Jul 1892; she was 5.

516. Ivey Hampton Liggett (Elizabeth Annie Harris[8], William Lindsey[7], David[6], Lewis[5], David[4], William[3], William[2], Thomas[1]). Born on 5 Feb 1888 in Marshall County, TN. Ivey Hampton died in Marshall County, TN, in Mar 1978; she was 90.

Information about the marriage is from WorldConnect.

On 19 Oct 1910 when Ivey Hampton was 22, she married Carl Douglas Phillips, in Marshall County, TN. Born on 9 May 1889. Carl Douglas died in Lawrence County, TN, on 19 Jul 1974; he was 85.

---

517. John Joyce Harris (Andrew Curran[9], Robert Giles[8], Giles Turner[7], Edmond[6], Giles[5], David[4], William[3], William[2], Thomas[1]). Born on 11 Dec 1915. John Joyce died on 16 Apr 1981; he was 65.

Information about the marriage is from Maury Co. Cemetery Records (Website).

In 1952 when John Joyce was 36, he married Elizabeth Short. Born on 1 Mar 1920 in Rutherford County, TN.

518. Albert L. Kern (Helen M. Harris[9], Tandy[8], John Claiborn[7], Claiborne[6], Giles[5], David[4], William[3], William[2], Thomas[1]). Born on 23 Nov 1900 in Virginia. Albert L. died on 28 Aug 1963; he was 62.

519. William M. Kern (Helen M. Harris[9], Tandy[8], John Claiborn[7], Claiborne[6], Giles[5], David[4], William[3], William[2], Thomas[1]). Born on 29 Aug 1903 in Virginia. William M. died on 9 Oct 1963; he was 60.

520. Marvin H. Kern (Helen M. Harris[9], Tandy[8], John Claiborn[7], Claiborne[6], Giles[5], David[4], William[3], William[2], Thomas[1]). Born on 18 May 1906 in Virginia. Marvin H. died in Fairfax County, VA, on 16 Apr 1978; he was 71.

521. Fara E. Kern (Helen M. Harris[9], Tandy[8], John Claiborn[7], Claiborne[6], Giles[5], David[4], William[3], William[2], Thomas[1]). Born on 5 Oct 1911 in Virginia. Fara E. died ? .

522. Verna A. Kern (Helen M. Harris[9], Tandy[8], John Claiborn[7], Claiborne[6], Giles[5], David[4], William[3], William[2], Thomas[1]). Born on 26 May 1915 in Virginia. Verna A. died in Nelson County, VA, in Jan 1988; she was 72.

523. John T. Kern (Helen M. Harris[9], Tandy[8], John Claiborn[7], Claiborne[6], Giles[5], David[4], William[3], William[2], Thomas[1]). Born on 6 Jun 1919 in Virginia. John T. died ? .

524. Claude M. Harris Jr. (Claude M.[9], Austin Dabney[8], William Austin[7], Giles[6], Lewis[5], David[4], William[3], William[2], Thomas[1]). Born ca 1908 in Louisiana. Claude M. died ? .

525. Reginald W. Harris (Claude M.[9], Austin Dabney[8], William Austin[7], Giles[6], Lewis[5], David[4], William[3], William[2], Thomas[1]). Born ca 1901 in Louisiana. Reginald W. died ? .

526. Aubyn Harris (Claude M.[9], Austin Dabney[8], William Austin[7], Giles[6], Lewis[5], David[4], William[3], William[2], Thomas[1]). Born ca 1905 in Louisiana. Aubyn died ? .

527. Janie Clara McFall (Sarah Martha "Mattie" Harris[9], Gideon Lewis[8], David Rice[7], Gideon[6], Lewis[5], David[4], William[3], William[2], Thomas[1]). Born on 3 Dec 1887 in Florida. Janie Clara died on 1 Dec 1950; she was 62.

Information about the marriage is from WorldConnect.

On 5 Jun 1912 when Janie Clara was 24, she married Malcolm McAuley MacLeod. Born on 31 Aug 1887. Malcolm McAuley died ? .

528. John Harold McFall (Sarah Martha "Mattie" Harris[9], Gideon Lewis[8], David Rice[7], Gideon[6], Lewis[5], David[4], William[3], William[2],

Thomas[1]). Born on 11 Jul 1890 in Florida. John Harold died ?
.

Information about the marriage is from WorldConnect.

On 9 Nov 1935 when John Harold was 45, he married
Elizabeth Beals Daniel. Born on 16 Oct 1904. Elizabeth died
? .

529. Andrew Norris McFall (Sarah Martha "Mattie" Harris[9],
Gideon Lewis[8], David Rice[7], Gideon[6], Lewis[5], David[4], William[3],
William[2], Thomas[1]). Born on 9 Dec 1892 in Florida. Andrew
Norris died on 17 Oct 1928; he was 35.

Information about the marriage is from WorldConnect.

On 19 Jan 1925 when Andrew Norris was 32, he married
Marian Hilda Davis. Born on 19 Nov 1903. Marian Hilda
died ? .

530. Robert Trice McFall (Sarah Martha "Mattie" Harris[9],
Gideon Lewis[8], David Rice[7], Gideon[6], Lewis[5], David[4], William[3],
William[2], Thomas[1]). Born on 17 Mar 1896 in Florida. Robert
Trice died ? .

Information about the marriage is from WorldConnect.

On 7 Jan 1921 when Robert Trice was 24, he married
Victoria Ann Serbs. Born on 23 Apr 1903. Victoria Ann died
? .

531. Ned Harris Webb (Maude May Harris[9], Giles Tinsley[8],
David Rice[7], Gideon[6], Lewis[5], David[4], William[3], William[2], Thomas[1]).
Born on 26 Nov 1912. Ned Harris died on 16 Nov 1936; he
was 23.

532. William Carey Webb (Maude May Harris[9], Giles Tinsley[8], David Rice[7], Gideon[6], Lewis[5], David[4], William[3], William[2], Thomas[1]). Born on 21 Jul 1917.

Information about the marriage is from WorldConnect.

On 13 Jul 1937 when William Carey was 19, he married Grace Ruth Goblet. Born on 29 Oct 1917. Grace Ruth died ? .

533. Ralph T. Harris (Cecil Rice[9], Giles Tinsley[8], David Rice[7], Gideon[6], Lewis[5], David[4], William[3], William[2], Thomas[1]). Born on 12 Jun 1916. Ralph T. died ? .

Information about the marriage is from WorldConnect.

On 19 Apr 1940 when Ralph T. was 23, he married Frances Lucille Largen. Born on 3 Feb 1918.

534. Sarah C. Harris (Cecil Rice[9], Giles Tinsley[8], David Rice[7], Gideon[6], Lewis[5], David[4], William[3], William[2], Thomas[1]). Born in 1920 in Tennessee.

535. Elizabeth Lee Harris (William Lee[9], William Thomas[8], James Gilliam[7], Gideon[6], Lewis[5], David[4], William[3], William[2], Thomas[1]). Born ca 1908 in Tennessee. Elizabeth Lee died ? .

Information about the marriage is from WorldConnect.

On 7 Mar 1942 when Elizabeth Lee was 34, she married Raven I. McDavid. Born ? . Raven I. died ? .

536. Thomas Ferrell Harris (William Lee[9], William Thomas[8], James Gilliam[7], Gideon[6], Lewis[5], David[4], William[3], William[2], Thomas[1]). Born ca 1911 in Tennessee. Thomas Ferrell died ? .

Information about the marriage is from WorldConnect.

On 20 Jun 1947 when Thomas Ferrell was 36, he married Ann Shannon. Born ? . Ann died ? .

537. Waller B. Harris (William Lee[9], William Thomas[8], James Gilliam[7], Gideon[6], Lewis[5], David[4], William[3], William[2], Thomas[1]). Born ca 1914 in Tennessee.

538. Grover Cisco Walker (James Thomas[9], Martha Elizabeth Harris[8], Gideon Lindsey[7], Gideon[6], Lewis[5], David[4], William[3], William[2], Thomas[1]). Born on 22 Jul 1886 in McNairy County, TN. Grover Cisco died in McNairy County, TN, on 2 Nov 1970; he was 84.

Information about the wife and daughter is from McNairy Co., TN, Census 1910.

Grover Cisco married Media A. ?. Born ca 1889 in Tennessee. Media A. died ? .

They had one child:

> **749** i. Parnie V. (ca1908-?)

539. Manson Rupert Walker (James Thomas[9], Martha Elizabeth Harris[8], Gideon Lindsey[7], Gideon[6], Lewis[5], David[4], William[3], William[2], Thomas[1]). Born on 14 May 1888 in McNairy County, TN. Manson Rupert died on 3 Jun 1948; he was 60.

540. Duel Rastus Walker (James Thomas[9], Martha Elizabeth Harris[8], Gideon Lindsey[7], Gideon[6], Lewis[5], David[4], William[3], William[2], Thomas[1]). Born on 19 Jun 1890 in Tennessee. Duel Rastus died in Jackson, TN, on 24 Sep 1975; he was 85.

541. Everette Cecil Walker (James Thomas[9], Martha Elizabeth Harris[8], Gideon Lindsey[7], Gideon[6], Lewis[5], David[4], William[3], William[2], Thomas[1]). Born on 1 Jun 1894 in McNairy County,

TN. Everette Cecil died in McNairy County, TN, on 19 Dec 1987; he was 93.

542. Irma Walker (Joseph Anthony[9], Martha Elizabeth Harris[8], Gideon Lindsey[7], Gideon[6], Lewis[5], David[4], William[3], William[2], Thomas[1]). Born ca 1905 in Tennessee. Irma died ? .

543. Ella May Harris (William Marion[9], Giles Claiborne[8], Gideon Lindsey[7], Gideon[6], Lewis[5], David[4], William[3], William[2], Thomas[1]). Born on 23 Oct 1886 in McNairy County, TN. Ella May died in Santa Cruz County, CA, on 22 Jan 1967; she was 80.

Information about the marriage is from WorldConnect; information about the children is from McNairy Co., TN, Census 1910 and Clay Co., AR, Census 1920.

On 22 Oct 1903 when Ella May was 16, she married Charlie Fred Walker, in Jackson, TN. Born on 4 Sep 1877 in McNairy County, TN. Charlie Fred died in Santa Cruz County, CA, in Jul 1957; he was 79.

They had the following children:

750	i.	Lilburn T. (1904-1976)
751	ii.	Hazel (1907-?)
752	iii.	Zahelia (1909-?)
753	iv.	Norman Fay (1913-1986)
754	v.	Mildred (ca1916-?)
755	vi.	Don (ca1919-)

544. Dulber Odell Harris (Gideon Simpson[9], Giles Claiborne[8], Gideon Lindsey[7], Gideon[6], Lewis[5], David[4], William[3], William[2],

Thomas[1]). Born on 13 Nov 1886 in McNairy County, TN. Dulber Odell died in Detroit, MI, on 14 Feb 1929; he was 42.

Information about the marriage is from WorldConnect.

On 27 Aug 1911 when Dulber Odell was 24, he married Retta Maude Killian. Born on 8 Feb 1882. Retta Maude died ? in Detroit, MI.

545. Nolus Guy Harris (Gideon Simpson[9], Giles Claiborne[8], Gideon Lindsey[7], Gideon[6], Lewis[5], David[4], William[3], William[2], Thomas[1]). Born on 30 Apr 1887 in McNairy County, TN. Nolus Guy died in San Mateo, CA, on 12 Nov 1941; he was 54.

Information about the marriage and son is from WorldConnect.

On 23 Apr 1916 when Nolus Guy was 28, he married Irene Beatrice Hawkins, in Memphis, TN. Born on 16 Jul 1895 in Allegan County, MI. Irene Beatrice died in San Francisco, CA, on 24 May 1981; she was 85.

They had one child:

> **756**   i.   Winston Howard (1917-1992)

546. Cordia Licurgus Harris (Gideon Simpson[9], Giles Claiborne[8], Gideon Lindsey[7], Gideon[6], Lewis[5], David[4], William[3], William[2], Thomas[1]). Born on 6 Nov 1889 in Memphis, TN. Cordia Licurgus died in Dunklin County, MO, on 30 Nov 1961; he was 72.

Information about the marriage is from Dunklin Co., MO, website; information about the children is from Dunklin Co., MO, Census 1930.

On 13 Oct 1906 when Cordia Licurgus was 16, he married Lela Harvey. Born on 30 Sep 1888. Lela died in Dunklin County, MO, on 14 Nov 1957; she was 69.

They had the following children:

757	i.	Carl B. (1907-1970)
758	ii.	George S. (1911-1981)
759	iii.	Mildred D. (1913-1979)
760	iv.	Roy (1916-1963)
761	v.	Darl T. (ca1921-)
762	vi.	Billy W. (ca1924-)

547. Vander Eason Harris (Gideon Simpson[9], Giles Claiborne[8], Gideon Lindsey[7], Gideon[6], Lewis[5], David[4], William[3], William[2], Thomas[1]). Born on 8 Jan 1892 in McNairy County, TN. Vander Eason died in Dunklin County, MO, on 10 Jun 1962; he was 70.

Information about the marriage is from Dunklin Co., MO, Website; information about the children is from Dunklin Co., MO, Census 1930.

On 28 Dec 1913 when Vander Eason was 21, he married Delpha Jane Thompson, in Dunklin County, MO. Born on 3 Dec 1895 in Dunklin County, MO. Delpha Jane died ? .

They had the following children:

763	i.	Beauford I. (1915-1978)
764	ii.	Winston B. (ca1918-)
765	iii.	Imogene (ca1923-)
766	iv.	Jesse F. (ca1925-)
767	v.	Mary S. (ca1927-)

548. William Goss Harris (Gideon Simpson[9], Giles Claiborne[8], Gideon Lindsey[7], Gideon[6], Lewis[5], David[4], William[3], William[2], Thomas[1]). Born on 4 Feb 1894 in Tennessee. William Goss died in Memphis, TN, on 21 Oct 1968; he was 74.

Information about the marriage is from WorldConnect.

On 15 Nov 1926 when William Goss was 32, he married Allie Beatrice Brazier, in Dunklin County, MO. Born on 23 Jul 1901 in Dyer County, TN. Allie Beatrice died ? .

549. Sallie Gladys Harris (Gideon Simpson[9], Giles Claiborne[8], Gideon Lindsey[7], Gideon[6], Lewis[5], David[4], William[3], William[2], Thomas[1]). Born on 19 Apr 1895 in McNairy County, TN. Sallie Gladys died in Memphis, TN, in 1966; she was 70.

Information about the marriage is from WorldConnect; information about the childen is from Crockett, TN, Census 1930. Apparently, Howard is the son of a previous marriage.

On 29 Apr 1916 when Sallie Gladys was 21, she married Walter Benjamin Hay, in Missouri. Born on 3 Dec 1873 in Crockett County, TN. Walter Benjamin died in Crockett County, TN, in 1957; he was 83.

They had the following children:

768	i.	Howard L. (ca1908-)
769	ii.	Grace Owen (1917-)
770	iii.	Mary E. (ca1920-)
771	iv.	Iria N. (ca1922-)
772	v.	Rachel C. (ca1926-)
773	vi.	Rebecca J. (ca1927-)

550. Robert Taylor Harris (Gideon Simpson[9], Giles Claiborne[8], Gideon Lindsey[7], Gideon[6], Lewis[5], David[4], William[3], William[2], Thomas[1]). Born on 10 Jun 1898 in McNairy County, TN. Robert Taylor died in Kern County, CA, on 13 Aug 1972; he was 74.

Information about the marriage is from WorldConnect; information about the daughter is from Kern Co., California, Census 1930.

On 21 Dec 1921 when Robert Taylor was 23, he married Fernie Idella Ridgeway, in Dunklin County, MO. Born on 26 Mar 1900 in Dunklin County, MO. Fernie Idella died ? in Kern County, CA.

They had one child:

| 774 | i. | Joyce (ca1930-) |

551. Alfred Taylor Harris (Gideon Simpson[9], Giles Claiborne[8], Gideon Lindsey[7], Gideon[6], Lewis[5], David[4], William[3], William[2], Thomas[1]). Born on 10 Jun 1898 in McNairy County, TN. Alfred Taylor died in Kern County, CA, on 28 Jun 1980; he was 82.

Information about the marriage is from WorldConnect; information about the son is from Kern Co., California, Census 1930.

On 14 Jan 1923 when Alfred Taylor was 24, he married Melissa Ruth Ridgeway, in Dunklin County, MO. Born on 16 Nov 1903 in Dunklin County, MO. Melissa Ruth died in Kern County, CA, on 14 Aug 1993; she was 89.

They had one child:

775   i.   Elwood B. (ca1927-)

552. Ervin Lafayette Harris (Gideon Simpson[9], Giles Claiborne[8], Gideon Lindsey[7], Gideon[6], Lewis[5], David[4], William[3], William[2], Thomas[1]). Born on 25 Nov 1900 in McNairy County, TN. Ervin Lafayette died in Marion County, OR, on 24 Nov 1964; he was 63.

Information about the marriage is from WorldConnect.

On 18 May 1919 when Ervin Lafayette was 18, he married Elnora Cary. Born on 13 Oct 1902. Elnora died ? .

553. Jewel Thedus Harris (Gideon Simpson[9], Giles Claiborne[8], Gideon Lindsey[7], Gideon[6], Lewis[5], David[4], William[3], William[2], Thomas[1]). Born on 12 Feb 1902 in McNairy County, TN. Jewel Thedus died in Flint, MI, on 29 Dec 1974; he was 72.

Information about the marriage and son is from LDS.

On 19 Sep 1920 when Jewel Thedus was 18, he married Ida Mahalye Kinnett, in Dunklin County, MO. Born on 7 Jan 1900 in Atlanta, GA. Ida Mahalye died in Fenton, MI, on 21 May 1988; she was 88.

They had one child:

776   i.   Jewel Winfred (1931-1951)

554. Claude Pascal English (Mahalye Jane Harris[9], Giles Claiborne[8], Gideon Lindsey[7], Gideon[6], Lewis[5], David[4], William[3], William[2], Thomas[1]). Born on 11 Feb 1886 in McNairy County, TN. Claude Pascal died in Little Rock, AR, in 1954; he was 67.

Information about the marriage is from Shelby Co., TN, Census 1920. Carra's father and mother are members of the household in 1920.

In 1914 when Claude Pascal was 27, he married Carra I. Carrol. Born ? . Carra I. died ? .

555. Ernest Buster English (Mahalye Jane Harris[9], Giles Claiborne[8], Gideon Lindsey[7], Gideon[6], Lewis[5], David[4], William[3], William[2], Thomas[1]). Born on 8 Nov 1887 in McNairy County, TN. Ernest Buster died in Nov 1953; he was 65.

Information about the marriage is from WorldConnect.

On 21 Feb 1912 when Ernest Buster was 24, he married Eba Jane Carroll. Born on 18 Apr 1894 in Gibson County, TN. Eba Jane died in Leachville, AR, in Jul 1971; she was 77.

556. Ova Agatha English (Mahalye Jane Harris[9], Giles Claiborne[8], Gideon Lindsey[7], Gideon[6], Lewis[5], David[4], William[3], William[2], Thomas[1]). Born on 28 Dec 1889 in McNairy County, TN. Ova Agatha died in Hardin County, TN, on 21 Jun 1978; she was 88.

Information about the marriage is from Ancestry.

On 23 Jan 1913 when Ova Agatha was 23, she married Ronayne Blanchard White, son of Neil Soules White & Mary Jane Littlefield, in McNairy County, TN. Born on 13 Nov 1876 in Hardin County, TN. Ronayne Blanchard died in Hardin County, TN, on 30 Jul 1930; he was 53.

557. Doran J. English (Mahalye Jane Harris[9], Giles Claiborne[8], Gideon Lindsey[7], Gideon[6], Lewis[5], David[4], William[3], William[2], Thomas[1]). Born on 6 Sep 1891 in McNairy County, TN. Doran J. died in Memphis, TN, on 3 May 1960; he was 68.

558. Eva M. English (Mahalye Jane Harris[9], Giles Claiborne[8], Gideon Lindsey[7], Gideon[6], Lewis[5], David[4], William[3], William[2], Thomas[1]). Born on 13 May 1893 in McNairy County, TN. Eva M. died in McNairy County, TN, on 28 Aug 1923; she was 30.

Information about the marriage is from WorldConnect.

On 23 Dec 1912 when Eva M. was 19, she married William C. Donaldson, in McNairy County, TN. Born on 19 Dec 1889 in Hardin County, TN. William C. died in McNairy County, TN, in Dec 1980; he was 90.

559. George Harter English (Mahalye Jane Harris[9], Giles Claiborne[8], Gideon Lindsey[7], Gideon[6], Lewis[5], David[4], William[3], William[2], Thomas[1]). Born on 19 Feb 1896 in McNairy County, TN. George Harter died in Memphis, TN, in Sep 1986; he was 90.

Information about the wife is from WorldConnect.

George Harter married Anna Mary Cook. Born ? . Anna Mary died ? .

560. Sally M. English (Mahalye Jane Harris[9], Giles Claiborne[8], Gideon Lindsey[7], Gideon[6], Lewis[5], David[4], William[3], William[2], Thomas[1]). Born on 19 Apr 1898 in McNairy County, TN. Sally M. died in McNairy County, TN, on 6 May 1998; she was 100.

Information about the marriage is from WorldConnect.

On 8 Oct 1916 when Sally M. was 18, she married Jaby Linton Tidwell, in McNairy County, TN. Born on 28 Jul 1895 in McNairy County, TN. Jaby Linton died in Jackson, TN, in Feb 1946; he was 50.

561. Mary English (Mahalye Jane Harris[9], Giles Claiborne[8], Gideon Lindsey[7], Gideon[6], Lewis[5], David[4], William[3], William[2], Thomas[1]). Born on 17 Aug 1900 in McNairy County, TN. Mary died in Jackson, TN, on 26 Dec 1974; she was 74.

Information about the marriage is from McNairy Co., TN, Census 1930. George and Mahalia English are members of the household in 1930.

Ca 1922 when Mary was 21, she married Fred Sanders, son of John C. Sanders & Melvina J. ?, in McNairy County, TN. Born on 15 Jan 1893. Fred died in Montgomery County, TN, in Jun 1985; he was 92.

562. Columbus Gavin Harris (John Madison[9], Giles Claiborne[8], Gideon Lindsey[7], Gideon[6], Lewis[5], David[4], William[3], William[2], Thomas[1]). Born on 16 Oct 1889 in McNairy County, TN. Columbus Gavin died in Pinellas County, FL, on 22 Mar 1977; he was 87.

Information about the marriage is from WorldConnect; information about the children is from Flint Co., MI, Census 1920.

On 1 Sep 1909 when Columbus Gavin was 19, he married Elma Elizabeth Smith, in Dunklin County, MO. Born on 13 Oct 1892 in Woodruff County, AR. Elma Elizabeth died in Alcona County, MI, on 24 Oct 1986; she was 94.

They had the following children:

> **777**   i.   Lovy B. (1914-1984)
>
> **778**   ii.   Fanader G. (ca1919-)

563. Willie Ilah Harris (John Madison[9], Giles Claiborne[8], Gideon Lindsey[7], Gideon[6], Lewis[5], David[4], William[3], William[2], Thomas[1]). Born on 15 Jun 1904 in Dunklin County, MO. Willie Ilah died in Flint, MI, on 7 Aug 1964; she was 60.

Information about the marriage is from WorldConect; information about the daughter is from Genesee Co., MI, Census 1930.

On 20 Jan 1928 when Willie Ilah was 23, she married Herman Kruse, in Flint, MI. Born on 16 Jan 1905 in Duluth County, MN. Herman died in Bay County, MI, on 3 Aug 1975; he was 70.

They had one child:

> **779**   i.   Joyce (1930-)

564. Clyde Pascal Harris (John Madison[9], Giles Claiborne[8], Gideon Lindsey[7], Gideon[6], Lewis[5], David[4], William[3], William[2], Thomas[1]). Born on 9 Apr 1910 in Dunklin County, MO.

Clyde Pascal died in Kern County, CA, on 24 Jun 1997; he was 87.

Information about the marriage is from WorldConnect.

On 5 Mar 1933 when Clyde Pascal was 22, he married Hazel Alma Mayo, in Flint, MI. Born on 9 Dec 1915 in Muncie, IN. Hazel Alma died in Kern County, CA, on 15 Nov 1989; she was 73.

565. F. L. Harris (John Madison[9], Giles Claiborne[8], Gideon Lindsey[7], Gideon[6], Lewis[5], David[4], William[3], William[2], Thomas[1]). Born on 13 Jul 1913 in Clay County, AR.

Information about the marriage is from WorldConnect.

On 1 Apr 1934 when F. L. was 20, he married Marjorie Tracy Hull, in Flint, MI. Born on 23 Apr 1917 in Flint, MI.

566. Minnie Nagle (Lucy Elizabeth Harris[9], Giles Claiborne[8], Gideon Lindsey[7], Gideon[6], Lewis[5], David[4], William[3], William[2], Thomas[1]). Born on 29 Sep 1885. Minnie died in Tishomingo County, MS, on 20 Oct 1947; she was 62.

567. Millard Nagle (Lucy Elizabeth Harris[9], Giles Claiborne[8], Gideon Lindsey[7], Gideon[6], Lewis[5], David[4], William[3], William[2], Thomas[1]). Born on 30 May 1887 in Tishomingo County, MS. Millard died in Tishomingo County, MS, on 10 Sep 1977; he was 90.

568. Fayette Nagle (Lucy Elizabeth Harris[9], Giles Claiborne[8], Gideon Lindsey[7], Gideon[6], Lewis[5], David[4], William[3], William[2], Thomas[1]). Born on 14 Nov 1890 in Tishomingo County, MS. Fayette died in Tishomingo County, MS, on 5 Sep 1988; he was 97.

569. Maudie Nagle (Lucy Elizabeth Harris^9, Giles Claiborne^8, Gideon Lindsey^7, Gideon^6, Lewis^5, David^4, William^3, William^2, Thomas^1). Born on 5 Sep 1895. Maudie died ? .

570. William V. Riggs (Sarah Frances Harris^9, Giles Claiborne^8, Gideon Lindsey^7, Gideon^6, Lewis^5, David^4, William^3, William^2, Thomas^1). Born on 27 Feb 1888 in McNairy County, TN. William V. died in Leachville, AR, on 26 Mar 1936; he was 48.

571. Eber H. Riggs (Sarah Frances Harris^9, Giles Claiborne^8, Gideon Lindsey^7, Gideon^6, Lewis^5, David^4, William^3, William^2, Thomas^1). Born on 6 Jun 1890 in McNairy County, TN. Eber H. died in McNairy County, TN, on 10 Nov 1904; he was 14.

572. William C. Butler (Amanda Catherine Harris^9, Giles Claiborne^8, Gideon Lindsey^7, Gideon^6, Lewis^5, David^4, William^3, William^2, Thomas^1). Born on 16 Jan 1891 in McNairy County, TN. William C. died on 13 Apr 1969; he was 78.

573. Zula M. Butler (Amanda Catherine Harris^9, Giles Claiborne^8, Gideon Lindsey^7, Gideon^6, Lewis^5, David^4, William^3, William^2, Thomas^1). Born on 10 Mar 1893 in McNairy County, TN. Zula M. died in Corinth, MS, in Aug 1981; she was 88.

574. Plaught Butler (Amanda Catherine Harris^9, Giles Claiborne^8, Gideon Lindsey^7, Gideon^6, Lewis^5, David^4, William^3, William^2, Thomas^1). Born on 17 Feb 1895 in McNairy County, TN. Plaught died in Corinth, MS, on 5 Mar 1972; he was 77.

575. Sally I. Butler (Amanda Catherine Harris^9, Giles Claiborne^8, Gideon Lindsey^7, Gideon^6, Lewis^5, David^4, William^3, William^2,

Thomas[1]). Born on 6 Aug 1899 in McNairy County, TN.
Sally I. died in Corinth, MS, on 7 Mar 1980; she was 80.

576. Eura Harris (George Calvin[9], Giles Claiborne[8], Gideon
Lindsey[7], Gideon[6], Lewis[5], David[4], William[3], William[2], Thomas[1]).
Born on 30 Oct 1894 in McNairy County, TN. Eura died in
Dunklin County, MO, on 30 Jun 1994; she was 99.

Information about the marriage is from WorldConnect;
information about the daughter is from Dunklin Co., MO,
Census 1920.

On 5 Dec 1915 when Eura was 21, she married James Odell
Fuzzell, in Dunklin County, MO. Born on 6 May 1893 in
Carroll County, TN. James Odell died in Dunklin County,
MO, on 16 Dec 1981; he was 88.

They had one child:

> **780**   i.   Evelyn A. (1917-1996)

577. Straudy Harris (George Calvin[9], Giles Claiborne[8], Gideon
Lindsey[7], Gideon[6], Lewis[5], David[4], William[3], William[2], Thomas[1]).
Born on 13 May 1896 in McNairy County, TN. Straudy died
in Dunklin County, MO, on 19 Nov 1997; she was 101.

Information about the marriage is from WorldConnect.

On 9 Dec 1918 when Straudy was 22, she married Wade
Field Manley, son of Jacob B Manley & Mary G. ?, in
Dunklin County, MO. Born on 12 Sep 1897 in Friendship,
TN. Wade Field died in Dunklin County, MO, on 4 Apr
1962; he was 64.

578. Bessie Harris (George Calvin[9], Giles Claiborne[8], Gideon
Lindsey[7], Gideon[6], Lewis[5], David[4], William[3], William[2], Thomas[1]).

Born on 26 Nov 1900 in Dunklin County, MO. Bessie died in Cape Girardeau, MO, on 7 Jun 1996; she was 95.

Information about the marriage is from WorldConnect.

On 30 Aug 1924 when Bessie was 23, she married Albert Monroe Estes, in Jackson, MO. Born on 21 Aug 1901 in Millersville, MO. Albert Monroe died in Cape Girardeau, MO, on 18 Apr 1974; he was 72.

579. Joseph Harris (George Calvin[9], Giles Claiborne[8], Gideon Lindsey[7], Gideon[6], Lewis[5], David[4], William[3], William[2], Thomas[1]). Born on 28 Nov 1902 in McNairy County, TN. Joseph died in Dunklin County, MO, on 30 Nov 1992; he was 90.

Information about the marriage is from WorldConnect.

On 22 Feb 1928 when Joseph was 25, he married Tavia May Loftin, in Memphis, TN. Born on 28 Dec 1907 in Tate County, MS. Tavia May died in St. Louis, MO, on 26 Feb 1979; she was 71.

580. Verna L. Harris (George Calvin[9], Giles Claiborne[8], Gideon Lindsey[7], Gideon[6], Lewis[5], David[4], William[3], William[2], Thomas[1]). Born on 29 Oct 1909 in Dunklin County, MO. Verna L. died in Dunklin County, MO, on 29 Jan 1997; she was 87.

Information about the marriage is from Dunklin Co., MO, Website.

On 10 Jun 1934 when Verna L. was 24, she married Arthur Estes Cummins, in Dunklin County, MO. Born on 27 Dec 1909 in Attala County, MS. Arthur Estes died in Dunklin County, MO, on 30 Apr 1994; he was 84.

581. Nina M. Harris (George Calvin[9], Giles Claiborne[8], Gideon Lindsey[7], Gideon[6], Lewis[5], David[4], William[3], William[2], Thomas[1]). Born on 9 Aug 1911 in Dunklin County, MO. Nina M. died ? .

Information about the marriage is from WorldConnect.

On 18 Aug 1934 when Nina M. was 23, she married Roy Audry Berry, in Stoddard County, MO. Born on 12 Feb 1907 in Bollinger County, MO. Roy Audry died in St. Louis, MO, on 5 May 1982; he was 75.

582. Edwin R. Harris (George Calvin[9], Giles Claiborne[8], Gideon Lindsey[7], Gideon[6], Lewis[5], David[4], William[3], William[2], Thomas[1]). Born on 21 Jan 1914 in Dunklin County, MO. Edwin R. died in Dunklin County, MO, on 4 Nov 1987; he was 73.

Information about the marriage and daughter is from Dunklin Co., MO, Website.

On 2 Jan 1938 when Edwin R. was 23, he married Dorothy Ione Graves, in Greene County, AR. Born on 11 Aug 1916 in Dunklin County, MO. Dorothy Ione died on 29 Oct 2003; she was 87.

They had one child:

    781 i.   Eleanor Graves

583. Paul C. Harris (George Calvin[9], Giles Claiborne[8], Gideon Lindsey[7], Gideon[6], Lewis[5], David[4], William[3], William[2], Thomas[1]). Born on 3 Sep 1916 in Dunklin County, MO. Paul C. died on 10 Jan 1975; he was 58.

Information about the marriage is from WorldConnect.

On 20 May 1933 when Paul C. was 16, he married Mavis Krone, in Greene County, AR. Born on 7 Feb 1916 in Dunklin County, MO.

584. G. C. Harris (George Calvin[9], Giles Claiborne[8], Gideon Lindsey[7], Gideon[6], Lewis[5], David[4], William[3], William[2], Thomas[1]). Born ca 1925 in Missouri.

585. Rosa Smith (Julia Kinnell Harris[9], Giles Claiborne[8], Gideon Lindsey[7], Gideon[6], Lewis[5], David[4], William[3], William[2], Thomas[1]). Born on 7 Oct 1893 in McNairy County, TN. Rosa died in Trousdale County, TN, on 5 Nov 1958; she was 65.

Information about the husband is from WorldConnect.

Rosa married Mitchell Wright. Born on 20 Jul 1889. Mitchell died in Trousdale County, TN, on 7 Nov 1957; he was 68.

586. Roxia Smith (Julia Kinnell Harris[9], Giles Claiborne[8], Gideon Lindsey[7], Gideon[6], Lewis[5], David[4], William[3], William[2], Thomas[1]). Born on 23 Mar 1896 in Parker County, TX. Roxia died in Memphis, TN, in Oct 1982; she was 86.

Information about the marriage is from WorldConnect.

On 8 Dec 1912 when Roxia was 16, she married Leslie Donohoe Gammons. Born on 24 Nov 1893 in Henry County, TN. Leslie Donohoe died in Owensboro, KY, on 29 Aug 1953; he was 59.

587. Donald McClanahan (Julia Kinnell Harris[9], Giles Claiborne[8], Gideon Lindsey[7], Gideon[6], Lewis[5], David[4], William[3], William[2], Thomas[1]). Born on 22 Sep 1905 in Trousdale County, TN. Donald died in Nashville, TN, on 25 Nov 1988; he was 83.

588. Gladys McClanahan (Julia Kinnell Harris[9], Giles Claiborne[8], Gideon Lindsey[7], Gideon[6], Lewis[5], David[4], William[3], William[2], Thomas[1]). Born on 24 Oct 1908 in Trousdale County, TN. Gladys died in Wilson County, TN, in Mar 1993; she was 84.

589. Mamie McClanahan (Julia Kinnell Harris[9], Giles Claiborne[8], Gideon Lindsey[7], Gideon[6], Lewis[5], David[4], William[3], William[2], Thomas[1]). Born on 2 Apr 1910 in Trousdale County, TN. Mamie died in Nashville, TN, on 21 Jul 1928; she was 18.

590. Eugene McClanahan (Julia Kinnell Harris[9], Giles Claiborne[8], Gideon Lindsey[7], Gideon[6], Lewis[5], David[4], William[3], William[2], Thomas[1]). Born on 16 Jul 1912 in Trousdale County, TN. Eugene died in Wilson County, TN, in Apr 1986; he was 73.

591. Talmage McClanahan (Julia Kinnell Harris[9], Giles Claiborne[8], Gideon Lindsey[7], Gideon[6], Lewis[5], David[4], William[3], William[2], Thomas[1]). Born on 19 May 1916 in Trousdale County, TN. Talmage died in Trousdale County, TN, on 12 Sep 1924; he was 8.

592. Viola Harris (Jeptha Virgil[9], Giles Claiborne[8], Gideon Lindsey[7], Gideon[6], Lewis[5], David[4], William[3], William[2], Thomas[1]). Born on 1 Oct 1908 in Dunklin County, MO. Viola died in Santa Fe, NM, on 4 Apr 1961; she was 52.

On 3 Oct 1929 when Viola was 21, she married Thetus Pritchard. Born on 14 Oct 1903 in Carroll County, TN. Thetus died in Carroll County, TN, on 24 Apr 1970; he was 66.

593. J. R. Harris (Jeptha Virgil[9], Giles Claiborne[8], Gideon Lindsey[7], Gideon[6], Lewis[5], David[4], William[3], William[2], Thomas[1]). Born on 14 Feb 1913 in Clay County, AR. J. R. died in Clay County, AR, on 4 Feb 1923; he was 9.

594. Thelma Nadine Harris (Jeptha Virgil[9], Giles Claiborne[8], Gideon Lindsey[7], Gideon[6], Lewis[5], David[4], William[3], William[2], Thomas[1]). Born on 17 Sep 1917 in Dunklin County, MO.

Information about the marriage is from WorldConnect.

On 16 Sep 1939 when Thelma Nadine was 21, she married Hubert Elmer Flynt, in Clay County, AR. Born on 10 Oct 1915 in Navarro County, TX. Hubert Elmer died in Clay County, AR, on 10 Dec 2004; he was 89.

595. James O. Littlefield (Lucy Jane Harris[9], David Thomas[8], Gideon Lindsey[7], Gideon[6], Lewis[5], David[4], William[3], William[2], Thomas[1]). Born on 7 Mar 1888 in Tennessee. James O. died in Hardin County, TN, on 14 Oct 1909; he was 21.

596. Aryte M. Littlefield (Lucy Jane Harris[9], David Thomas[8], Gideon Lindsey[7], Gideon[6], Lewis[5], David[4], William[3], William[2], Thomas[1]). Born on 15 Jul 1890 in Tennessee. Aryte M. died in 1954; she was 63.

597. Luther R. Littlefield (Lucy Jane Harris[9], David Thomas[8], Gideon Lindsey[7], Gideon[6], Lewis[5], David[4], William[3], William[2], Thomas[1]). Born on 20 Jul 1893 in McNairy County, TN. Luther R. died in Hardin County, TN, on 14 Oct 1909; he was 16.

598. Altha M. Littlefield (Lucy Jane Harris[9], David Thomas[8], Gideon Lindsey[7], Gideon[6], Lewis[5], David[4], William[3], William[2], Thomas[1]). Born on 10 Jul 1896 in McNairy County, TN.

Altha M. died in McNairy County, TN, on 26 Mar 1923; she was 26.

599. William P. Littlefield (Lucy Jane Harris[9], David Thomas[8], Gideon Lindsey[7], Gideon[6], Lewis[5], David[4], William[3], William[2], Thomas[1]). Born on 16 Feb 1899 in McNairy County, TN. William P. died in McNairy County, TN, in Nov 1979; he was 80.

600. Lizzie E. Littlefield (Lucy Jane Harris[9], David Thomas[8], Gideon Lindsey[7], Gideon[6], Lewis[5], David[4], William[3], William[2], Thomas[1]). Born on 22 Feb 1902 in McNairy County, TN. Lizzie E. died in Jackson, TN, on 7 Feb 1995; she was 92.

601. Mable Harris (James Marley[9], David Thomas[8], Gideon Lindsey[7], Gideon[6], Lewis[5], David[4], William[3], William[2], Thomas[1]). Born on 11 Oct 1890 in McNairy County, TN. Mable died ?.

Information about the marriage is from WorldConnect.

On 11 Aug 1909 when Mable was 18, she married Otie Keith. Born on 8 Apr 1889. Otie died on 23 Sep 1923; he was 34.

602. Leonard Erskin Harris (Clayborne Franklin[9], David Thomas[8], Gideon Lindsey[7], Gideon[6], Lewis[5], David[4], William[3], William[2], Thomas[1]). Born on 10 Jan 1901 in McNairy County, TN. Leonard Erskin died aft 1950; he was 48.

Information about the marriage is from Ancestry.

On 18 Sep 1919 when Leonard Erskin was 18, he married Geraldine Slaughter, in Montgomery County, TX. Born on 27 Jan 1903. Geraldine died ?.

603. Herschell Warren Barron (Dorothy Lee Harris[9], David Thomas[8], Gideon Lindsey[7], Gideon[6], Lewis[5], David[4], William[3], William[2], Thomas[1]). Born on 30 Dec 1903 in McNairy County, TN. Herschell Warren died on 17 Sep 1942; he was 38.

604. Thelma Lee Barron (Dorothy Lee Harris[9], David Thomas[8], Gideon Lindsey[7], Gideon[6], Lewis[5], David[4], William[3], William[2], Thomas[1]). Born on 29 Dec 1905 in McNairy County, TN. Thelma Lee died in Henderson County, TN, on 7 Aug 1998; she was 92.

605. Alma Elizabeth Barron (Dorothy Lee Harris[9], David Thomas[8], Gideon Lindsey[7], Gideon[6], Lewis[5], David[4], William[3], William[2], Thomas[1]). Born on 9 Jan 1909 in McNairy County, TN. Alma Elizabeth died in McNairy County, TN, on 5 Apr 1928; she was 19.

606. Pauline Wright (Mittie Ophelia Harris[9], David Thomas[8], Gideon Lindsey[7], Gideon[6], Lewis[5], David[4], William[3], William[2], Thomas[1]). Born ca 1917 in Tennessee. Pauline died ? .

607. Artis Glenn Harris (Ocie Bedford[9], David Thomas[8], Gideon Lindsey[7], Gideon[6], Lewis[5], David[4], William[3], William[2], Thomas[1]). Born on 3 Jun 1915. Artis Glenn died ? .

Information about the marriage is from WorldConnect.

On 26 Nov 1932 when Artis Glenn was 17, he married Oval Benita Dallas. Born on 15 Apr 1916. Oval Benita died ? .

608. Cleyta Harris (Ocie Bedford[9], David Thomas[8], Gideon Lindsey[7], Gideon[6], Lewis[5], David[4], William[3], William[2], Thomas[1]). Born ca 1920 in Tennessee.

609. Harold Augustus Harris (Lewis Gideon[9], Gideon Lindsey[8], Gideon Lindsey[7], Gideon[6], Lewis[5], David[4], William[3], William[2], Thomas[1]). Born on 17 Oct 1894 in McNairy County, TN. Harold Augustus died ? .

Information about the marriage is from McNairy Co., TN, Website; information about the children is from the Shelby Co., TN, Census 1930.

On 23 Dec 1914 when Harold Augustus was 20, he married Bessie Belgium Lee, in McNairy County, TN. Born on 16 Oct 1894. Bessie Belgium died ? .

They had the following children:

> **782** i. Theta May (1916-1962)
>
> **783** ii. Leon (ca1919-)
>
> **784** iii. Lafory H. (ca1921-)
>
> **785** iv. Charlie L. (ca1927-)

610. Furman Harris (Lewis Gideon[9], Gideon Lindsey[8], Gideon Lindsey[7], Gideon[6], Lewis[5], David[4], William[3], William[2], Thomas[1]). Born ca 1894 in Tennessee. Furman died ? .

611. James Gideon Landreth (Rebecca Elizabeth Harris[9], Gideon Lindsey[8], Gideon Lindsey[7], Gideon[6], Lewis[5], David[4], William[3], William[2], Thomas[1]). Born on 16 Aug 1890 in McNairy County, TN. James Gideon died in McNairy County, TN, on 23 May 1903; he was 12.

612. Otto Levan Landreth (Rebecca Elizabeth Harris[9], Gideon Lindsey[8], Gideon Lindsey[7], Gideon[6], Lewis[5], David[4], William[3],

William[2], Thomas[1]). Born on 12 Mar 1893 in McNairy County, TN. Otto Levan died ? .

613. Thomas Odell Landreth (Rebecca Elizabeth Harris[9], Gideon Lindsey[8], Gideon Lindsey[7], Gideon[6], Lewis[5], David[4], William[3], William[2], Thomas[1]). Born on 2 Nov 1897 in McNairy County, TN. Thomas Odell died ? .

Information about the marriage is from WorldConnect.

On 18 Dec 1919 when Thomas Odell was 22, he married Ersa May Cook, daughter of Archie B. Cook & Martha ?. Born on 16 Feb 1896. Ersa May died ? .

614. Paul Gipson Landreth (Rebecca Elizabeth Harris[9], Gideon Lindsey[8], Gideon Lindsey[7], Gideon[6], Lewis[5], David[4], William[3], William[2], Thomas[1]). Born on 21 Mar 1916 in McNairy County, TN. Paul Gipson died ? .

615. Archie Herschell Harris (Giles Furman[9], Gideon Lindsey[8], Gideon Lindsey[7], Gideon[6], Lewis[5], David[4], William[3], William[2], Thomas[1]). Born on 3 Feb 1907. Archie Herschell died on 23 May 1953; he was 46.

616. J. W. Harris (Giles Furman[9], Gideon Lindsey[8], Gideon Lindsey[7], Gideon[6], Lewis[5], David[4], William[3], William[2], Thomas[1]). Born in 1920 in Texas.

617. Effie Jane Harris (May Augustus[9], Gideon Lindsey[8], Gideon Lindsey[7], Gideon[6], Lewis[5], David[4], William[3], William[2], Thomas[1]). Born on 31 Jul 1907 in McNairy County, TN. Effie Jane died on 16 Jan 1942; she was 34.

Information about the marriage is from McNairy Co., TN, Website.

On 6 Apr 1925 when Effie Jane was 17, she married Cozmo Nicholoff. Born on 23 Jul 1895. Cozmo died on 11 Feb 1928; he was 32.

618. Ruby Demova Harris (May Augustus[9], Gideon Lindsey[8], Gideon Lindsey[7], Gideon[6], Lewis[5], David[4], William[3], William[2], Thomas[1]). Born on 25 Jul 1908 in McNairy County, TN. Ruby Demova died ? .

Information about the marriage is from WorldConnect.

On 30 Jul 1933 when Ruby Demova was 25, she married Robert Kermit Brewer, in McNairy County, TN. Born on 25 Sep 1909 in McNairy County, TN. Robert Kermit died in McNairy County, TN, on 13 Mar 1993; he was 83.

619. Malcolm Hobert Harris (May Augustus[9], Gideon Lindsey[8], Gideon Lindsey[7], Gideon[6], Lewis[5], David[4], William[3], William[2], Thomas[1]). Born on 21 Jul 1909 in McNairy County, TN. Malcolm Hobert died on 3 Jun 1934; he was 24.

Information about the marriage is from WorldConnect; information about the son is from the McNairy Co., TN, Census 1930.

On 25 Dec 1928 when Malcolm Hobert was 19, he married Hettie Pearl Elliott. Born on 18 Jan 1912. Hettie Pearl died ? .

They had one child:

        786   i.   John R. (ca1929-)

620. Urbane Eustace Harris (May Augustus[9], Gideon Lindsey[8], Gideon Lindsey[7], Gideon[6], Lewis[5], David[4], William[3], William[2], Thomas[1]). Born on 18 Dec 1912 in McNairy County, TN.

Urbane Eustace died in Memphis, TN, in Jun 1980; he was 67.

Information about the marriage is from WorldConnect.

On 20 Nov 1946 when Urbane Eustace was 33, he married Annie Nell Kerr. Born on 25 Mar 1913. Annie Nell died in Memphis, TN, on 14 Jun 1999; she was 86.

621. Eva Inez Harris (May Augustus[9], Gideon Lindsey[8], Gideon Lindsey[7], Gideon[6], Lewis[5], David[4], William[3], William[2], Thomas[1]). Born on 11 Mar 1915 in McNairy County, TN.

Information about the marriage is from WorldConnect.

On 20 Aug 1938 when Eva Inez was 23, she married Clyde Sherman Treece, in McNairy County, TN. Born on 9 Sep 1917 in McNairy County, TN. Clyde Sherman died in McNairy County, TN, on 1 May 1992; he was 74.

622. Ruth Harris (May Augustus[9], Gideon Lindsey[8], Gideon Lindsey[7], Gideon[6], Lewis[5], David[4], William[3], William[2], Thomas[1]). Born ca 1921 in Tennessee.

623. Lewis Harris (May Augustus[9], Gideon Lindsey[8], Gideon Lindsey[7], Gideon[6], Lewis[5], David[4], William[3], William[2], Thomas[1]). Born ca 1923 in Tennessee.

624. Roy Harris (May Augustus[9], Gideon Lindsey[8], Gideon Lindsey[7], Gideon[6], Lewis[5], David[4], William[3], William[2], Thomas[1]). Born ca 1924 in Tennessee.

625. Ray Harris (May Augustus[9], Gideon Lindsey[8], Gideon Lindsey[7], Gideon[6], Lewis[5], David[4], William[3], William[2], Thomas[1]). Born ca 1925 in Tennessee.

626. Hassie B. Pyron (Sidney Augustus[9], Sarah Francis "Frankie" Harris[8], Gideon Lindsey[7], Gideon[6], Lewis[5], David[4], William[3], William[2], Thomas[1]). Born ca 1897 in Tennessee. Hassie B. died ? .

627. DeWitt Pyron (Sidney Augustus[9], Sarah Francis "Frankie" Harris[8], Gideon Lindsey[7], Gideon[6], Lewis[5], David[4], William[3], William[2], Thomas[1]). Born ca 1899 in Tennessee. DeWitt died ? .

628. Ory O. Pyron (Sidney Augustus[9], Sarah Francis "Frankie" Harris[8], Gideon Lindsey[7], Gideon[6], Lewis[5], David[4], William[3], William[2], Thomas[1]). Born ca 1901 in Tennessee. Ory O. died ? .

629. William C. Pyron (Sidney Augustus[9], Sarah Francis "Frankie" Harris[8], Gideon Lindsey[7], Gideon[6], Lewis[5], David[4], William[3], William[2], Thomas[1]). Born ca 1905 in Tennessee. William C. died ? .

630. Effie M. Pyron (Sidney Augustus[9], Sarah Francis "Frankie" Harris[8], Gideon Lindsey[7], Gideon[6], Lewis[5], David[4], William[3], William[2], Thomas[1]). Born ca 1908 in Tennessee. Effie M. died ? .

631. Fred Edward Hardin (Lucy Artimus Harris[9], William Ashley[8], Gideon Lindsey[7], Gideon[6], Lewis[5], David[4], William[3], William[2], Thomas[1]). Born on 7 Sep 1890 in McNairy County, TN. Fred Edward died in Texas on 24 Apr 1967; he was 76.

632. William Inloe Hardin (Lucy Artimus Harris[9], William Ashley[8], Gideon Lindsey[7], Gideon[6], Lewis[5], David[4], William[3], William[2], Thomas[1]). Born on 6 Jan 1892 in McNairy County,

TN. William Inloe died in Tarrant County, TX, on 8 Apr 1968; he was 76.

633. Della Frances Hardin (Lucy Artimus Harris[9], William Ashley[8], Gideon Lindsey[7], Gideon[6], Lewis[5], David[4], William[3], William[2], Thomas[1]). Born on 9 Dec 1893 in McNairy County, TN. Della Frances died in Tarrant County, TX, on 26 Jan 1971; she was 77.

634. Versie Aldora Hardin (Lucy Artimus Harris[9], William Ashley[8], Gideon Lindsey[7], Gideon[6], Lewis[5], David[4], William[3], William[2], Thomas[1]). Born on 18 Oct 1898 in Jack County, TX. Versie Aldora died in San Diego, CA, on 10 Dec 1977; she was 79.

635. Reta Belle Hardin (Lucy Artimus Harris[9], William Ashley[8], Gideon Lindsey[7], Gideon[6], Lewis[5], David[4], William[3], William[2], Thomas[1]). Born on 28 Feb 1899 in Jack County, TX. Reta Belle died ? .

636. Ethel Mae Hardin (Lucy Artimus Harris[9], William Ashley[8], Gideon Lindsey[7], Gideon[6], Lewis[5], David[4], William[3], William[2], Thomas[1]). Born on 3 May 1901 in Jack County, TX. Ethel Mae died in Los Angeles, CA, on 24 Jan 1976; she was 74.

637. Luther Joseph Hardin (Lucy Artimus Harris[9], William Ashley[8], Gideon Lindsey[7], Gideon[6], Lewis[5], David[4], William[3], William[2], Thomas[1]). Born on 23 Apr 1903 in Jack County, TX. Luther Joseph died ? .

638. Fant George Hardin (Lucy Artimus Harris[9], William Ashley[8], Gideon Lindsey[7], Gideon[6], Lewis[5], David[4], William[3], William[2], Thomas[1]). Born on 24 May 1905 in Jack County,

TX. Fant George died in Fresno, CA, on 7 May 1984; he was 78.

639. Herbert Doyle Hardin (Lucy Artimus Harris[9], William Ashley[8], Gideon Lindsey[7], Gideon[6], Lewis[5], David[4], William[3], William[2], Thomas[1]). Born on 14 Feb 1908 in Jack County, TX. Herbert Doyle died in Tarrant County, TX, in Mar 1975; he was 67.

640. William Earl Harris (James David[9], William Ashley[8], Gideon Lindsey[7], Gideon[6], Lewis[5], David[4], William[3], William[2], Thomas[1]). Born on 8 Aug 1895 in McNairy County, TN. William Earl died in Montezuma County, CO, on 5 Jan 1967; he was 71.

Information about the marriage is from LDS; information about the children is from Bailey Co., TX, Census 1930.

On 12 Dec 1915 when William Earl was 20, he married Orpha Antonia Hazel Garvin, in Parker County, TX. Born on 11 Nov 1895 in Jack County, TX. Orpha Antonia Hazel died in Montezuma County, CO, on 21 Dec 1979; she was 84.

They had the following children:

787	i.	Lucile Elmira (1917-1996)
788	ii.	Billie E. (ca1920-)
789	iii.	Hazel (ca1922-)
790	iv.	James D. (ca1924-)
791	v.	Ruby J. (ca1925-)
792	vi.	Bettie Lou (ca1927-)

641. Alvin Luther Harris (James David[9], William Ashley[8], Gideon Lindsey[7], Gideon[6], Lewis[5], David[4], William[3], William[2], Thomas[1]). Born on 20 Feb 1897 in McNairy County, TN. Alvin Luther died in Baylor County, TX, on 1 Sep 1969; he was 72.

Information about the marriage is from LDS.

On 4 Aug 1918 when Alvin Luther was 21, he married Molly Lutisha Armes, in Jack County, TX. Born on 3 Sep 1899 in Wise County, TX. Molly Lutisha died in Parmer County, TX, on 28 Sep 1982; she was 83.

642. Retie Ceulia Harris (James David[9], William Ashley[8], Gideon Lindsey[7], Gideon[6], Lewis[5], David[4], William[3], William[2], Thomas[1]). Born on 3 Nov 1898 in McNairy County, TN. Retie Ceulia died in Willacy County, TX, on 25 Oct 1989; she was 90.

Information about the marriage is from LDS.

On 17 Aug 1919 when Retie Ceulia was 20, she married Harvey D. Cash, in Clay County, TX. Born on 18 Feb 1901 in Bowie County, TX. Harvey D. died in Willacy County, TX, on 8 Mar 1983; he was 82.

They had the following children:

793	i.	Milton Keon (1921-1985)
794	ii.	David Lavelle (1931-1996)
795	iii.	Aaron Lloyd (1938-1984)

643. Margie Patie Harris (James David[9], William Ashley[8], Gideon Lindsey[7], Gideon[6], Lewis[5], David[4], William[3], William[2], Thomas[1]). Born on 4 Sep 1900 in McNairy County, TN. Margie Patie died in Stephens County, OK, on 22 Dec 1974; she was 74.

Information about the marriage and daughter is from LDS.

On 4 Jan 1918 when Margie Patie was 17, she married Earl Marion Hix, in Clay County, TX. Born on 13 Apr 1896 in Arkansas. Earl Marion died in Stephens County, OK, on 2 Aug 1967; he was 71.

They had one child:

> **796**   i.   Wilma Louise (1923-1973)

644. Ollin Littlefield Harris (James David[9], William Ashley[8], Gideon Lindsey[7], Gideon[6], Lewis[5], David[4], William[3], William[2], Thomas[1]). Born on 30 Dec 1903 in McNairy County, TN. Ollin Littlefield died in Montgomery County, TX, on 14 Mar 1985; he was 81.

Information about the marriage is from WorldConnect.

On 6 Nov 1930 when Ollin Littlefield was 26, he married Edna May Ball, in Stephens County, OK. Born on 11 Jan 1910 in Denton County, TX. Edna May died in Montgomery County, TX, on 27 Apr 1988; she was 78.

645. Avie Elizabeth Harris (James David[9], William Ashley[8], Gideon Lindsey[7], Gideon[6], Lewis[5], David[4], William[3], William[2], Thomas[1]). Born on 11 Apr 1906 in Parker County, TX. Avie Elizabeth died in Caldwell County, TX, in 1979; she was 72.

Information about the marriage is from WorldConnect.

On 7 Sep 1924 when Avie Elizabeth was 18, she married Benjamin Tillman Williams, in Stephens County, OK. Born on 14 Jun 1901 in Bryan County, Oklahoma Indian Territory. Benjamin Tillman died in Caldwell County, TX, on 18 Jul 1994; he was 93.

646. Nona Agatha Harris (James David[9], William Ashley[8], Gideon Lindsey[7], Gideon[6], Lewis[5], David[4], William[3], William[2], Thomas[1]). Born on 17 Jun 1908 in Parker County, TX. Nona Agatha died in Comanche County, OK, on 1 Jun 1984; she was 75.

Information about the marriage is from WorldConnect.

On 13 Jun 1926 when Nona Agatha was 17, she married William Temple Clay, in Stephens County, OK. Born on 16 Jan 1905 in Oklahoma Indian Territory. William Temple died in Caddo County, OK, on 22 Jan 1986; he was 81.

647. Leta May Harris (James David[9], William Ashley[8], Gideon Lindsey[7], Gideon[6], Lewis[5], David[4], William[3], William[2], Thomas[1]). Born on 9 Jul 1910 in Wise County, TX. Leta May died in Cameron County, TX, on 10 Jun 2004; she was 93.

Information about the marriage is from LDS.

On 3 Feb 1929 when Leta May was 18, she married James Benjamin Pinson, in Stephens County, OK. Born on 26 Sep 1907 in Mills County, TX. James Benjamin died in Cameron County, TX, on 6 Nov 2001; he was 94.

648. James Leland Harris (James David[9], William Ashley[8], Gideon Lindsey[7], Gideon[6], Lewis[5], David[4], William[3], William[2], Thomas[1]). Born on 4 Oct 1912 in Jack County, TX. James

Leland died in Willacy County, TX, on 23 Apr 1999; he was 86.

This was a second marriage (WorldConnect).

On 1 Oct 1977 when James Leland was 64, he married Lela Mae Stapp, in Cameron County, TX. Born on 17 May 1916 in Cooke County, TX. Lela Mae died in Cameron County, TX, on 20 Feb 1992; she was 75.

649. Theola Pyron Harris (James David[9], William Ashley[8], Gideon Lindsey[7], Gideon[6], Lewis[5], David[4], William[3], William[2], Thomas[1]). Born on 25 Nov 1916 in Clay County, TX.

Information about the marriage is from WorldConnect.

On 25 Jul 1937 when Theola Pyron was 20, she married Harold Leslie Keller, in Stephens County, OK. Born on 23 Oct 1915 in Calgary, Alberta, Canada. Harold Leslie died in Galveston, TX, on 15 Apr 1942; he was 26.

650. Jewel Harris (William Franklin[9], William Ashley[8], Gideon Lindsey[7], Gideon[6], Lewis[5], David[4], William[3], William[2], Thomas[1]). Born on 17 Apr 1896 in McNairy County, TN. Jewel died in Gibson County, TN, on 15 Apr 1992; she was 95.

Information about the marriage is from WorldConnect.

In 1919 when Jewel was 22, she married Hugh Avery Keenan, in Gibson County, TN. Born on 11 Jun 1897. Hugh Avery died on 6 Oct 1965; he was 68.

651. Louis Gilbert Harris (William Franklin[9], William Ashley[8], Gideon Lindsey[7], Gideon[6], Lewis[5], David[4], William[3], William[2], Thomas[1]). Born on 15 Oct 1904 in Oklahoma. Louis Gilbert died in Tulare County, CA, on 9 Mar 1986; he was 81.

Information about the marriage is from WorldConnect.

On 4 Aug 1930 when Louis Gilbert was 25, he married Bertha Oleta Wallace. Born on 30 Mar 1913. Bertha Oleta died in Tulare County, CA, on 14 Apr 1999; she was 86.

652. Russell Elbert Harris (William Franklin[9], William Ashley[8], Gideon Lindsey[7], Gideon[6], Lewis[5], David[4], William[3], William[2], Thomas[1]). Born on 16 Jun 1906 in Oklahoma. Russell Elbert died in Tulare County, CA, on 20 Dec 1991; he was 85.

653. Reba Iola Harris (William Franklin[9], William Ashley[8], Gideon Lindsey[7], Gideon[6], Lewis[5], David[4], William[3], William[2], Thomas[1]). Born on 1 Apr 1909 in Oklahoma. Reba Iola died in Grady County, OK, in May 1984; she was 75.

Information about the marriage is from WorldConnect.

On 24 Dec 1928 when Reba Iola was 19, she married James Truman Guest. Born on 24 Jul 1907 in Arkansas. James Truman died in Glendora, CA, on 22 Nov 1986; he was 79.

654. Ruby Viola Harris (William Franklin[9], William Ashley[8], Gideon Lindsey[7], Gideon[6], Lewis[5], David[4], William[3], William[2], Thomas[1]). Born on 31 Mar 1911 in Oklahoma. Ruby Viola died in Dakota County, MN, on 19 Oct 2005; she was 94.

Information about the marriage is from WorldConnect.

On 23 Jul 1931 when Ruby Viola was 20, she married James Melt Campbell. Born on 1 Aug 1904. James Melt died ? .

655. Lillie Pearl Harris (William Franklin[9], William Ashley[8], Gideon Lindsey[7], Gideon[6], Lewis[5], David[4], William[3], William[2], Thomas[1]). Born on 19 Mar 1914. Lillie Pearl died in Grady County, OK, in Mar 1984; she was 69.

Information about the marriage is from WorldConnect.

On 28 Oct 1933 when Lillie Pearl was 19, she married Jasper Robert Lumpkin, in Oklahoma. Born on 20 Apr 1913. Jasper Robert died in Caddo County, OK, in Apr 1975; he was 61.

656. William Nelton Harris (William Franklin[9], William Ashley[8], Gideon Lindsey[7], Gideon[6], Lewis[5], David[4], William[3], William[2], Thomas[1]). Born on 15 Mar 1917 in Oklahoma. William Nelton died in Glendora, CA, on 20 Aug 1992; he was 75.

657. Haskel Garwin Harris (William Franklin[9], William Ashley[8], Gideon Lindsey[7], Gideon[6], Lewis[5], David[4], William[3], William[2], Thomas[1]). Born on 5 Apr 1919 in McNairy County, TN. Haskel Garwin died on 5 Jul 1921; he was 2.

658. Vivian Milborn Harris (John Lindon[9], William Ashley[8], Gideon Lindsey[7], Gideon[6], Lewis[5], David[4], William[3], William[2], Thomas[1]). Born on 4 Jul 1907 in McNairy County, TN. Vivian Milborn died in McNairy County, TN, on 3 Oct 1907; she was <1.

659. Bivian Lafayette Harris (John Lindon[9], William Ashley[8], Gideon Lindsey[7], Gideon[6], Lewis[5], David[4], William[3], William[2], Thomas[1]). Born on 8 Sep 1908 in McNairy County, TN. Bivian Lafayette died in McNairy County, TN, on 8 Sep 1908; he was <1.

660. Raymond Garland Harris (John Lindon[9], William Ashley[8], Gideon Lindsey[7], Gideon[6], Lewis[5], David[4], William[3], William[2], Thomas[1]). Born on 17 Aug 1910 in McNairy County, TN. Raymond Garland died in McNairy County, TN, in May 1987; he was 76.

Information about the marriage is from LDS.

On 26 Dec 1931 when Raymond Garland was 21, he married Iva Drake, in McNairy County, TN. Born on 26 Nov 1907 in McNairy County, TN. Iva died in McNairy County, TN, on 7 Apr 1995; she was 87.

661. Dan Harris (Albert Royal[9], William Ashley[8], Gideon Lindsey[7], Gideon[6], Lewis[5], David[4], William[3], William[2], Thomas[1]). Born on 9 Apr 1906 in Texas. Dan died in Dallas County, TX, on 1 Feb 1987; he was 80.

662. William Harris (Albert Royal[9], William Ashley[8], Gideon Lindsey[7], Gideon[6], Lewis[5], David[4], William[3], William[2], Thomas[1]). Born ca 1908 in Tennessee. William died ? .

663. Beatrice Harris (Albert Royal[9], William Ashley[8], Gideon Lindsey[7], Gideon[6], Lewis[5], David[4], William[3], William[2], Thomas[1]). Born in 1910 in Tennessee. Beatrice died ? .

664. Walter Harris (Albert Royal[9], William Ashley[8], Gideon Lindsey[7], Gideon[6], Lewis[5], David[4], William[3], William[2], Thomas[1]). Born in 1911 in Texas. Walter died ? .

665. Price Edward Harris (Albert Royal[9], William Ashley[8], Gideon Lindsey[7], Gideon[6], Lewis[5], David[4], William[3], William[2], Thomas[1]). Born in 1914 in Texas. Price Edward died in Texas in 1989; he was 75.

666. Tenner M. Harris (Albert Royal[9], William Ashley[8], Gideon Lindsey[7], Gideon[6], Lewis[5], David[4], William[3], William[2], Thomas[1]). Born ca 1919 in Texas.

667. Mary G. Harris (Albert Royal[9], William Ashley[8], Gideon Lindsey[7], Gideon[6], Lewis[5], David[4], William[3], William[2], Thomas[1]). Born in 1920 in Texas.

668. Mary Florence Harris (Julius Andrew[9], William Ashley[8], Gideon Lindsey[7], Gideon[6], Lewis[5], David[4], William[3], William[2], Thomas[1]). Born on 10 Sep 1907 in McNairy County, TN. Mary Florence died in McNairy County, TN, on 22 Nov 1999; she was 92.

Information about the marriage is from McNairy Co., TN, Website.

On 15 Feb 1925 when Mary Florence was 17, she married Alfie Newton Weeks, in McNairy County, TN. Born on 11 Jan 1903 in McNairy County, TN. Alfie Newton died in McNairy County, TN, on 17 Jun 1985; he was 82.

669. Everett Sylvan Harris (Julius Andrew[9], William Ashley[8], Gideon Lindsey[7], Gideon[6], Lewis[5], David[4], William[3], William[2], Thomas[1]). Born on 25 Jan 1911 in McNairy County, TN. Everett Sylvan died in McNairy County, TN, on 6 Dec 1990; he was 79.

Information about the marriage is from LDS.

On 16 Aug 1935 when Everett Sylvan was 24, he married Orpha Mildred Gray, in McNairy County, TN. Born on 11 Feb 1916 in McNairy County, TN. Orpha Mildred died in McNairy County, TN, on 11 Dec 1997; she was 81.

670. Edward Bunyan Harris (Julius Andrew[9], William Ashley[8], Gideon Lindsey[7], Gideon[6], Lewis[5], David[4], William[3], William[2], Thomas[1]). Born on 9 Aug 1913 in McNairy County, TN.

Edward Bunyan died in McNairy County, TN, on 25 Oct 1987; he was 74.

Information about the marriage is from WorldConnect.

On 16 Jan 1937 when Edward Bunyan was 23, he married O. Inez Davis, in McNairy County, TN. Born ? . O. Inez died ? .

671. Lillie Faye Harris (Julius Andrew[9], William Ashley[8], Gideon Lindsey[7], Gideon[6], Lewis[5], David[4], William[3], William[2], Thomas[1]). Born ca 1914 in McNairy County, TN. Lillie Faye died in McNairy County, TN, on 16 Mar 1919; she was 5.

672. Troy Harris (Julius Andrew[9], William Ashley[8], Gideon Lindsey[7], Gideon[6], Lewis[5], David[4], William[3], William[2], Thomas[1]). Born on 14 Jan 1916 in McNairy County, TN. Troy died in McNairy County, TN, on 16 Apr 1919; he was 3.

673. Theatus Harris (Julius Andrew[9], William Ashley[8], Gideon Lindsey[7], Gideon[6], Lewis[5], David[4], William[3], William[2], Thomas[1]). Born on 10 Mar 1919 in Tennessee. Theatus died in California on 7 Aug 1972; he was 53.

674. Exie Harris (Julius Andrew[9], William Ashley[8], Gideon Lindsey[7], Gideon[6], Lewis[5], David[4], William[3], William[2], Thomas[1]). Born ca 1922 in Tennessee.

675. Millard Harris (Julius Andrew[9], William Ashley[8], Gideon Lindsey[7], Gideon[6], Lewis[5], David[4], William[3], William[2], Thomas[1]). Born ca 1929 in Tennessee. Millard died on 11 Aug 1997; he was 68.

676. Roxie Theola Walker (Mary Percilla Harris[9], William Ashley[8], Gideon Lindsey[7], Gideon[6], Lewis[5], David[4], William[3], William[2], Thomas[1]). Born on 3 Sep 1905 in McNairy County,

TN. Roxie Theola died in McNairy County, TN, on 23 Jan 1906; she was <1.

677. Scleeta Aldonia Walker (Mary Percilla Harris[9], William Ashley[8], Gideon Lindsey[7], Gideon[6], Lewis[5], David[4], William[3], William[2], Thomas[1]). Born on 14 Nov 1908 in McNairy County, TN. Scleeta Aldonia died in Weakley County, TN, on 25 Nov 1997; she was 89.

678. Everett Virdell Walker (Mary Percilla Harris[9], William Ashley[8], Gideon Lindsey[7], Gideon[6], Lewis[5], David[4], William[3], William[2], Thomas[1]). Born on 25 Jan 1911 in Texas. Everett Virdell died in McNairy County, TN, on 22 Oct 1991; he was 80.

679. Hardy Odell Walker (Mary Percilla Harris[9], William Ashley[8], Gideon Lindsey[7], Gideon[6], Lewis[5], David[4], William[3], William[2], Thomas[1]). Born on 10 Feb 1913 in McNairy County, TN. Hardy Odell died in Weakley County, TN, on 18 Aug 1992; he was 79.

680. Luther Wilburn Walker (Mary Percilla Harris[9], William Ashley[8], Gideon Lindsey[7], Gideon[6], Lewis[5], David[4], William[3], William[2], Thomas[1]). Born on 10 Nov 1914 in McNairy County, TN. Luther Wilburn died in McNairy County, TN, in May 1986; he was 71.

681. John Virgle Walker (Mary Percilla Harris[9], William Ashley[8], Gideon Lindsey[7], Gideon[6], Lewis[5], David[4], William[3], William[2], Thomas[1]). Born on 26 Oct 1916 in McNairy County, TN. John Virgle died in McNairy County, TN, on 26 Apr 1988; he was 71.

682. Mary U. Walker (Mary Percilla Harris[9], William Ashley[8], Gideon Lindsey[7], Gideon[6], Lewis[5], David[4], William[3], William[2], Thomas[1]). Born ca 1920 in Tennessee.

683. Rayburn Walker (Mary Percilla Harris[9], William Ashley[8], Gideon Lindsey[7], Gideon[6], Lewis[5], David[4], William[3], William[2], Thomas[1]). Born ca 1922 in Tennessee.

684. Larance L. Walker (Mary Percilla Harris[9], William Ashley[8], Gideon Lindsey[7], Gideon[6], Lewis[5], David[4], William[3], William[2], Thomas[1]). Born ca 1924 in Tennessee.

685. Merlin Flynn Harris (Thurman Lindsey[9], William Ashley[8], Gideon Lindsey[7], Gideon[6], Lewis[5], David[4], William[3], William[2], Thomas[1]). Born on 7 May 1915 in McNairy County, TN. Merlin Flynn died in Milton, FL, on 5 May 1976; he was 60.

Information about the marriage is from WorldConnect; information about the son is from LDS.

On 24 Jun 1934 when Merlin Flynn was 19, he married Altha Lorraine Stephens, in McNairy County, TN. Born on 26 Aug 1917 in Tennessee.

They had one child:

> **797**   i.   Michael Flynn (1949-1965)

686. Thomas Clifford Harris (Thurman Lindsey[9], William Ashley[8], Gideon Lindsey[7], Gideon[6], Lewis[5], David[4], William[3], William[2], Thomas[1]). Born on 28 Jan 1917 in McNairy County, TN. Thomas Clifford died in Memphis, TN, on 6 Sep 1996; he was 79.

687. Norris Harris (Thurman Lindsey[9], William Ashley[8], Gideon Lindsey[7], Gideon[6], Lewis[5], David[4], William[3], William[2], Thomas[1]). Born ca 1926.

688. Audra Evelyn Harris (Bunyan Stephens[9], William Ashley[8], Gideon Lindsey[7], Gideon[6], Lewis[5], David[4], William[3], William[2], Thomas[1]). Born on 19 Sep 1913 in McNairy County, TN. Audra Evelyn died in McNairy County, TN, on 12 Jul 1995; she was 81.

Information about the marriage is from LDS.

On 5 Feb 1933 when Audra Evelyn was 19, she married Clyde Blackward Rogers, in McNairy County, TN. Born on 28 Jul 1908 in McNairy County, TN. Clyde Blackward died in McNairy County, TN, on 27 Sep 1999; he was 91.

689. William Harlin Harris (Bunyan Stephens[9], William Ashley[8], Gideon Lindsey[7], Gideon[6], Lewis[5], David[4], William[3], William[2], Thomas[1]). Born on 26 Apr 1917 in McNairy County, TN. William Harlin died ? in Louisiana.

690. Alva Zela Harris (Mannon Lindsey[9], Doctor Franklin "Docky"[8], Gideon Lindsey[7], Gideon[6], Lewis[5], David[4], William[3], William[2], Thomas[1]). Born on 22 Apr 1901 in McNairy County, TN. Alva Zela died bef 1930; she was 28.

Information about the marriage is from WorldConnect.

Alva Zela married Burris N. Newell. Born on 24 Aug 1888 in McNairy County, TN. Burris N. died ? .

They had one child:

798   i.   Bulis (ca1916-)

691. Doris Harris (Tolbert Dalton[9], Doctor Franklin "Docky"[8], Gideon Lindsey[7], Gideon[6], Lewis[5], David[4], William[3], William[2], Thomas[1]). Born ca 1925 in Texas.

692. Wilma Sue Harris (Hubert Vernon[9], Doctor Franklin "Docky"[8], Gideon Lindsey[7], Gideon[6], Lewis[5], David[4], William[3], William[2], Thomas[1]). Born on 13 Jan 1917 in Mississippi.

693. Vera G. Harris (Hubert Vernon[9], Doctor Franklin "Docky"[8], Gideon Lindsey[7], Gideon[6], Lewis[5], David[4], William[3], William[2], Thomas[1]). Born ca 1923 in Louisiana.

694. Hubert V. Harris (Hubert Vernon[9], Doctor Franklin "Docky"[8], Gideon Lindsey[7], Gideon[6], Lewis[5], David[4], William[3], William[2], Thomas[1]). Born ca 1927 in Louisiana.

695. Raybun N. Walker (Sarah Myrtle Harris[9], Doctor Franklin "Docky"[8], Gideon Lindsey[7], Gideon[6], Lewis[5], David[4], William[3], William[2], Thomas[1]). Born ca 1920 in Tennessee.

696. Varnie M. Walker (Sarah Myrtle Harris[9], Doctor Franklin "Docky"[8], Gideon Lindsey[7], Gideon[6], Lewis[5], David[4], William[3], William[2], Thomas[1]). Born ca 1922 in Tennessee.

697. Nellie C. Walker (Sarah Myrtle Harris[9], Doctor Franklin "Docky"[8], Gideon Lindsey[7], Gideon[6], Lewis[5], David[4], William[3], William[2], Thomas[1]). Born ca 1926 in Tennessee.

698. A. Doral Dalton (Alice Harris[9], Thomas Gideon[8], Giles Claiborne[7], Gideon[6], Lewis[5], David[4], William[3], William[2], Thomas[1]). Born in May 1881 in Tennessee. A. Doral died ? .

699. J. Suler Dalton (Alice Harris[9], Thomas Gideon[8], Giles Claiborne[7], Gideon[6], Lewis[5], David[4], William[3], William[2], Thomas[1]). Born in Apr 1883 in Illinois. J. Suler died ? .

700. B. Sela Dalton (Alice Harris[9], Thomas Gideon[8], Giles Claiborne[7], Gideon[6], Lewis[5], David[4], William[3], William[2], Thomas[1]). Born in Apr 1883 in Illinois. B. Sela died ? .

701. B. Irah Dalton (Alice Harris[9], Thomas Gideon[8], Giles Claiborne[7], Gideon[6], Lewis[5], David[4], William[3], William[2], Thomas[1]). Born in Apr 1885 in Illinois. B. Irah died ? .

702. L. Elzie Dalton (Alice Harris[9], Thomas Gideon[8], Giles Claiborne[7], Gideon[6], Lewis[5], David[4], William[3], William[2], Thomas[1]). Born in May 1886 in Illinois. L. Elzie died ? .

703. M. Hertie Dalton (Alice Harris[9], Thomas Gideon[8], Giles Claiborne[7], Gideon[6], Lewis[5], David[4], William[3], William[2], Thomas[1]). Born in Mar 1888 in Illinois. M. Hertie died ? .

704. M. Ivy Dalton (Alice Harris[9], Thomas Gideon[8], Giles Claiborne[7], Gideon[6], Lewis[5], David[4], William[3], William[2], Thomas[1]). Born in Aug 1889 in Tennessee. M. Ivy died ? .

705. A. Bertha Dalton (Alice Harris[9], Thomas Gideon[8], Giles Claiborne[7], Gideon[6], Lewis[5], David[4], William[3], William[2], Thomas[1]). Born in Apr 1891 in Tennessee. A. Bertha died ? .

706. William Conrad Butts (Dolly Lucy Catherine Harris[9], William Tinsley[8], Giles Claiborne[7], Gideon[6], Lewis[5], David[4], William[3], William[2], Thomas[1]). Born on 25 Feb 1895. William Conrad died ? .

707. Denver Bertrand Butts (Dolly Lucy Catherine Harris[9], William Tinsley[8], Giles Claiborne[7], Gideon[6], Lewis[5], David[4], William[3], William[2], Thomas[1]). Born on 21 Aug 1897. Denver Bertrand died ? .

708. Ima Elizabeth Butts (Dolly Lucy Catherine Harris[9], William Tinsley[8], Giles Claiborne[7], Gideon[6], Lewis[5], David[4], William[3], William[2], Thomas[1]). Born on 14 Sep 1900. Ima Elizabeth died ? .

709. Pauline Butts (Dolly Lucy Catherine Harris[9], William Tinsley[8], Giles Claiborne[7], Gideon[6], Lewis[5], David[4], William[3], William[2], Thomas[1]). Born on 31 Mar 1904. Pauline died ? .

710. Minnie Noreen Butts (Dolly Lucy Catherine Harris[9], William Tinsley[8], Giles Claiborne[7], Gideon[6], Lewis[5], David[4], William[3], William[2], Thomas[1]). Born on 7 Aug 1906. Minnie Noreen died ? .

711. Willie D. Gibson (Minnie Jane Harris[9], William Tinsley[8], Giles Claiborne[7], Gideon[6], Lewis[5], David[4], William[3], William[2], Thomas[1]). Born ca 1898 in Alabama. Willie D. died ? .

712. Dee O. Gibson (Minnie Jane Harris[9], William Tinsley[8], Giles Claiborne[7], Gideon[6], Lewis[5], David[4], William[3], William[2], Thomas[1]). Born ca 1903 in Alabama. Dee O. died ? .

713. Katie M. Gibson (Minnie Jane Harris[9], William Tinsley[8], Giles Claiborne[7], Gideon[6], Lewis[5], David[4], William[3], William[2], Thomas[1]). Born ca 1907 in Alabama. Katie M. died ? .

714. Bettie C. Gibson (Minnie Jane Harris[9], William Tinsley[8], Giles Claiborne[7], Gideon[6], Lewis[5], David[4], William[3], William[2], Thomas[1]). Born ca 1911 in Alabama. Bettie C. died ? .

715. Joe C. Gibson (Minnie Jane Harris[9], William Tinsley[8], Giles Claiborne[7], Gideon[6], Lewis[5], David[4], William[3], William[2], Thomas[1]). Born ca 1914 in Alabama. Joe C. died ? .

716. Minnie Annie Gibson (Minnie Jane Harris[9], William Tinsley[8], Giles Claiborne[7], Gideon[6], Lewis[5], David[4], William[3], William[2], Thomas[1]). Born on 5 Mar 1917 in Lawrence County, AL.

Information about the marriage is from WorldConnect.

On 9 Mar 1935 when Minnie Annie was 18, she married Lenard Virgil Long, in Franklin, KY. Born on 22 Oct 1914 in Chester County, TN. Lenard Virgil died ? .

717. Nellie M. Harris (William T.[9], Robert Wiseman[8], Giles Claiborne[7], Gideon[6], Lewis[5], David[4], William[3], William[2], Thomas[1]). Born on 29 Dec 1893 in Sumner County, TN. Nellie M. died in Scottsville, KY, on 25 Jul 1990; she was 96.

Information about the marriage and daughter is from family records.

On 26 Sep 1914 when Nellie M. was 20, she married Orbin Clifton Cook, son of Robert Wilson Cook & Permelia Alice Follis, in Gallatin, TN. Born on 13 Dec 1894 in Allen County, KY. Orbin Clifton died in Barren County, KY, on 30 May 1953; he was 58.

They had one child:

> **799**   i.   Nina Loyce (1915-2004)

718. Willie W. Harris (William T.[9], Robert Wiseman[8], Giles Claiborne[7], Gideon[6], Lewis[5], David[4], William[3], William[2], Thomas[1]). Born on 8 Aug 1896 in Macon County, TN. Willie W. died in Allen County, KY, on 7 Mar 1988; she was 91.

Information about the husband and son is from family records.

Willie W. married Roy D. Cline, son of Joe Cline & Dora Meador. Born on 16 Jan 1892. Roy D. died on 3 Jan 1975; he was 82.

They had one child:

      800   i.   Harris C. (1918-1996)

719. Paul Nimmo Harris (Giles Bledsoe[9], Robert Wiseman[8], Giles Claiborne[7], Gideon[6], Lewis[5], David[4], William[3], William[2], Thomas[1]). Born in Aug 1899 in Macon County, TN. Paul Nimmo died in 1948; he was 48.

Information about the marriage is from the Sumner Co. Website; information about the children is from Sumner Co. Census 1930.

On 2 Nov 1918 when Paul Nimmo was 19, he married Caminet Moncrief (727), daughter of Gideon Paul Moncrief & Mattie Anna Harris (469), in Sumner County, TN. Born in 1898. Caminet died ? .

They had the following children:

      801   i.   Virginia (ca1920-)

      802   ii.   Aubra (ca1922-)

      803   iii.   Roy (ca1924-)

720. James Blanton Harris (Giles Bledsoe[9], Robert Wiseman[8], Giles Claiborne[7], Gideon[6], Lewis[5], David[4], William[3], William[2], Thomas[1]). Born on 21 Dec 1903 in Sumner County, TN. James Blanton died on 25 Nov 1986; he was 82.

721. Selma Weatherford (Sarah Tennie Harris[9], Robert Wiseman[8], Giles Claiborne[7], Gideon[6], Lewis[5], David[4], William[3], William[2], Thomas[1]). Born ca 1907 in Tennessee. Selma died ? .

722. Willie Weatherford (Sarah Tennie Harris[9], Robert Wiseman[8], Giles Claiborne[7], Gideon[6], Lewis[5], David[4], William[3], William[2], Thomas[1]). Born ca 1908 in Tennessee. Willie died bef 1920; he was 12.

723. Hilery Harris Weatherford (Sarah Tennie Harris[9], Robert Wiseman[8], Giles Claiborne[7], Gideon[6], Lewis[5], David[4], William[3], William[2], Thomas[1]). Born on 27 May 1910 in Tennessee. Hilery Harris died in Florida on 5 May 2000; he was 89.

Information about the wives is from WorldConnect.

Hilery Harris first married Mary Ella Crosby. Born ? . Mary Ella died ? .

Hilery Harris second married Karene Wills. Born ? . Karene died ? .

724. Cordell Weatherford (Sarah Tennie Harris[9], Robert Wiseman[8], Giles Claiborne[7], Gideon[6], Lewis[5], David[4], William[3], William[2], Thomas[1]). Born ca 1913 in Tennessee. Cordell died ? .

725. Annie L. Gilliam (Mattie Anna Harris[9], Robert Wiseman[8], Giles Claiborne[7], Gideon[6], Lewis[5], David[4], William[3], William[2], Thomas[1]). Born ca 1904 in Tennessee. Annie L. died ? .

726. Orby Moncrief (Mattie Anna Harris[9], Robert Wiseman[8], Giles Claiborne[7], Gideon[6], Lewis[5], David[4], William[3], William[2], Thomas[1]). Born ca 1905 in Tennessee. Orby died ? .

727. Caminet Moncrief (Mattie Anna Harris[9], Robert Wiseman[8], Giles Claiborne[7], Gideon[6], Lewis[5], David[4], William[3], William[2], Thomas[1]). Born in 1898. Caminet died ? .

On 2 Nov 1918 when Caminet was 20, she married Paul Nimmo Harris (719), son of Giles Bledsoe Harris (465) & Nellie Nimmo, in Sumner County, TN. Born in Aug 1899 in Macon County, TN. Paul Nimmo died in 1948; he was 48.

They had the following children:

801	i.	Virginia (ca1920-)
802	ii.	Aubra (ca1922-)
803	iii.	Roy (ca1924-)

728. Venlist Moncrief (Mattie Anna Harris[9], Robert Wiseman[8], Giles Claiborne[7], Gideon[6], Lewis[5], David[4], William[3], William[2], Thomas[1]). Born ca 1909 in Tennessee. Venlist died ? .

729. Mary E. Harris (Rice Odell[9], Robert Wiseman[8], Giles Claiborne[7], Gideon[6], Lewis[5], David[4], William[3], William[2], Thomas[1]). Born ca 1907 in Tennessee. Mary E. died ? .

730. Bettie Lou Harris (Rice Odell[9], Robert Wiseman[8], Giles Claiborne[7], Gideon[6], Lewis[5], David[4], William[3], William[2], Thomas[1]). Born ca 1912 in Tennessee. Bettie Lou died ? .

731. Edna Roark (Bessie N. Harris[9], Robert Wiseman[8], Giles Claiborne[7], Gideon[6], Lewis[5], David[4], William[3], William[2], Thomas[1]). Born ca 1901 in Tennessee. Edna died ? .

732. William F. Roark (Bessie N. Harris[9], Robert Wiseman[8], Giles Claiborne[7], Gideon[6], Lewis[5], David[4], William[3], William[2], Thomas[1]). Born ca 1912 in Tennessee. William F. died ? .

733. Robert D. Roark (Bessie N. Harris[9], Robert Wiseman[8], Giles Claiborne[7], Gideon[6], Lewis[5], David[4], William[3], William[2], Thomas[1]). Born ca 1915 in Tennessee. Robert D. died ? .

734. William I. Harris (Henry H.[9], John Sumpter[8], Giles Claiborne[7], Gideon[6], Lewis[5], David[4], William[3], William[2], Thomas[1]). Born in Aug 1899 in Macon County, TN. William I. died in 1965; he was 65. Buried in Rocky Mound Cemetery, Macon Co., TN.

Information about the marriage is from Bronner, *Macon Co. Marriages*, v. 1.

On 23 Nov 1919 when William I. was 20, he married Gracie Lund, in Macon County, TN. Born in 1902. Gracie died on 7 Sep 1984; she was 82.

735. Elisha O. Harris (Henry H.[9], John Sumpter[8], Giles Claiborne[7], Gideon[6], Lewis[5], David[4], William[3], William[2], Thomas[1]). Born on 28 Aug 1902 in Macon County, TN. Elisha O. died on 1 Jan 1983; he was 80. Buried in Pleasant Grove Methodist Cemetery, Sumner Co., TN.

Information about the wife and sons is from the Sumner Co., TN, Census 1930.

Elisha O. married Nola B. ?. Born on 15 May 1903. Nola B. died on 8 Mar 1977; she was 73.

They had the following children:

804	i.	A. J. (ca1926-)
805	ii.	Carlis (ca1927-)

736. Lillie Pearl Harris (Henry H.[9], John Sumpter[8], Giles Claiborne[7], Gideon[6], Lewis[5], David[4], William[3], William[2], Thomas[1]). Born ca 1905 in Macon County, TN. Lillie Pearl died ? .

737. Vercil Claudie Harris (Henry H.[9], John Sumpter[8], Giles Claiborne[7], Gideon[6], Lewis[5], David[4], William[3], William[2], Thomas[1]). Born on 17 Aug 1908 in Macon County, TN. Vercil Claudie died on 26 May 1976; he was 67. Buried in Rocky Mound Cemetery, Macon Co., TN.

Information about the marriage is from Bronner, *Macon Co. Marriages*, v. 1.

On 25 Apr 1926 when Vercil Claudie was 17, he married Pauline Creasey, in Macon County, TN. Born in 1910 in Kentucky.

738. Cordell Harris (Giles S.[9], John Sumpter[8], Giles Claiborne[7], Gideon[6], Lewis[5], David[4], William[3], William[2], Thomas[1]). Born on 5 Sep 1913 in Tennessee. Cordell died on 20 Jan 1976; he was 62. Buried in Pleasant Grove Methodist Cemetery, Sumner Co., TN.

739. Elgie Irwin Harris (Wiley A.[9], David Lawson[8], William Lindsey[7], David[6], Lewis[5], David[4], William[3], William[2], Thomas[1]). Born on 14 Aug 1900 in Marshall County, TN. Elgie Irwin died in Marshall County, TN, in May 1981; he was 80.

Information about the marriage is from WorldConnect.

On 6 Dec 1929 when Elgie Irwin was 29, he married Mary Camilla Bryant, in Marshall County, TN. Born on 8 Mar 1898. Mary Camilla died in Marshall County, TN, on 5 Jan 1989; she was 90.

740. Hazel Harris (Wiley A.[9], David Lawson[8], William Lindsey[7], David[6], Lewis[5], David[4], William[3], William[2], Thomas[1]). Born on 13 Oct 1904 in Marshall County, TN. Hazel died in Marshall County, TN, on 15 Dec 1993; she was 89.

Information about the marriage is from WorldConnect; information about the daughter is from Marshall Co., TN, Census 1930.

On 26 Oct 1923 when Hazel was 19, she married Sam Hardison Tennison, son of Hiram Tennison & Mattie ?, in Marshall County, TN. Born on 20 Sep 1898. Sam Hardison died in Marshall County, TN, on 30 Oct 1988; he was 90.

They had one child:

> **806**   i.   Myrte V. (ca1928-)

741. David Harris (Wiley A.[9], David Lawson[8], William Lindsey[7], David[6], Lewis[5], David[4], William[3], William[2], Thomas[1]). Born on 26 Mar 1907. David died on 12 Mar 1974; he was 66.

Information about the marriage is from WorldConnect.

On 26 Nov 1936 when David was 29, he married Evelyn Ruth Hill. Born on 28 May 1911. Evelyn Ruth died on 28 Apr 1965; she was 53.

742. William Lawson Harris (Riggs Tidwell[9], David Lawson[8], William Lindsey[7], David[6], Lewis[5], David[4], William[3], William[2], Thomas[1]). Born on 25 Jan 1905 in Illinois. William Lawson died on 25 Jan 1954; he was 49.

Information about the marriage is from WorldConnect; in 1930 William Lawson and Gladys are in Evansville, IN.

On 11 Apr 1927 when William Lawson was 22, he married Gladys Simpson. Born on 26 Jan 1906 in Illinois. Gladys died ? .

743. Joseph Linn Harris (Riggs Tidwell[9], David Lawson[8], William Lindsey[7], David[6], Lewis[5], David[4], William[3], William[2], Thomas[1]). Born on 9 Oct 1906 in Illinois. Joseph Linn died ? .

Information about the marriage is from WorldConnect.

On 20 Aug 1938 when Joseph Linn was 31, he married Ruth E. Cundiff. Born on 13 Dec 1904. Ruth E. died ? .

744. Goodrum Hardison (Jesse Reed Harris[9], David Lawson[8], William Lindsey[7], David[6], Lewis[5], David[4], William[3], William[2], Thomas[1]). Born on 31 Aug 1903 in Tennessee. Goodrum died ? .

Information about the marriage is from WorldConnect.

On 30 Jun 1926 when Goodrum was 22, he married Lillian Murphy Twitty. Born on 5 Mar 1905. Lillian Murphy died ? .

745. Magneus Hardison (Jesse Reed Harris[9], David Lawson[8], William Lindsey[7], David[6], Lewis[5], David[4], William[3], William[2], Thomas[1]). Born on 28 Mar 1905 in Tennessee. Magneus died ? .

Information about the marriage is from WorldConnect.

On 6 Dec 1935 when Magneus was 30, he married Nellie Josephine Davis. Born on 23 Jan 1905. Nellie Josephine died ? .

746. Cecil Hardison (Jesse Reed Harris[9], David Lawson[8], William Lindsey[7], David[6], Lewis[5], David[4], William[3], William[2], Thomas[1]).

Born on 24 Mar 1907 in Tennessee. Cecil died in Marshall County, TN, in Oct 1983; he was 76.

Information about the marriage is from WorldConnect.

On 9 May 1942 when Cecil was 35, he married Mignonette Burch. Born ? . Mignonette died ? .

747. James E. Harris (Lewis J.[9], James Patterson[8], William Lindsey[7], David[6], Lewis[5], David[4], William[3], William[2], Thomas[1]). Born on 24 Mar 1911. James E. died in Feb 1976; he was 64.

Information about the marriage is from Worldconnect.

On 8 Jan 1933 when James E. was 21, he married Waneta Beisheim. Born on 9 Sep 1911. Waneta died on 17 Jul 1971; she was 59.

748. Christine Harris (J. Fount[9], James Patterson[8], William Lindsey[7], David[6], Lewis[5], David[4], William[3], William[2], Thomas[1]). Born on 26 Jun 1915.

Information about the marriage is from McNairy Co., TN, Website.

On 21 Apr 1935 when Christine was 19, she married John Raifford Sharp. Born on 31 Oct 1907 in Tennessee. John Raifford died in McNairy County, TN, on 19 Sep 2002; he was 94.

---

749. Parnie V. Walker (Grover Cisco[10], James Thomas[9], Martha Elizabeth Harris[8], Gideon Lindsey[7], Gideon[6], Lewis[5], David[4], William[3], William[2], Thomas[1]). Born ca 1908 in Tennessee. Parnie V. died ? .

750. Lilburn T. Walker (Ella May Harris[10], William Marion[9], Giles Claiborne[8], Gideon Lindsey[7], Gideon[6], Lewis[5], David[4], William[3], William[2], Thomas[1]). Born on 31 Jul 1904 in Jackson, TN. Lilburn T. died in Kern County, CA, on 3 Jun 1976; he was 71.

751. Hazel Walker (Ella May Harris[10], William Marion[9], Giles Claiborne[8], Gideon Lindsey[7], Gideon[6], Lewis[5], David[4], William[3], William[2], Thomas[1]). Born on 21 Jan 1907 in Jackson, TN. Hazel died ? .

752. Zahelia Walker (Ella May Harris[10], William Marion[9], Giles Claiborne[8], Gideon Lindsey[7], Gideon[6], Lewis[5], David[4], William[3], William[2], Thomas[1]). Born on 13 Jan 1909 in McNairy County, TN. Zahelia died ? .

753. Norman Fay Walker (Ella May Harris[10], William Marion[9], Giles Claiborne[8], Gideon Lindsey[7], Gideon[6], Lewis[5], David[4], William[3], William[2], Thomas[1]). Born on 14 Apr 1913 in Clay County, AR. Norman Fay died in Sanger, CA, in Jul 1986; he was 73.

754. Mildred Walker (Ella May Harris[10], William Marion[9], Giles Claiborne[8], Gideon Lindsey[7], Gideon[6], Lewis[5], David[4], William[3], William[2], Thomas[1]). Born ca 1916 in Arkansas. Mildred died ?.

755. Don Walker (Ella May Harris[10], William Marion[9], Giles Claiborne[8], Gideon Lindsey[7], Gideon[6], Lewis[5], David[4], William[3], William[2], Thomas[1]). Born ca 1919 in Arkansas.

756. Winston Howard Harris (Nolus Guy[10], Gideon Simpson[9], Giles Claiborne[8], Gideon Lindsey[7], Gideon[6], Lewis[5], David[4], William[3], William[2], Thomas[1]). Born on 24 Apr 1917 in Memphis, TN. Winston Howard died in Sonoma, CA, on 17 Jul 1992; he was 75.

757. Carl B. Harris (Cordia Licurgus[10], Gideon Simpson[9], Giles Claiborne[8], Gideon Lindsey[7], Gideon[6], Lewis[5], David[4], William[3], William[2], Thomas[1]). Born on 12 Jul 1907 in Missouri. Carl B. died in Dunklin County, MO, on 7 Jul 1970; he was 62.

On 3 Jan 1934 when Carl B. was 26, he married Lois Irene Pitts. Born on 11 Jun 1911.

758. George S. Harris (Cordia Licurgus[10], Gideon Simpson[9], Giles Claiborne[8], Gideon Lindsey[7], Gideon[6], Lewis[5], David[4], William[3], William[2], Thomas[1]). Born on 19 Aug 1911 in Missouri. George S. died in Dunklin County, MO, in Dec 1981; he was 70.

Information about the marriage is from WorldConnect.

On 3 Dec 1939 when George S. was 28, he married Lillian Nail. Born on 10 Jun 1922.

759. Mildred D. Harris (Cordia Licurgus[10], Gideon Simpson[9], Giles Claiborne[8], Gideon Lindsey[7], Gideon[6], Lewis[5], David[4], William[3], William[2], Thomas[1]). Born on 24 Sep 1913 in Missouri. Mildred D. died in Dunklin County, MO, on 24 Mar 1979; she was 65.

Information about the marriage is from WorldConnect.

In 1931 when Mildred D. was 17, she married Homer Lawless. Born ? .

760. Roy Harris (Cordia Licurgus[10], Gideon Simpson[9], Giles Claiborne[8], Gideon Lindsey[7], Gideon[6], Lewis[5], David[4], William[3], William[2], Thomas[1]). Born on 17 Jan 1916 in Missouri. Roy died in Dunklin County, MO, on 15 Mar 1963; he was 47.

Information about the marriage is from Worldconnect.

On 30 Jan 1945 when Roy was 29, he married Thelma B. Kelley. Born ? .

761. Darl T. Harris (Cordia Licurgus[10], Gideon Simpson[9], Giles Claiborne[8], Gideon Lindsey[7], Gideon[6], Lewis[5], David[4], William[3], William[2], Thomas[1]). Born ca 1921 in Missouri.

762. Billy W. Harris (Cordia Licurgus[10], Gideon Simpson[9], Giles Claiborne[8], Gideon Lindsey[7], Gideon[6], Lewis[5], David[4], William[3], William[2], Thomas[1]). Born ca 1924 in Missouri.

763. Beauford I. Harris (Vander Eason[10], Gideon Simpson[9], Giles Claiborne[8], Gideon Lindsey[7], Gideon[6], Lewis[5], David[4], William[3], William[2], Thomas[1]). Born on 12 Oct 1915 in Dunklin County, MO. Beauford I. died in Dunklin County, MO, on 21 Jul 1978; he was 62.

Information about the marriage is from WorldConnect.

On 21 Jun 1937 when Beauford I. was 21, he married Stella Lorraine Smith, in Blytheville, AR. Born on 27 Dec 1920 in Dunklin County, MO.

764. Winston B. Harris (Vander Eason[10], Gideon Simpson[9], Giles Claiborne[8], Gideon Lindsey[7], Gideon[6], Lewis[5], David[4], William[3], William[2], Thomas[1]). Born ca 1918 in Missouri.

765. Imogene Harris (Vander Eason[10], Gideon Simpson[9], Giles Claiborne[8], Gideon Lindsey[7], Gideon[6], Lewis[5], David[4], William[3], William[2], Thomas[1]). Born ca 1923 in Missouri.

766. Jesse F. Harris (Vander Eason[10], Gideon Simpson[9], Giles Claiborne[8], Gideon Lindsey[7], Gideon[6], Lewis[5], David[4], William[3], William[2], Thomas[1]). Born ca 1925 in Missouri.

767. Mary S. Harris (Vander Eason[10], Gideon Simpson[9], Giles Claiborne[8], Gideon Lindsey[7], Gideon[6], Lewis[5], David[4], William[3], William[2], Thomas[1]). Born ca 1927 in Missouri.

768. Howard L. Hay (Sallie Gladys Harris[10], Gideon Simpson[9], Giles Claiborne[8], Gideon Lindsey[7], Gideon[6], Lewis[5], David[4], William[3], William[2], Thomas[1]). Born ca 1908 in Tennessee.

769. Grace Owen Hay (Sallie Gladys Harris[10], Gideon Simpson[9], Giles Claiborne[8], Gideon Lindsey[7], Gideon[6], Lewis[5], David[4], William[3], William[2], Thomas[1]). Born on 6 May 1917 in Crockett County, TN.

770. Mary E. Hay (Sallie Gladys Harris[10], Gideon Simpson[9], Giles Claiborne[8], Gideon Lindsey[7], Gideon[6], Lewis[5], David[4], William[3], William[2], Thomas[1]). Born ca 1920 in Tennessee.**771. Iria N. Hay** (Sallie Gladys Harris[10], Gideon Simpson[9], Giles Claiborne[8], Gideon Lindsey[7], Gideon[6], Lewis[5], David[4], William[3], William[2], Thomas[1]). Born ca 1922 in Tennessee.

772. Rachel C. Hay (Sallie Gladys Harris^{10}, Gideon Simpson^9, Giles Claiborne^8, Gideon Lindsey^7, Gideon^6, Lewis^5, David^4, William^3, William^2, Thomas^1). Born ca 1926 in Tennessee.

773. Rebecca J. Hay (Sallie Gladys Harris^{10}, Gideon Simpson^9, Giles Claiborne^8, Gideon Lindsey^7, Gideon^6, Lewis^5, David^4, William^3, William^2, Thomas^1). Born ca 1927 in Tennessee.

774. Joyce Harris (Robert Taylor^{10}, Gideon Simpson^9, Giles Claiborne^8, Gideon Lindsey^7, Gideon^6, Lewis^5, David^4, William^3, William^2, Thomas^1). Born ca 1930 in Kern County, CA.

775. Elwood B. Harris (Alfred Taylor^{10}, Gideon Simpson^9, Giles Claiborne^8, Gideon Lindsey^7, Gideon^6, Lewis^5, David^4, William^3, William^2, Thomas^1). Born ca 1927 in California.

776. Jewel Winfred Harris (Jewel Thedus^{10}, Gideon Simpson^9, Giles Claiborne^8, Gideon Lindsey^7, Gideon^6, Lewis^5, David^4, William^3, William^2, Thomas^1). Born on 29 May 1931 in Flint, MI. Jewel Winfred died in Korea on 16 Sep 1951; he was 20.

777. Lovy B. Harris (Columbus Gavin^{10}, John Madison^9, Giles Claiborne^8, Gideon Lindsey^7, Gideon^6, Lewis^5, David^4, William^3, William^2, Thomas^1). Born on 17 Jul 1914 in Clay County, AR. Lovy B. died on 2 Feb 1984; she was 69.

778. Fanader G. Harris (Columbus Gavin^{10}, John Madison^9, Giles Claiborne^8, Gideon Lindsey^7, Gideon^6, Lewis^5, David^4, William^3, William^2, Thomas^1). Born ca 1919 in Missouri.

779. Joyce Kruse (Willie Ilah Harris^{10}, John Madison^9, Giles Claiborne^8, Gideon Lindsey^7, Gideon^6, Lewis^5, David^4, William^3, William^2, Thomas^1). Born in 1930 in Flint, MI.

780. Evelyn A. Fuzzell (Eura Harris[10], George Calvin[9], Giles Claiborne[8], Gideon Lindsey[7], Gideon[6], Lewis[5], David[4], William[3], William[2], Thomas[1]). Born on 7 Feb 1917 in Dunklin County, MO. Evelyn A. died in Dunklin County, MO, on 2 Mar 1996; she was 79.

781. Eleanor Graves Harris (Edwin R.[10], George Calvin[9], Giles Claiborne[8], Gideon Lindsey[7], Gideon[6], Lewis[5], David[4], William[3], William[2], Thomas[1]). Born ? .

Information about the husband and children is from Dunklin Co., MO, Website.

Eleanor Graves married Elton Dalton. Born ? .

They had the following children:

807	i.	Kyle
808	ii.	Elizabeth

782. Theta May Harris (Harold Augustus[10], Lewis Gideon[9], Gideon Lindsey[8], Gideon Lindsey[7], Gideon[6], Lewis[5], David[4], William[3], William[2], Thomas[1]). Born on 21 Dec 1916. Theta May died on 10 Apr 1962; she was 45.

Information about the marriage is from LDS. On 22 Aug 1933 when Theta May was 16, she married Ward Edwin Dawkins, in Marion, AR. Born on 6 Jul 1915. Ward Edwin died ? .

783. Leon Harris (Harold Augustus[10], Lewis Gideon[9], Gideon Lindsey[8], Gideon Lindsey[7], Gideon[6], Lewis[5], David[4], William[3], William[2], Thomas[1]). Born ca 1919 in Tennessee.

784. Lafory H. Harris (Harold Augustus[10], Lewis Gideon[9], Gideon Lindsey[8], Gideon Lindsey[7], Gideon[6], Lewis[5], David[4], William[3], William[2], Thomas[1]). Born ca 1921 in Tennessee.

785. Charlie L. Harris (Harold Augustus[10], Lewis Gideon[9], Gideon Lindsey[8], Gideon Lindsey[7], Gideon[6], Lewis[5], David[4], William[3], William[2], Thomas[1]). Born ca 1927 in Tennessee.

786. John R. Harris (Malcolm Hobert[10], May Augustus[9], Gideon Lindsey[8], Gideon Lindsey[7], Gideon[6], Lewis[5], David[4], William[3], William[2], Thomas[1]). Born ca 1929 in Tennessee.

787. Lucile Elmira Harris (William Earl[10], James David[9], William Ashley[8], Gideon Lindsey[7], Gideon[6], Lewis[5], David[4], William[3], William[2], Thomas[1]). Born on 27 Apr 1917 in Clay County, TX. Lucile Elmira died in Dolores County, CO, on 4 Dec 1996; she was 79.

788. Billie E. Harris (William Earl[10], James David[9], William Ashley[8], Gideon Lindsey[7], Gideon[6], Lewis[5], David[4], William[3], William[2], Thomas[1]). Born ca 1920 in Oklahoma.

789. Hazel Harris (William Earl[10], James David[9], William Ashley[8], Gideon Lindsey[7], Gideon[6], Lewis[5], David[4], William[3], William[2], Thomas[1]). Born ca 1922 in Oklahoma.

790. James D. Harris (William Earl[10], James David[9], William Ashley[8], Gideon Lindsey[7], Gideon[6], Lewis[5], David[4], William[3], William[2], Thomas[1]). Born ca 1924 in Oklahoma.

791. Ruby J. Harris (William Earl[10], James David[9], William Ashley[8], Gideon Lindsey[7], Gideon[6], Lewis[5], David[4], William[3], William[2], Thomas[1]). Born ca 1925 in Oklahoma.

792. Bettie Lou Harris (William Earl[10], James David[9], William Ashley[8], Gideon Lindsey[7], Gideon[6], Lewis[5], David[4], William[3], William[2], Thomas[1]). Born ca 1927 in Oklahoma.

93. Milton Keon Cash (Retie Ceulia Harris[10], James David[9], William Ashley[8], Gideon Lindsey[7], Gideon[6], Lewis[5], David[4], William[3], William[2], Thomas[1]). Born on 6 Mar 1921 in Oklahoma. Milton Keon died in Texas on 13 Apr 1985; he was 64.

794. David Lavelle Cash (Retie Ceulia Harris[10], James David[9], William Ashley[8], Gideon Lindsey[7], Gideon[6], Lewis[5], David[4], William[3], William[2], Thomas[1]). Born on 8 Oct 1931 in Oklahoma. David Lavelle died in Texas on 14 Mar 1996; he was 64.

795. Aaron Lloyd Cash (Retie Ceulia Harris[10], James David[9], William Ashley[8], Gideon Lindsey[7], Gideon[6], Lewis[5], David[4], William[3], William[2], Thomas[1]). Born on 28 Jul 1938 in Texas. Aaron Lloyd died in Texas on 12 Jan 1984; he was 45.

796. Wilma Louise Hix (Margie Patie Harris[10], James David[9], William Ashley[8], Gideon Lindsey[7], Gideon[6], Lewis[5], David[4], William[3], William[2], Thomas[1]). Born on 20 Aug 1923 in Oklahoma. Wilma Louise died in Nov 1973; she was 50.

797. Michael Flynn Harris (Merlin Flynn[10], Thurman Lindsey[9], William Ashley[8], Gideon Lindsey[7], Gideon[6], Lewis[5], David[4], William[3], William[2], Thomas[1]). Born on 4 Jul 1949 in Columbus, MS. Michael Flynn died in Milton, FL, on 15 Jun 1965; he was 15.

798. Bulis Newell (Alva Zela Harris[10], Mannon Lindsey[9], Doctor Franklin "Docky"[8], Gideon Lindsey[7], Gideon[6], Lewis[5], David[4], William[3], William[2], Thomas[1]). Born ca 1916 in Tennessee.

799. Nina Loyce Cook (Nellie M. Harris[10], William T.[9], Robert Wiseman[8], Giles Claiborne[7], Gideon[6], Lewis[5], David[4], William[3], William[2], Thomas[1]). Born on 17 Aug 1915 in Allen County, KY. Nina Loyce died in Sumner County, TN, on 15 May 2004; she was 88.

Information about the marriages and children is from family records.

In 1933 when Nina Loyce was 17, she first married Aubrey G. Witt, in Glasgow, KY. Born on 30 Jul 1912 in Allen County, KY. Aubrey G. died in Allen County, KY, on 25 Oct 1986; he was 74.

They had one child:

> **809**   i.   Robert W. (1937-)

Nina Loyce second married Randall R. Jackson. Born in Jul 1920 in Allen County, KY. Randall R. died in Warren County, KY, in Jan 1991; he was 70.

> **810**   i.   Teresa Gail (1953-1981)

> **811**   ii.   Jennifer Sue (1955-)

800. Harris C. Cline (Willie W. Harris[10], William T.[9], Robert Wiseman[8], Giles Claiborne[7], Gideon[6], Lewis[5], David[4], William[3], William[2], Thomas[1]). Born on 29 Jul 1918. Harris C. died in Allen County, KY, on 28 Mar 1996; he was 77.

Information about the marriage and son is from family records and Allen County, KY, Family History.

On 25 Dec 1938 when Harris C. was 20, he married Lois Napier, daughter of Owsley Benson Napier & Clytie Mae Howell. Born on 28 Aug 1920. Lois died on 21 May 1988; she was 67.

They had one child:

> **812**   i.   Robert Harris (1942-)

801. Virginia Harris (Paul Nimmo[10], Giles Bledsoe[9], Robert Wiseman[8], Giles Claiborne[7], Gideon[6], Lewis[5], David[4], William[3], William[2], Thomas[1]). Born ca 1920 in Tennessee.

802. Aubra Harris (Paul Nimmo[10], Giles Bledsoe[9], Robert Wiseman[8], Giles Claiborne[7], Gideon[6], Lewis[5], David[4], William[3], William[2], Thomas[1]). Born ca 1922 in Tennessee.

803. Roy Harris (Paul Nimmo[10], Giles Bledsoe[9], Robert Wiseman[8], Giles Claiborne[7], Gideon[6], Lewis[5], David[4], William[3], William[2], Thomas[1]). Born ca 1924 in Tennessee.

804. A. J. Harris (Elisha O.[10], Henry H.[9], John Sumpter[8], Giles Claiborne[7], Gideon[6], Lewis[5], David[4], William[3], William[2], Thomas[1]). Born ca 1926.

805. Carlis Harris (Elisha O.[10], Henry H.[9], John Sumpter[8], Giles Claiborne[7], Gideon[6], Lewis[5], David[4], William[3], William[2], Thomas[1]). Born ca 1927.

Information about the marriage is from Bronner, *Macon Marriages*, v. 2.

On 27 Jun 1942 when Carlis was 15, he married Ruby Dell Brawner, in Macon County, TN. Born ? .**806. Myrte V. Tennison** (Hazel Harris[10], Wiley A.[9], David Lawson[8], William Lindsey[7], David[6], Lewis[5], David[4], William[3], William[2], Thomas[1]). Born ca 1928 in Tennessee.

---

807. Kyle Dalton (Eleanor Graves Harris[11], Edwin R.[10], George Calvin[9], Giles Claiborne[8], Gideon Lindsey[7], Gideon[6], Lewis[5], David[4], William[3], William[2], Thomas[1]). Born ? .

808. Elizabeth Dalton (Eleanor Graves Harris[11], Edwin R.[10], George Calvin[9], Giles Claiborne[8], Gideon Lindsey[7], Gideon[6], Lewis[5], David[4], William[3], William[2], Thomas[1]). Born ? .

809. Robert W. Witt (Nina Loyce Cook[11], Nellie M. Harris[10], William T.[9], Robert Wiseman[8], Giles Claiborne[7], Gideon[6], Lewis[5], David[4], William[3], William[2], Thomas[1]). Born on 26 Mar 1937 in Allen County, KY.

810. Teresa Gail Jackson (Nina Loyce Cook[11], Nellie M. Harris[10], William T.[9], Robert Wiseman[8], Giles Claiborne[7], Gideon[6], Lewis[5], David[4], William[3], William[2], Thomas[1]). Born on 5 Apr 1953 in Scottsville, KY. Teresa Gail died in Scottsville, KY, on 26 Nov 1981; she was 28.

Information about the husband and sons is from family records.

Teresa Gail married Michael Mayhew. Born on 24 Nov 1945.

They had the following children:

813	i.	Alan (1975-1996)
814	ii.	John (1978-)

811. Jennifer Sue Jackson (Nina Loyce Cook[11], Nellie M. Harris[10], William T.[9], Robert Wiseman[8], Giles Claiborne[7], Gideon[6], Lewis[5], David[4], William[3], William[2], Thomas[1]). Born on 22 Nov 1955 in Scottsville, KY.

Information about the husbands and daughter is from family records.

Jennifer Sue first married Mark Hood. Born on 11 Sep 1953 in Allen County, KY.

They had one child:

>**815** i. Angela Beth (1973-)

Jennifer Sue second married Michael Hardy. Born on 17 Mar 1947.

812. Robert Harris Cline (Harris C.[11], Willie W. Harris[10], William T.[9], Robert Wiseman[8], Giles Claiborne[7], Gideon[6], Lewis[5], David[4], William[3], William[2], Thomas[1]). Born on 27 Apr 1942.

Information about the marriage and sons is from Allen County, KY, Family History. On 24 Jun 1972 when Robert Harris was 30, he married Linda Whitlow, daughter of Robert H. Whitlow & Jeanette Stovall, in Allen County, KY. Born on 4 Jul 1944.

They had the following children:

>**816** i. Robert Harris (1973-)
>
>**817** ii. JoeDan Benson (1979-)

---

813. Alan Mayhew (Teresa Gail Jackson[12], Nina Loyce Cook[11], Nellie M. Harris[10], William T.[9], Robert Wiseman[8], Giles Claiborne[7], Gideon[6], Lewis[5], David[4], William[3], William[2], Thomas[1]). Born on 21 Apr 1975 in Warren County, KY. Alan died in Allen County, KY, on 13 Oct 1996; he was 21.

814. John Mayhew (Teresa Gail Jackson[12], Nina Loyce Cook[11], Nellie M. Harris[10], William T.[9], Robert Wiseman[8], Giles Claiborne[7], Gideon[6], Lewis[5], David[4], William[3], William[2], Thomas[1]). Born on 2 Jul 1978 in Warren County, KY.

815. Angela Beth Hood (Jennifer Sue Jackson[12], Nina Loyce Cook[11], Nellie M. Harris[10], William T.[9], Robert Wiseman[8], Giles Claiborne[7], Gideon[6], Lewis[5], David[4], William[3], William[2], Thomas[1]). Born on 26 Dec 1973 in Allen County, KY.

Angela Beth married Ricky Swygart. Born on 26 Apr 1970.

They had the following children:

818	i.	Ally Shannon (1999-)
819	ii.	Riley Beth (2004-)
820	iii.	Tanner Hayden (2007-)

816. Robert Harris Cline Jr. (Robert Harris[12], Harris C.[11], Willie W. Harris[10], William T.[9], Robert Wiseman[8], Giles Claiborne[7], Gideon[6], Lewis[5], David[4], William[3], William[2], Thomas[1]). Born on 12 Dec 1973.

817. JoeDan Benson Cline (Robert Harris[12], Harris C.[11], Willie W. Harris[10], William T.[9], Robert Wiseman[8], Giles Claiborne[7], Gideon[6], Lewis[5], David[4], William[3], William[2], Thomas[1]). Born on 23 May 1979.

---

818. Ally Shannon Swygart (Angela Beth Hood[13], Jennifer Sue Jackson[12], Nina Loyce Cook[11], Nellie M. Harris[10], William T.[9], Robert Wiseman[8], Giles Claiborne[7], Gideon[6], Lewis[5], David[4], William[3], William[2], Thomas[1]). Born in 1999 in Warren County, KY.

819. Riley Beth Swygart (Angela Beth Hood[13], Jennifer Sue Jackson[12], Nina Loyce Cook[11], Nellie M. Harris[10], William T.[9], Robert Wiseman[8], Giles Claiborne[7], Gideon[6], Lewis[5], David[4], William[3], William[2], Thomas[1]). Born in 2004 in Warren County, KY.

820. Tanner Hayden Swygart (Angela Beth Hood[13], Jennifer Sue Jackson[12], Nina Loyce Cook[11], Nellie M. Harris[10], William T.[9], Robert Wiseman[8], Giles Claiborne[7], Gideon[6], Lewis[5], David[4], William[3], William[2], Thomas[1]). Born on 28 Feb 2007 in Warren County, KY.

Index

PO = parent of

SO = spouse of

John PO SO 68
John H. 112
Lindsey 115
Margaret Elizabeth 113
Mary "Polly" T. 114
Rhoda SO 63
Aycock
Narcissus SO 99
Baldridge
Emmett SO 399
Baldwin
Agnes SO 58
Elizabeth SO 59
John PO SO 58
John PO SO 59
Ball
Edna May SO 644
Ballard
Ellen Jane PO SO 155
Barnes
Rena SO 421
Barron
Alma Elizabeth 605
Herschell Warren 603
James Warren SO 417
Thelma Lee 604
Bates
Eliza Amelia 372
Giles Lee Blount 371
Kittie Lucille 370
Samuel Lee spouse of 204
William Howard 369
Baxter
Amanda Jane 254
Bessie Sue SO 510
Edmond S. 259

James N. 256
John F. 260
Martha N. 261
Montgomery H. 258
Robert G. 257
William Fletcher SO 125
William Fletcher SO 124
William H. 255
Beals Daniel
Elizabeth SO 528
Beard
Eugenia Malenia SO 344
Beaty
L. Crab SO 216
Beisheim
Waneta SO 747
Berry
Elizabeth PO SO 116
Roy Audry SO 581
Binford
Frank SO 149
Katherine 277
Bond
Elmo SO 511
Bransford
Benjamin PO SO 81
Martha Williamson "Patsy"
SO 81
Brasher
Myrtle Jane SO 357
Brawner
Ruby Dell SO 805
Brazier
Allie Beatrice SO 548
Brewer
Robert Kermit SO 618

Britt
  George Smith   341
Brooder
  Cornelia   394
Brooks
  Hezekiah Simpson SO398
Brown
  Emily PO SO   195
  Emily PO SO   199
  Jefferson H. SO   215
  Sarah PO SO   63
  Sarah PO SO   68
Bryant
  Lavenia Laemon SO 193
  Mary Camilla SO   739
Burch
  Mignonette SO   746
Burge
  Edna SO   295
  James W. SO   293
  William Fletcher PO SO
                          293
Burn
  Malcolm Patterson SO
                          368
Butler
  Plaught   574
  Sally I.   575
  William Bennett PO SO
                          406
  William C.   572
  William Calvin SO   406
  Zula M.   573
Butts
  Claude SO   462
  Denver Bertrand   707

  Ima Elizabeth   708
  Minnie Noreen   710
  Pauline   709
  William Conrad   706
  Cary SO   34
  Michael SO   201
Caldwell
  Aurelia   303
Byrd
  Caliborne   302
  Constance   304
  John Archer SO   157
  William Christopher 305
Campbell
  James Melt SO   654
Carothers
  Bonnie Esther SO   450
  Zella SO   456
Carr
  Naomi SO   242
Carrington
  Nathaniel SO   93
Carrol
  Carra I. SO   554
Carroll
  Eba Jane SO   555
Cary
  Elnora SO   552
Cash
  Aaron Lloyd   795
  David Lavelle   794
  Harvey D. SO   642
  Milton Keon   793
Chandler
  Ann E. Gray SO   49
Cheatham

Annes Edith 508
James Theodore SO 265
Luther M. 510
Mary Ora 511
William Thomas 509
Cheek
Permelia PO SO 122
Chenault
Burleigh SO 299
Claunch
Minnie SO 444
Clay
William Temple SO 646
Cline
Harris C. 800
Joe PO SO 718
JoeDan Benson 817
Robert Harris 812
Robert Harris Jr. 816
Roy D. SO 718
Cobb
Samuel D. SO 395
Coleman
Emily F. PO SO 293
Mattie Ann PO SO 295
Cook
Anna Mary SO 559
Archie B. PO SO 613
Ersa May SO 613
Nina Loyce 799
Orbin Clifton SO 717
Robert Wilson PO SO
717
Cox
Frank Wallace SO 347
Creasey
Pauline SO 737

Crosby
Mary Ella SO 723
Crowe
Gouldman Amanda SO
83
Crowell
Sarah Eva SO 458
Cude
Cecil Haywood SO 364
Cummins
Arthur Estes SO 580
Cundiff
Ruth E. SO 743
Dallas
Mary Jane SO 235
Mary Jane PO SO 393
Oval Benita SO 607
Dalton
A. Bertha 705
A. Doral 698
B. Irah 701
B. Sela 700
Elizabeth 808
Elton SO 781
J. Suler 699
Joseph Robert SO 461
Kyle 807
L. Elzie 702
M. Hertie 703
M. Ivy 704
Shelton PO SO 461
Daniel
Caroline SO 79
Dark
Harris SO 216
Daughtery

Ewing
 Sammie Gideon SO 506
Ezell
 Frances PO SO   272
Farrar
 Thomas SO   7
Ferguson
 Allan Blanchard PO SO 295
 Anna Louise SO   295
Ferrell
 Nell Dale SO   381
Flynt
 Hubert Elmer PO SO 594
Follis
 Permelia Alice PO SO 717
Fowler
 ? SO   87
 Sallie Sanderson SO 86
Fox
 Sarah Jane SO   502
Frayser
 Frederick Harris   278
 Giles Harris   286
 Jessamine   284
 Judith Bransford   279
 Martha Bransford   287
 Mary Susan   281
 Sarah Catherine   283
 Sidney Anderson   288
 Thomas Hatcher SO 150
 Thomas Hatcher Jr. 282
 Virginia   280
 William   285
Fuzzell
 Evelyn A.   780
 James Odell SO   576

Gammon
 Addie May SO   251
Gammons
 Leslie Donohoe SO 586
Gannaway
 Gregory PO SO   64
 Mary "Polly" SO   64
Garrett
 Martha Elizabeth SO 226
Garvin
 Orpha Antonia Hazel SO
                     640
Gibson
 Bettie C.   714
 Bluit Pruit SO   463
 Dee O.   712
 Joe C.   715
 Katie M.   713
 Minnie Annie   716
 Nancy SO   223
 Willie D.   711
Gilbert
 Minerva Ann SO   178
Giles
 Mary SO   10
Gilliam
 Annie L.   725
 Herschell SO   469
 James PO SO   70
 Martha Taylor SO   70
 Sarah Frances PO SO 121
Gilmore
 Frances PO SO   121
Glenn
 Lydia May PO SO   392
Goblet

273

Grace Ruth SO	532	G. Frank SO	503
Gooding		Goodrum	744
Etta SO	297	Magneus	745
Goodwin		Thomas R. PO SO	503
Fred Allen SO	352	**Hardy**	
Graves		Michael SO	811
Dorothy Ione SO	582	**Harris**	
Paddy Paul SO	214	A. J.	804
Gray		Albert Royal	447
Orpha Mildred SO	669	Alfred Taylor	551
Thomas SO	62	Alice	352
Gray Harrison		Alice	145
Margaret SO	120	Alice	461
Greene		Alva Zela	690
Frances SO	36	Alvin Luther	641
Mary SO	35	Amanda	159
Guest		Amanda Catherine	406
James Truman SO	653	Ammon	92
Hall		Andrew Curran	272
Elizabeth SO	40	Ann	56
Hancock		Anne	20
Robert SO	8	Annie	331
Hardin		Archie Herschell	615
Della Frances	633	Artemas Duren	455
Ethel Mae	636	Arthur Cleatus	458
Fant George	638	Arthur Giles	325
Fred Edward	631	Artis Glenn	607
Herbert Doyle	639	Aubra	802
Luther Joseph	637	Aubyn	526
Mary B. PO SO	254	Audra Evelyn	688
Reta Belle	635	Augustus	97
Siras Bell SO	442	Augustus G.	179
Versie Aldora	634	Aurelia Ann	222
William Inloe	632	Austin	329
Hardison		Austin Dabney	182
Cecil	746	Avie Elizabeth	645

Edward	21	Exie	674
Edward	53	F. L.	565
Edward	11	Fanader G.	778
Edward Bunyan	670	Fletch	485
Edward Olley	379	Florence Aurelia	411
Edwin R.	582	Frances Caroline	221
Effie Jane	617	Francis Hopkins	116
Eleanor Graves	781	Frederick Giles	151
Elgie Irwin	739	Furman	610
Elisha O.	735	G. C.	584
Elizabeth	30	George	60
Elizabeth	203	George	16
Elizabeth	324	George Calvin	407
Elizabeth	94	George Madison	435
Elizabeth	76	George S.	758
Elizabeth	111	Gertrude V.	501
Elizabeth	14	Gideon	70
Elizabeth SO	50	Gideon Lewis	218
Elizabeth	51	Gideon Lewis	196
Elizabeth Annie	266	Gideon Lewis	358
Elizabeth Lee	535	Gideon Lindsey Jr.	235
Elizabeth Lewis "Betsy"		Gideon Lindsey Jr. PO SO	
	118		393
Elizabeth Lindsey	217	Gideon Lindsey	120
Ella May	543	Gideon Simpson	401
Elwood B.	775	Giles	88
Emily	170	Giles Hunter	356
Emma Frances	326	Giles Rice	249
Ervin Lafayette	552	Giles S.	482
Esther R.	300	Giles	81
Ethel C.	483	Giles	49
Eura	576	Giles	166
Eura Magruder	348	Giles	66
Eva Inez	621	Giles Bledsoe	465
Evaline N.	185	Giles Bledsoe PO SO 727	
Everett Sylvan	669	Giles Claiborne	232

Giles Claiborne	121	James D.	790
Giles Furman	436	James David	443
Giles Tinsley	200	James E.	747
Giles Turner	79	James Gilliam	119
Giles Ward	96	James Leland	648
Giles Ward	178	James Lindsey	230
Gilliam Garrett	383	James Lindsey	248
Glennon Porter	490	James Marley	413
Graves	59	James Patterson	264
Guy	269	James Patterson SO	373
Harold Augustus	609	James R.	481
Harriett F.	187	James R.	473
Harrison	82	James Virgil	380
Harrison	47	Jane	72
Haskel Garwin	657	Jane Lindsey	102
Hattie L.	296	Jasper	323
Hazel	789	Jeptha Virgil	409
Hazel	740	Jesse F.	766
Helen M.	292	Jesse Reed	503
Henry H.	479	Jetta Beatrice SO	354
Hettie	271	Jewel	650
Homer T.	389	Jewel Thedus	553
Honor Delpha	488	Jewel Winfred	776
Hubert V.	694	Joe Cletus	392
Hubert Vernon	456	John	108
Hunter Hill	384	John	164
I. Effie	474	John	24
Imogene	765	John	27
Isam Gilliam	446	John	67
J. Fount	507	John	18
J. R.	593	John PO SO	50
J. W.	616	John A. SO	156
James Blanton	720	John Blanchard	423
James C.	390	John Bryce	382
James C.	484	John Claiborn	83
James Clanton	223	John Gardner	236

John Gardner	122	Lewis Gideon	433
John Hopkins	219	Lewis J.	506
John (Jack)	100	Lewis Tinsley	127
John Joyce	517	Lillie Faye	671
John Lindon	445	Lillie M.	298
John Lindsey	228	Lillie N.	492
John Madison	403	Lillie Pearl	736
John R.	786	Lillie Pearl	655
John R.	195	Lonzy	486
John Sumpter	247	Louis Gilbert	651
Joseph	579	Lovy B.	777
Joseph	274	Lucile Elmira	787
Joseph B.	186	Lucy Almedia SO	393
Joseph Carrol	252	Lucy Almedia	432
Joseph Linn	743	Lucy Artimus	442
Josephine	173	Lucy Elizabeth	404
Joyce	774	Lucy Hatcher	148
Judith	23	Lucy Jane	410
Judith	31	Lula May	388
Judith	77	Luvinia	180
Julia Kinnell	408	Mable	601
Julius Andrew	448	Maggie L.	472
Kate	270	Mahalye Jane	402
L. W.	311	Malcolm Hobert	619
Lafory H.	784	Mallie E.	468
Lee	330	Malvina "Mallie" C.	250
Leon	783	Mannon Lindsey	452
Leonard Erskin	602	Margaret Elizabeth	
Leta May	647	"Maggie"	253
Lettice	62	Margaret Safronia	
Lewis	105	"Maggie"	201
Lewis	89	Margie Patie	643
Lewis	623	Marion A.	240
Lewis	69	Martha	103
Lewis	50	Martha Anna "Matt"	246
Lewis SO	51	Martha Elizabeth	231

Martha Elizabeth PO SO		Maude May	349
	432	May Augustus	437
Martha Jane	216	Merlin Flynn	685
Martha Jane	199	Michael Flynn	797
Martha Jane	125	Milam King	361
Martha Jane "Mattie"		Mildred D.	759
	241	Millard	675
Martha Virginia	153	Mina Dora	168
Mary	244	Minnie A.	495
Mary	2	Minnie Jane	463
Mary	55	Mittie Ophelia	420
Mary	144	Nancy	160
Mary	95	Nancy	110
Mary	169	Nancy	177
Mary C.	467	Nancy Bennett	220
Mary Catherine "Cassie"		Nancye	75
	234	Nellie M.	717
Mary Constance	157	Nina M.	581
Mary E.	729	Nolus Guy	545
Mary Elizabeth	174	Nona Agatha	646
Mary Elizabeth	156	Norris	687
Mary Florence	668	Obadiah	99
Mary G.	667	Obediah	65
Mary J.	215	Obediah	90
Mary J. PO SO	264	Ocie Bedford	422
Mary J.	183	Ollin Littlefield	644
Mary Katherine	265	P. H.	308
Mary Percilla	449	Patience Elizabeth	68
Mary "Polly"	109	Patsy	161
Mary Robertson "Molly"		Paul C	583
	149	Paul Nimmo	719
Mary S.	767	Paul Nimmo SO	727
Mary Tinsley	71	Penelope	175
Mary Tinsley	123	Peter	28
Mattie Anna	469	Philip Watkins	171
Mattie Anna PO SO 719		Phoebe	93

Price Edward	665	Ruth	622
R. A.	307	Ruth	353
Ralph	58	Ryman Abner	360
Ralph	333	Sallie Gladys	549
Ralph T.	533	Samuel	172
Ray	625	Samuel PO SO	156
Raymond Garland	660	Samuel Sneed	419
Reba Iola	653	Sarah	22
Rebecca Elizabeth	434	Sarah	197
Rebecca Rice	204	Sarah B.	184
Reginald W.	525	Sarah C.	534
Retie Ceulia	642	Sarah Catherine	150
Rhoda	87	Sarah Elizabeth	214
Rice Odell	470	Sarah Frances	405
Richard	54	Sarah Francis "Frankie"	
Richard W.	106		237
Riggs Tidwell	502	Sarah Giles	104
Robert	91	Sarah Giles	124
Robert	267	Sarah Jane	263
Robert Andrew	421	Sarah Martha "Mattie"	339
Robert C. R.	46	Sarah Myrtle	457
Robert Claiborne	227	Sarah Tennie	466
Robert Giles	140	Sherwood (Shureed)	29
Robert Lee	453	Snead	107
Robert Taylor	550	Stephen	19
Robert Taylor	357	Straudy	577
Robert Wiseman	245	Susan E.	188
Roberta Lee	293	Susan Elizabeth	152
Rowena	142	Susanna	167
Roy	803	Susie L.	299
Roy	624	T. J.	310
Roy	760	Tandy	155
Ruby Demova	618	Tandy D.	295
Ruby J.	791	Tenner M.	666
Ruby Viola	654	Theatus	673
Russell Elbert	652	Thelma Nadine	594

Theodoric Carter Gannaway		Walter E.	297
	84	Wiley A.	500
Theola Pyron	649	William	74
Theta May	782	William	162
Thomas	25	William	198
Thomas	13	William	662
Captain Thomas	1	William	139
Thomas	45	William	85
Thomas	9	William III	15
Thomas Blount	202	William II	10
Thomas Blount Jr.	359	William I	3
Thomas C.	391	William	48
Thomas Clifford	686	William	181
Thomas Earl	385	William Ashley	238
Thomas Ferrell	536	William Austin	101
Thomas Gideon	414	William B.	294
Thomas Gideon	242	William Bransford	147
Thomas Woodson	146	William Burl	355
Thurman Lindsey	450	William Carnath	489
Tinsley	98	William Earl	640
Tolbert Dalton	454	William Franklin	444
Troy	672	William Goss	548
Unnamed	224	William Harlin	689
Unnamed	225	William I.	734
Urbane Eustace	620	William Lawson	742
Vander Eason	547	William Lee	381
Vera G.	693	William Lindsey	126
Vercil Claudie	737	William Lindsey PO SO	
Verna L.	580		373
Viola	592	William Marion	400
Virginia	158	William Moore	154
Virginia	78	William Nelton	656
Virginia	801	William T.	464
Vivian Milborn	658	William Thomas	226
Waller B.	537	William Tinsley	416
Walter	664	William Tinsley	243

William W.	176	Wilma Louise	796
Willie Ilah	563	**Hoare**	
Willie W.	718	Audrey SO	1
Wilma Sue	692	Thomas PO SO	1
Winston B.	764	**Hobby**	
Winston Howard	756	Columbus Worth SO	504
Harvey		Green PO SO	504
Lela SO	546	**Holman**	
Hatcher		Beula SO	383
Lucy PO SO	81	Maude SO	401
Hawkins		**Holmes**	
Irene Beatrice SO	545	Almeda SO	171
Robert PO SO	121	**Hood**	
Sarah H. SO	121	Angela Beth	815
Hay		Mark SO	811
Grace Owen	769	**Hopkins**	
Howard L.	768	Frances PO SO	70
Iria N.	771	**Houston**	
Mary E.	770	Joseph Oscar SO	241
Rachel C.	772	Lessie	459
Rebecca J.	773	Talmage Ray	460
Walter Benjamin SO	549	**Howell**	
Henderson		Clytie Mae PO SO	800
Lillie Mae SO	454	**Hudson**	
Higgs		Anna	43
Thomas F. SO	508	Charles	44
Hight		Christopher	34
Leia SO	273	Cuthbert	40
Hill		David	39
Evelyn Ruth SO	248	Elizabeth	38
Susan Angaline SO	119	George	33
William B. SO	113	John SO	14
Hines		John	35
Ella SO	251	Mary	41
Hix		Rebecca	42
Earl Marion SO	643		

Loftin

Tavia May SO   579

London

John PO SO   122

Rosannah SO   122

Long

Lenard Virgil SO   716

Lowrance

Jane Melissa SO   119

Lumpkin

Jasper Robert SO   655

Lund

Gracie SO   734

MacLeod

Malcolm McAuley SO 527

Malone

Edgar Bruce   505

Martha Ann "Mattie" 504

Murdock McKenzie SO 263

Manley

Jacob B PO SO   577

Wade Field SO   577

Marks

Hudson Watkins PO SO

    155

Roberta Alice SO   155

Martyn

Emma Ruth SO   423

Massengill

Sarah SO   232

Matthews

Susan SO   83

Mayberry

Lula Lee SO   229

Mayhew

Alan   813

John   814

Michael SO   810

Mayo

Hazel Alma SO   564

Mays

Charles SO   298

McBride

Mary Elizabeth SO   421

Mollie Mary SO   433

McClanahan

Bailey Peyton SO   408

Donald   587

Eugene   590

Gladys   588

Mamie   589

Talmage   591

McCord

William SO   75

McDaniel

Catherine SO   120

McDavid

Raven I. SO   535

McDonald

Andrew SO   110

Andrew   189

Elizabeth A.   190

McFall

Andrew Norris   529

Janie Clara   527

John Harold   528

John Sullivan SO   339

Robert Trice   530

Meador

Dora PO SO   718

Frances Catherine SO 121

Thomas S. PO SO   121

Meek
Minnie SO   451

Miles
Emmer L. SO   481

Milner
Rebecca SO   182

Mitchell
Samuel SO   102

Moncrief
Caminet SO   719
Caminet   727
Gideon Paul SO   469
Gideon Paul PO SO   719
Orby   726
Venlist   728

Moore
Elisha   194
Gideon Lindsey   192
James Giles   275
Robert Hawkins   193
Robert N. SO   142
Robert Nathaniel   276
Samuel PO SO   116
William Ashley SO   116

Mount
Robert Andrew SO   513

Myrick
William SO   104

Nagle
Fayette   568
Marion Patrick George
Anderson SO   404
Maudie   569
Millard   567

Minnie   566

Nail
Lillian SO   758

Napier
Lois SO   800
Owsley Benson PO SO 800

Neeley
Florence Annis SO   514
Lee PO SO   140
Martha R. SO   140

Newell
Bulis   798
Burris N. SO   690
Letha Jewel "Dee" SO 422

Nicholoff
Cozmo SO   617

Nichols
Joe Henry   363
Will Vivian   362
William Washington SO
    203

Nimmo
Grau PO SO   465
Nellie SO   465
Nellie PO SO   727

Nolan
Sammil SO   359

Norwood
Maggie Doshie SO   444

Oglesby
David Jr. SO   87

Owen
? SO   183

Pack
Nora Gertrude SO   325

Parrish

Cora Edna	428	Charlie Lewis SO	246
Cordie Crittenden	425	Clayborn	475
Eber Nathaniel	430	Dary	477
Gilliam Harris	431	James PO SO	246
James Clayborn	424	James PO SO	246
Jesse Jordon SO	234	Mallie C.	476
Jordon PO SO	234	William W. SO	246

Cora Edna 428
Cordie Crittenden 425
Eber Nathaniel 430
Gilliam Harris 431
James Clayborn 424
Jesse Jordon SO 234
Jordon PO SO 234
Jordon Augustus 426
Lucy Elizabeth 427
Matilda Ann SO 233
Willie Baxter 429
Patrick
Susannah SO 44
Patterson
James PO SO 126
Mary Ann SO 126
Mary Ann PO SO 373
Peak
Susannah PO SO 58
Susannah PO SO 59
Peeler
Jasper Newton SO 222
Perry
Maggie May SO 252
Mary Ann "Polly" SO 227
William SO 75
William SO 78
Persons
Carl Phillip SO 353
Peters
Hallie Josephine SO 369
Phillips
Carl Douglas SO 516
Roxanna Nora SO 228
Pike
Ally 478

Charlie Lewis SO 246
Clayborn 475
Dary 477
James PO SO 246
James PO SO 246
Mallie C. 476
William W. SO 246
Pinkston
Walter Ewing SO 387
Pinson
James Benjamin SO 647
Pitts
Lois Irene SO 757
Plunk
Etta Jane SO 448
Ida Leona SO 437
Prewitt
John Brantley 128
Kirk SO 76
Pritchard
Thetus SO 592
Pryor
Jesse SO 31
Pyron
Aurelia Aquilla 440
Calista Ann SO 445
DeWitt 627
Docia Bell SO 443
Effie M. 630
Gideon Lindsey 438
Hassie B. 626
James Clayborne 441
John Riley SO 237
Ory O. 628
Sidney Augustus 439
William C. 629

Philip A. 321

Skruggs

Vannale Bell SO 360

Slaughter

Geraldine SO 602

Sloan

Ella B. SO 479

Smith

? SO 80

Annice Belle SO 436

Elma Elizabeth SO 562

Hettie PO SO 140

J. P. SO 191

Rosa 585

Roxia 586

Ruby SO 294

Stella Lorraine SO 763

William Perry SO 408

Stapp

Lela Mae SO 648

Starbuck

Daniel SO 340

Steele

Martha Elizabeth 191

Stephens

Altha Lorraine SO 685

Stewart

Alice SO 3

Lucy SO 3

Stout

Mary Lena SO 447

Stovall

Jeanette PO SO 812

Strickland

Cynthia SO 101

Strohmeyer

Charles Frederick PO SO
392

Olive SO 392

Swygart

Ally Shannon 818

Riley Beth 819

Tanner Hayden 820

Tennison

Hiram PO SO 740

Myrte V. 806

Sam Hardison SO 740

Tharue

Laura SO 141

Thomas

Henrietta Ann SO 243

Thompson

Delpha Jane SO 547

Thurman

Elizabeth SO 66

Tidwell

Jaby Linton SO 560

Mildred Nancy SO 262

Tilford

Fany SO 107

Tinsley

Mary SO 18

Mary PO SO 50

Tooley

Elizabeth PO SO 246

Elizabeth PO SO 246

Treece

Clyde Sherman SO 621

Triplett

Julyan PO SO 1

Twitty

Lillian Murphy SO 744

Twoney
Ada Pearl SO — 350

Vaughn
John William SO — 370

Venable
? SO — 94

Vibert
Jane SO — 247

Vincent
Elizabeth — 205
Emma V. — 213
Iowa Florida — 210
James Anderson — 209
Joane SO — 1
John David SO — 118
John H. — 207
Martha — 206
Robert F. — 212
Sarah J. — 208
William H. — 211

Vinson
Lula Pearl SO — 452

Walker
Charlie Fred SO — 543
Don — 755
Duel Rastus — 540
Everett Virdel — 1
Everette Cecil — 541
Grover Cisco — 538
Hardy Odell — 679
Hazel — 751
Irma — 542
James Thomas — 393
James Thomas SO — 432
John SO — 231
John PO SO — 432

John PO SO — 457
John Gideon — 396
John Robert SO — 457
John Virgle — 681
Joseph Anthony — 394
Larance L. — 684
Lilburn T. — 750
Lucinda Catherine — 398
Luther Albert SO — 449
Luther Wilburn — 680
Manson Rupert — 539
Mary F. — 397
Mary Frances — 395
Mary U. — 682
Mattie Ann Belle — 399
Mildred — 754
Nellie C. — 697
Norman Fay — 753
Parnie V. — 749
Raybun N. — 695
Rayburn — 683
Roxie Theola — 676
Scleeta Aldonia — 677
Varnie M. — 696
Zahelia — 752

Wallace
Bertha Oleta SO — 651
Rosa Lee SO — 407
Selena Palestine SO — 403

Walthall
Elizabeth SO — 6

Ward
? SO — 66
Henry SO — 109

Watkins
Ann — 52

Elizabeth "Betty" SO 65
Mary Ann Smith SO 92

Weatherford
Cordell	724
Hilery Harris	723
Hilery J. PO SO	466
Robert Yancy SO	466
Selma	721
Willie	722

Weaver
Nannie Tennison SO	251

Webb
Ita SO	366
Larimore spouse of	349
Ned Harris	531
William Carey	532

Weeks
Alfie Newton SO	668

Wheatly
Mary Catherine SO	509

White
Neil Soules PO SO	556
Ronayne Blanchard SO	556

Whitesell
Zillah Emma SO	507

Whitlow
Linda SO	812
Robert H. PO SO	812

Wilburn
William Wiley SO	201

Wilkes
Ann Eliza	131
Benjamin Leroy	134
Franklin C.	130

George Washington	135
James Horace	137
John Summerfield	138
Josephine Castera	136
Martha Virginia	132
Richard Ambrose SO	77
Richard Sparks	133
William Henderson	129

Williams
Annabell SO	361
Benjamin Tillman SO	645
Pearl A. SO	171

Wills
Karene SO	723

Wilson
Daisy Dean SO	332

Winn
Elizabeth SO	67

Witt
Aubrey G. SO	799
Robert W.	809

Wood Davis
Elizabeth Catherine SO	121

Woodward
Jessie Sewell SO	512

Worsham
Mary SO	4

Wright
Anna SO	69
Manual L. SO	420
Mitchell SO	585
Pauline	606

Sources Cited

Allen County, Kentucky, Historical Society. *Allen County, Kentucky, Family History.* Paducah, KY: Turner Publishing Co., 2004.

Boddie, John Bennett. *Virginia Historical Genealogies.* Baltimore: Genealogical Pub. Co., 1965.

Bronner, Jimmy G. and Lorraine E. Macon County, Tennessee, Marriages. Unpublished Document, housed in the Macon County, Tennessee, Library, Lafayette, TN.

County Websites can be accessed at *The US Genweb Project* <usgenweb.org>.

Davis, Rosalie Edith. *Hanover County, Virginia, Deeds, 1783-1792.* Manchester, MO: Heritage Trails, 1980.

Foley, Louise Pledge Heath. *Early Virginia Families.* Baltimore: Genealogical Pub. Co., 1979.

GenForum/Harris <genforum.genealogy.com>. No longer available online.

Harris, Thomas Henry. *Harris Family of Virginia.* [n.p.], 1914.

Harris, W. Lee. Captain Thomas Harris, 1586-1658. Unpublished Manuscript housed in the Lebanon Library, Lebanon, TN.

Jamerson, Vicki. *Appomattox County Marriages, 1854-1890.* Appomattox, VA: Jamerson, 1979.

Kidd, Randy and Jeanne Stinson. *Lost Marriages of Buckingham County, Virginia.* Athens, GA: Iberian, 1992.

Knorr, Catherine Lindsey. *Marriage Bonds and Ministers' Returns of Prince Edward County, Virginia, 1754-1810.* Easley, SC: Southern Historical Press, 1982.

LDS Website <www.familysearch.org>.

Lindsay, Joyce H. *Marriages of Henrico County, Virginia, 1680-1808.* Richmond, VA: [n.p.], 1960.

Lucas, S. Emmett. *Marriages from Early Tennessee Newspapers, 1794-1851.* Easley, SC: Southern Historical Press, 1978.

Macon County, Tennessee, Historical Society. *Macon County, Tennessee, History and Families.* Paducah, KY: Turner Publishing Co., 2001.

Lightfoot, Marise Parrish and Evelyn B. Shackelford. *Maury County, Tennessee, Records.* [n.p.], 1964.

Parish Register of St. Peters, New Kent County, Virginia. Baltimore: Genealogical Publishing Co., 1966.

Partlow, Thomas E. *Wilson County, Tennessee, Deed Books C-M, 1793-1829.* Easley, SC: Southern Historical Press, 1984.

-----. *Wilson County, Tennessee, Miscellaneous Records, 1800-1875.* Easley, SC: Southern Historical Press, 1982.

-----. *Wilson County, Tennessee, Tax Lists, 1803-1807.* Baltimore: Genealogical Publishing, 1981.

-----. *Wilson County, Tennessee, Will Books 1-13, 1802-1850.* Easley, SC: Southern Historical Press, 1981.

Porch, Diane. *Marriage Records, Marshall County, Tennessee, 1836-1870.* Franklin, TN: Louise G. Lynch, 1976.

Stinson, Era W. and Elizabeth Sue Spurlock. *Sumner County, Tennessee, Marriages, 1839-1895.* Bowling Green, KY: E. W. Stinson and E. W. Spurlock, 1985.

Ward, Roger G. *Land Tax Summaries and Implied Deeds.* Athens, GA: Iberian Pub. Co., 1993-1995.

Weisger, Benjamin B. *Colonial Wills of Henrico County, Virginia.* Richmond, VA: Weisger, 1976-77.

-----. *Henrico County, Virginia, Deeds, 1706-1717.* Richmond, VA: B. B. Weisger, 1985-86.

Whitley, Edythe Johns Rucker. *Marriages of Maury County, Tennessee.* Baltimore: Genealogical Pub. Co., 1982.

-----. *Marriages of Sumner County, Tennessee, 1787-1838.* Baltimore: Genealogical Pub. Co.,1982.

-----. *Tennessee Genealogical Records.* Baltimore: Genealogical Pub. Co., 1980.

www.ingramcontent.com/pod-product-compliance
Lightning Source LLC
Chambersburg PA
CBHW061718270326
41928CB00011B/2024